AUTHENTICITY GUARANTEED

AUTHENTICITY GUARANTEED

Masculinity and the Rhetoric of
Anti-Consumerism in American Culture

SALLY ROBINSON

University of Massachusetts Press
Amherst and Boston

ISBN 978-1-62534-353-6 (paper); 352-9 (hardcover)

Designed by Sally Nichols
Set in Monotype Dante and Josefin Sans
Printed and bound by Maple Press, Inc.

Cover design by Patricia Duque Campos
Cover photo: *Repetition,* courtesy of Yui Sotzaki.

Library of Congress Cataloging-in-Publication Data
Names: Robinson, Sally, 1959– author.
Title: Authenticity guaranteed : masculinity and the rhetoric of
anti-consumerism in American culture / Sally Robinson.
Description: Amherst : University of Massachusetts Press, [2018] | Includes
bibliographical references and index. |
Identifiers: LCCN 2017050260 (print) | LCCN 2017054511 (ebook) | ISBN
9781613765944 (e-book) | ISBN 9781613765951 (e-book) | ISBN 9781625343529
(hardcover) | ISBN 9781625343536 (pbk.)
Subjects: LCSH: Consumption (Economics)—Social aspects—United States. |
Masculinity—United States.
Classification: LCC HC110.C6 (ebook) | LCC HC110.C6 R628 2018 (print) | DDC
306.30973—dc23
LC record available at https://lccn.loc.gov/2017050260

British Library Cataloguing-in-Publication Data
A catalog record for this book is available from the British Library.

A portion of chapter 2 was previously published in *Salinger's "The Catcher in the
Rye,"* edited by Sarah Graham, for Routledge Study Guides (2007), 69–76; a portion
of chapter 3 was published in *Genders,* no. 53 (2011); and a portion of chapter 4 was
published in *Postmodern Culture* 23, no. 2 (2014).

CONTENTS

For Stan Raleigh

PREFACE

This project began in 1999 at a movie theater in College Station, Texas, where I purchased a ticket to watch a commercial Hollywood film that savaged American commercialism by trotting out a well-worn narrative about gender and consumer culture. That film was *Fight Club,* and underlying its plot was a narrative about how consumer culture is a *feminizing* force that robs men of their individuality, autonomy, and authenticity and, further, transforms the United States into a nation of mindless, valueless shoppers. This film rubbed me the wrong way, to say the least. However, I was not bothered so much by the violence the film imagines to be a "cure" for what ails men and U.S. culture as by its story about how masculinity is endangered by women, by feminism, and by the multiple emasculations demanded by a contemporary American culture. My irritation only grew when it became evident that audiences, reviewers, and even scholars responding to the film bought its premise, hook, line, and sinker. Was it really possible, at the turn of the twenty-first century, decades after feminist theory and criticism have been institutionalized in universities and absorbed by popular culture, that this narrative could still have the power to explain the workings of consumer capitalism? Do people really still buy the premise that men are robbed of their masculinity by a feminizing consumer culture? What is it about this shopworn narrative that makes it so irresistible?

This book attempts to answer these questions and to account for the surprising persistence of a narrative that really should have disappeared decades ago. This narrative positions men and the masculine on the side of rebellion and women and femininity on the side of conformity, and it is characterized by a moralizing tone and an elitist tendency to divide the world into insiders and outsiders. My argument is that consumerism becomes a convenient target for social critics who wish to register anxieties about perceived attacks on masculinity, individualism, and authenticity. But in insisting that consumer culture is *feminizing,* anti-consumerism makes masculine protest the most potent form of social criticism and, further, reinforces a very traditional gender system based on essential and ahistorical difference. My archive for this project includes not only literary texts and popular culture but also widely read works from sociologists, marketers, and all kinds of writers interested in diagnosing the perils of American consumer culture. One of the most surprising things I have found as I worked with this archive is the emotional tenor of anti-consumerism, its hostility and anger not only toward shopping and other consumer activities but also toward *consumers* (who, of course, are most often represented as feminine). And one of the most exciting things I have found as I have worked on this book is that when I talk about this American "feminization" narrative, women often respond with an enthusiastic "Yes!" Recently reading through a library book called *Women Who Shop Too Much,* I was delighted to find a Post-It note expressing shock and perhaps anger at the "truth" of the premise that shopping is a feminine activity and female shoppers the perfect dupes of consumer culture, unable to control their impulses: "Shopaholics—always referred to as being women!!" I like to think of this Post-It comment as witnessing in some young woman, perhaps a marketing major, an "aha!" moment, one I have often witnessed in my students. It rarely occurs to these students to challenge the commonsense idea that shopping is a feminine activity or that consumer culture feminizes men. Nor have any of us, really, been provoked to think about how this formulation depends on the self-evident truth that all things "feminine" are trivial, out of control, prone to weakness, and so on.

Many students have helped shape this book, but I have also had many more casual conversations with non-academics who have encouraged me to develop these ideas—not least Stan, Emma, and Lucy Raleigh. I wish to thank Dana Lawrence, research assistant extraordinaire, for her work collecting material for chapter 2. Becca Harris and Brian Yost were excellent sparring partners whose very different perspectives on contemporary American culture helped me to articulate my own. Scores of undergraduate students who have taken my courses on consumerism in American culture and my class Art or Trash? have lent their insights and made this a better book. A number of colleagues have responded to various parts of this book in formal and informal settings; thanks to Mary Ann O'Farrell, David McWhirter, Vanita Reddy, Larry J. Reynolds, Claudia Nelson, Anne Morey, Emily Johansen, and Nandra Perry. Early encouragement came from Marlon Ross. I wish also to thank the Melbern G. Glasscock Center for Humanities Research at Texas A&M for early support.

AUTHENTICITY GUARANTEED

INTRODUCTION

Complaints about consumerism have a long history in American culture. From the middle of the nineteenth century to the beginning of the twenty-first, critics of, and rebels against, consumerism have contributed chapters to a long-running narrative about how consumer culture endangers authenticity, destroys individuality, and subjects the individual to forces that sap his creativity and commodify his personality. This narrative depends on a construction of gender that places masculinity on the side of the individual who is both subjected to consumer forces and authorized to complain about them, and femininity on the side of the social mechanisms, systems, and conventions that aim to curtail masculine agency and authenticity. Protests against consumer culture also reveal a stubborn elitism that continues to haunt American culture, legible in variations on "hip" anti-consumerism. This often smug anti-consumerism pops up throughout the second half of the twentieth century and shows little sign of dying out in the twenty-first. It is perfectly embodied in a bumper sticker that showed up in the 1970s, in such liberal enclaves as Northampton, Massachusetts, where I grew up and, later, in the 1990s, in Ann Arbor, Michigan, where I then worked. "Kill Your TV," this bumper sticker exhorted and, in doing so, addressed its audience as savvy, highbrow, and superior to the poor, deluded masses who waste so much time in front of "the box." This slogan stakes a claim to cultural resistance, but it is a cultural resistance that depends on an elitist desire to differentiate between insiders and outsiders, those in the know and those hopelessly unknowing. The meaning of the "Kill Your TV" bumper sticker is ensured by its placement in a familiar narrative about how rebellion against mass culture is a sign of intellectual superiority and a badge of honor.

A bumper sticker can say a lot, but we need to look elsewhere for a more fully developed articulation of this common posture on, and protest against, consumerism. The "Kill Your TV" slogan inserts its viewer into a narrative that rests on the self-evident premise that television, mass culture, and, indeed, consumer objects and practices in general endanger authenticity, genuine meaning, and real value. That narrative is so common as to be everywhere legible, in both high and popular culture. One of my favorite examples of elitist anti-consumerism, one that I often use on the first day of my classes on gender, class, and cultural hierarchy, comes from a *New York Times* column attacking the "Disneyfication" of high culture. What is particularly striking about this piece is the righteous indignation it attempts to stir up in its readers—or, more precisely, the righteous indignation it assumes its readers already possess. This article, like so many other journalistic and scholarly responses to the products of consumer culture, takes its force and its persuasiveness from a set of assumptions that have dominated American anti-consumerist critique since at least the middle of the nineteenth century: consumer or mass culture threatens authenticity, in the individual and the nation, because it "feminizes"—that is, renders weak, foolish, and trivial—the individual and the nation.

The piece, titled "Cuddling Up to Quasimodo and Friends," penned by Paul Goldberger in 1996, uses the language of a frightening consumption machine to produce anxiety about the destruction of cultural value heralded by the Disney corporation's desire to commodify (or cartoonify) the great works of Western literature. The particular object of Goldberger's hostility is the Disney film *The Hunchback of Notre Dame*. Without defending Disney's approach to Victor Hugo's novel, we can read in Goldberger's predictable response a familiar rhetoric that accuses mass or popular culture of endangering more authentic forms of culture and, worse, threatening to reduce high culture to mere commodities. Literalizing metaphors of consumption, Goldberger writes, "Our society's appetite for entertainment is now so vast that it has begun to plunder everything—including high culture—in search of material. The Disney version of 'The Hunchback of Notre Dame' is merely the latest and most spectacular evidence of how our popular culture is literally devouring itself, a maw that grinds all in its path into a form of commercial entertainment."

As Janice Radway has so persuasively argued in her analysis of the hostility that greeted the appearance of the Book-of-the-Month Club on the literary landscape, such metaphors of eating always invoke the specter of the feminine and, in particular, the maternal (*Feeling for Books* 210–11). Against the paternal legacy of the great works of Western culture is posed a threatening maternal presence that, in league with the masses, threatens to devour all in its path. Anyone at all familiar with Dwight MacDonald's infamous "Masscult and Midcult" screed will recognize that what is particularly threatening about the middlebrow is the loss of distinction between high and low, the familiar cultural hierarchy that keeps everything properly in place and, as I will argue here, the blurring of the distinction between masculinity and femininity—or, more precisely, the corruption of the masculine by the feminine. Anxiety about the blurring of cultural boundaries is clear in Goldberger's article, as he rehashes MacDonald's position: "Whatever the cause, Disney seems to be confusing popular and high culture, conflating the two into something altogether different. I'm not sure what this new product is. Certainly it is not high culture, with its tradition of complexity and ambiguity; yet it isn't quite pure, just-for-fun pop culture, either. Maybe we should call it Disingenuous Culture, for it pretends to a level of profundity while corrupting the very aspects of high culture it claims kinship with." The repetition, nearly a half century later, of a position that even in its moment smacked of snobbery and elitism demonstrates the surprising persistence of this rhetoric and this logic, its continued appeal to those who wish to police the boundaries of culture.

The language of "corruption" points to an unargued and, indeed, self-evident truism: art, or "genuine" culture, is pure and authentic, its purity and its authenticity secured by its distance from commercial culture and the marketplace. As Andreas Huyssen pointed out many years ago, the desire to partition art from mass culture is always also a desire to protect the masculine from contamination by the feminine. Further, such critiques of a feminizing consumer culture always flirt with elitism; invested in hierarchy, in arguing for the superiority of one form of culture over another, this anti-consumerism can often perpetuate class and racial, as well as gender, divisions. John Fiske, in his influential "Popular Discrimination," argued that evaluations of cultural forms slip easily into evaluations of the subjects who appreciate and consume those forms: "The concept of critical discrimination has always contained, however repressed, a dimension of social discrimination" (103). "Low culture" easily and seamlessly morphs into "low class," and cultural critics, thus, can fall into the elitism of the "Kill Your TV" variety. Worse, the often palpable hostility toward the forms and practices of consumer culture comes uncomfortably close to a hostility toward those persons who do not know the difference between high and low, or who come to embody various inappropriate forms of consumption.

The stance Goldberger and other critics of consumerism take is an essentially modernist one that positions the elite (male) artist against the feminized mass, and carries with it a depressingly familiar set of assumptions that seemed stubbornly to persist into the end of the twentieth century. As Joseph Heath and Andrew Potter have pointed out in their *Nation of Rebels,* many late-twentieth-century critiques of consumer culture recycle the mid-century critique of mass culture that worried about the damage to individualism done by conformity and so enshrined "rebellion" as the mark of authenticity. But, as any late-twentieth-century commentator would surely realize, the distinction between conformity and rebellion—and, more important, the equation of rebellion with anti-consumerism—has always been an illusion; as Heath and Potter argue, consumer culture has actually been fueled more by rebellion than by conformity (98–99).

The oppositions between mass and elite culture, between conformity and rebellion, between the marketplace and the uncommodified realm of art are all conventional, highly constructed, and ideological. That these are gendered oppositions does not concern Heath and Potter, but their choice of the two films *American Beauty* and *Fight Club* to exemplify this form of critique suggests pretty forcefully that the "crisis" of consumerism so happily decried by so many generations of rebellious scholars and culture makers is also and always a crisis of masculinity. And while it is clear that "authenticity" itself has long been commercialized and commodified, used in countless advertising (and political) campaigns, that does not mean that the fantasy of finding and securing authenticity has been delegitimated or abandoned. On the contrary, the greater the perceived threat to authenticity, the more pervasive and compelling the fantasy becomes. I call the search for authenticity a "fantasy" not because I want to chide anti-consumerist critics for naively believing in the possibility of authenticity in a world in which authenticity itself has been thoroughly commodified, but in order to underline the psychological pull of the concept of authenticity. Fantasies of authenticity operate as a protest against consumerism, but a protest that is becoming increasingly difficult to sustain.

The title *Authenticity Guaranteed* is meant to underline this difficulty and to describe both a persistent narrative within anti-consumerist discourses *and* that narrative's ironic relation to the consumer culture against which it protests. Within American culture, authenticity is "guaranteed" by the expression of a masculinity that positions itself against consumer culture and its feminizations—and, indeed, against any and all social systems imagined to impinge on the true expression of a (masculine) individualism. At the same time, "authenticity guaranteed" is a promise proffered not only by American ideologies of individualism and exceptionalism but also by the very consumer culture against which the authentic individual positions himself. At once a philosophical stance and a commercial come-on, "authenticity guaranteed" expresses a number of ironies within anti-consumerist rhetoric and discourses. The very existence of this irony makes the masculine protest against perceived threats to authenticity the more urgent, if also the more futile.

Although anti-consumerism is articulated from both the Left and the Right, my focus in this book is on the dominance of a certain left-liberal anti-consumerism that repeats, in different historical moments, a narrative about the feminizing effects of consumer culture, a narrative that has the effect of naturalizing the association of masculinity with authenticity. Critiques of consumerism from the Right and from religious conservatives tend to bemoan the narcissism of consumerist values and the materialism that distracts Americans and forces us to focus on the body and the self instead of the soul or some higher power. And while, increasingly, such critiques focus more on men than on women, as if men are being "feminized" through pursuing the vanities that women have always pursued, they do not typically position those who articulate anti-consumerist critique as rebellious or as rising above the more consumerist masses. Anti-consumerist rhetoric from the Left, in contrast, tends to draw attention to the subjects who rebel, resist, or define themselves against consumer culture even as they challenge the consumerist system itself. Even when articulated from within leftist or vanguardist paradigms, an anti-consumerism that invests in the hip and the cool often codes as "feminine" the forces against which a masculine rebellion unfolds.

Feminist critics have often pointed out the gender blind spots in progressive cultural studies. Lori Merish, for example, suggests that much scholarly anti-consumerist analysis "has been sexist and moralistic, informed as often by residual theological values as by a progressive political agenda. The extent to which critiques of consumerism have constituted a gendered discourse is itself telling, suggesting the inextricability of the discursive production of gender from discourses of consumption" (7). Building on Tania Modleski's important *Feminism without Women*, Susan Fraiman, in *Cool Men and the Second Sex*, analyzes the "gender exclusivity and the ideological incoherence of coolness as a mode of rebellion" (xv). Fraiman challenges the "cool men" who have earned reputations for progressive thinking, even while reproducing "rotten gender" paradigms (xvii). Taking particular aim at Andrew Ross, "bad boy" par excellence, Fraiman suggests that certain high-profile male critical rebels implicitly construct the "feminine" (and particularly the maternal) as the ground from which their critique is launched. Fraiman reads in Ross and others the "genderizing of class" and the "moralizing of gender" that poses a "heroic, masculinized working class against a corrupt, feminized middle class" (65), with the latter made to signify the threat to male rebellions against convention. This feminized middle class is imagined as in league with corporate, consumerist interests—as in Ross's effort to differentiate the "manly" sport of soccer from its "feminization by U.S. corporate" sponsors (xix), a "feminization" not unrelated to the fact that U.S. soccer includes women as well as men. Fraiman argues that narratives aiming to differentiate "good" from "bad" forms of entertainment and consumption often reveal a desire to safeguard for the masculine something like a "pure" space in which an authentic politics can unfold. "What troubles me," she writes, "is the way righteousness, rebellion, and athletic integrity are tied by this argument to an emphatically all-male sport, while domestication, gentrification, and commercialization are linked to the coeducated game presided over by the United States" (63–64).[1]

Why does a critique of the commercialization of an American sport need to draw support from an ideology of gender difference? What is gained by creating a signifying chain that links masculinity, rebellion, integrity, and class consciousness, on the one hand, and femininity, conformity, domestication, and commercialization, on the other? It will be my argument here that anti-consumerist rhetoric is fueled as much by a deep resistance to women and femininity as it is by a resistance to consumer culture and that the fantasy of authenticity betrayed by such rhetoric depends on an association of women with conformity, the consumerist "system," and other social forces that aim to limit the expression of male autonomy and individuality. Further, the conceptualization of femininity at the heart of anti-consumerist discourse is itself a construction of that discourse rather than some prediscursive, material "real." In fact, I will argue that anti-consumerist rhetoric depends on this constructed femininity as a prop for the elaboration of a masculine self whose authenticity is threatened by both the proximity to femininity and the feminizing forces of consumer culture.

This anti-consumerist narrative is so persistent that intellectuals, scholars, cultural commentators, novelists, movie critics, and media pundits do not feel the need to offer any *evidence* in support of their claims that consumer culture destroys authenticity, autonomy, and individualism. This view of consumerism, firmly entrenched in American thinking through the mid-century critique of "mass man" and "mass society," is everywhere assumed and rarely argued. In a recent book challenging the "commodification thesis," Colin C. Williams makes an argument similar to the one I will make here and demonstrates that the widespread belief that the world and its cultures are becoming ever more commodified is understood as such "an irrefutable and indisputable fact" that no thinker or writer even feels it necessary to argue its relevance and accuracy. Williams is not suggesting that commodification does not exist within capitalism, but he is questioning the "common-sense understanding . . . that the colonization of daily life by the market is so ubiquitous and obvious that no corroboration is required" (2). Calling the commodification thesis a "meta-narrative," Williams notes that it dominates thinking on both the Left and the Right; commodification is both lamented and celebrated; it is seen as both constructed and natural; and the commodification thesis unites neoliberal thinking and Marxist critique of that thinking. Williams concludes that there is little evidence to support a "linear and unidimensional" narrative about the inevitable movement toward increasing commodification (of work and of life) and, further, questions the logic by which "'non-capitalist' activities have been caricatured as a weak, primitive, traditional, stagnant, marginal and residual sphere that is dwindling and disappearing as the commodified realm becomes more powerful, pervasive, victorious, expansive, hegemonic and totalizing" (268–69). Although Williams is not pursuing the kind of rhetorical analysis I am undertaking here—he is not so much interested in how the meaning of commodification has been produced and reproduced through the use of language and imagery—his book does suggest that certain touchstones in late-twentieth-century economic and political theory and practice have for too long been granted the status of meta-narratives. Here, I will argue that anti-consumerism and the feminization thesis on which it depends have become just such a meta-narrative.

Central to this meta-narrative is the a priori belief that consumerism is not a social or public realm in the same way that production is and that consumption cannot itself be an active, productive form of agency. Daniel Miller frames his work on material culture (much of which focuses on shopping as cultural practice and social relation) by pointing to the "academic trends which have led to an overwhelming concentration on the area of production as the key generative arena for the emergence of the dominant social relations in contemporary societies, and a comparative neglect of consumption, together with a concomitant failure to observe the actual changes which have taken place over the last century in the balance of influence between these two forms of interactions with goods" (*Material Culture* 3). As Miller goes on to suggest, this bias toward production as the only important arena of social relations has the function not only of trivializing consumption but also of imagining consumption as false and inauthentic, based in illusions and manipulations. Likewise, Mica Nava has argued that "consumerism does not simply mirror production" and warns against the common assumption that all consumer practices mean the same thing. "Consumerism is a discourse," she writes, "through which disciplinary power is both exercised and contested. While not negating its relation to capitalism, we must refuse to return it always to questions of production" (168). My work in this book builds on these critiques, expanding them into the literary field and also challenging the claims of anti-consumerist discourse by subjecting its language, narrative structures, and underlying assumptions to a feminist rhetorical analysis.

In some ways, the heyday of rebellious anti-consumerism has passed, as consumer culture has grown both more concentrated and more diffuse— and with it the potential ways that individuals and collectives can both accept and resist the pleasures on offer and the disciplinary regimes such pleasures serve. Although this book traces a surprisingly consistent narrative about the dangers consumer culture poses to masculine authenticity on the level of the individual, and to American authenticity on the level of the cultural, this does not mean that other narratives seeking to challenge the dominance of consumer logics in twentieth-century life are not possible. But the logic that poses commercialization and feminization against authenticity and masculinity has been naturalized to the point that we no longer even see it working, no longer even see the subtle valuation of the masculine over the feminine it underwrites. This valuation is as complex as it is subtle, and it can be seen in conceptualizations of the individual in isolation from, and in tension with, the social; in the celebration of male rebellion and the linkage of conformity with women and femininity; and in the equation of authenticity with a set of values that has, historically and contemporaneously, been tied to the masculine.

The anti-consumerism I am tracking is a discourse, and it can appear in both fictional and nonfictional texts. My interest in anti-consumerism as a discourse is fueled by my conviction that the language in which we articulate cultural critique, and the narratives we construct to articulate the distinctions on which that critique is based, are the vehicles through which we create worldviews that have consequences in material terms. Reproducing the gender meanings that come along with the idea that consumer culture is feminizing means more than assenting to the cultural truth that women are consumers, while men are producers; it is also to consent to the idea that femininity endangers something, that the objects, practices, and identities that are associated with women are, by definition, at odds with what is real, true, and authentic in American culture. I want to make a distinction between anti-consumerist discourses that are focused primarily on *complaining* about the dominance of consumerism as an ideology and consumer activism as a practice aiming to expose harmful effects of specific products, unethical practices of the corporations, and the failures of government to properly regulate the consumer sphere and to protect the environment. Anti-consumerist discourse sometimes engages in consumer activism, but its agenda is often a thorough delegitimation of consumerism. Some forms of consumer activism are tempted by the rhetoric of masculine protest, however, and consumer activism can, at times, appear to be less about changing patterns of consumption, labor, and profit and more about securing a moral high ground for those who challenge those patterns. The theory and practice of "culture jamming," broadly conceived, is a case in point.

"Culture jamming" refers to a set of cultural practices that emerged in the 1990s as a response to media monopoly, the ubiquity of advertising, and the increasing presence of consumerism in every aspect of life. Its practitioners aimed to "jam" the system through guerrilla tactics of subversion—the most famous of which, perhaps, was the "revision" of Camel cigarette billboards to feature "Joe Cancer" instead of "Joe Camel." The early culture jammers positioned themselves as heroic outsiders who, in the words of Mark Dery's influential pamphlet, aimed to "hack, slash, and snipe" in the "Empire of Signs." As Dery reflected more than twenty years later, early culture jammers hovered on the edge of a "crankypants elitism and gloomy declinism" and could often sound like "vanguardist snobs whose disdain for the masses, so easily gulled by the hidden persuaders and subliminal seducers of Madison Avenue and Hollywood, was equaled only by their obliviousness to the conundrum at the heart of their argument: namely, if the media pulled the wool over our eyes, how had *they* managed to spy out the truth?" (foreword to *Culture Jamming* xi).

More recent practices have challenged this us-versus-them narrative, in part because network cultures have blurred the lines between producers and consumers and allowed for more participatory, less purely oppositional, forms of cultural engagement and critique. As a recent volume of essays on newer forms of culture jamming makes clear, the purely negative posturing of the early activists and artists has given way to more positivist modes of engagement and resistance. Henry Jenkins suggests "cultural acupuncture" as an updated version of culture jamming, arguing that while the early culture jammers were "antitechnological, seeking the authenticity of wheat paste and spray paint over the slick, corporate imagery associated with television" (133), cultural acupuncturists have developed new models of "attention-based activism" that eschew the knee-jerk anti-consumerist posturing that marks such organs as *Adbusters*. Jenkins discusses the Harry Potter Alliance (HPA),[2] an online community group composed of Harry Potter fans whose love for the series could be harnessed for activism. After many years of effort, the group succeeded in getting Warner Brothers to use only fair-trade chocolate for its widely marketed "chocolate frogs" and, thus, to do their small part in intervening in the use of child slave labor in West Africa. The campaign, titled "Not in Harry's Name," is distinguishable from the earlier culture jams in its embrace of the materials, methods, and tools of consumer culture; as Jenkins explains, HPA members are "still acting as fans even as they are also acting as activists" (146). While anti-consumerist purists have been known to criticize "fan activism" as "doing nothing more than fighting for their right to consume" (147), Jenkins points out that activism within consumption, fighting wrongs through an embrace of consumer culture, *is* political activism, rather than a lesser consumer-based version of it. Fan activism, like "commodity activism," does not depend on a clear separation between insiders and outsiders, between those who fight against consumerism and those who embrace it. Both are, perhaps, instantiations of neoliberalism, but both also offer the possibility of "new theoretical frameworks that refuse the traditional and nostalgic binaries that position politics in opposition to consumerism" (Mukherjee and Banet-Weiser 13).

In recent years, it has become standard within critical theory and cultural studies to identify as "neoliberal" the various forces that have caused a shift in both conceptualizations of the self and the role of the state. Neoliberalism is understood, to refer back to Colin Williams, as the "commodification of everything." Among the key premises of neoliberalism are the marketization of the liberal state, the commodification of the self, and the belief that consumption best provides freedom, citizenship rights, and human well-being. Much persuasive work has been done to elaborate on these concepts and to expose the corporate interests that quite literally fund this neoliberal order, and the scholars who are doing this work are enabling us to see just what is at stake in neoliberalism, particularly for the most vulnerable populations and for the future of the planet. But in some ways, critiques of neoliberal logics have become a new mode of anti-consumerism, complete with new fantasies of authenticity, and this twenty-first-century anti-consumerism can sometimes unproblematically import with it a gendered rhetoric and a cultural elitism that link it with the older anti-consumerism that began to take hold in the mid-twentieth century.

Brenda Weber's discussion of the shift from the "self-made man" to the "self-made*over* man" nicely encapsulates how an earlier form of anti-consumerism has morphed into an anti-neoliberalism that shares many of its premises. What Weber refers to as the "Makeover Mission" is a form of neoliberal rationality that functions to *feminize* the subject in both overt and covert ways, interpellating its subjects as engaged in a regime of "self-care," self-improvement, beautification—all performed for an "audience," not only of television viewers but also of others to whom the subject looks for support, encouragement, and approval. In language that echoes Susan Faludi's analysis of how celebrity culture or "ornamental" culture has turned erstwhile autonomous, rugged, hardworking men into men whose primary work and value are found in presenting the self as a commodity on the open market, Weber's account of men ensnared in the "Makeover Machine" details how these television shows "import neoliberal ideologies, which position the subject as an entrepreneur of the self" (39), placing men in a feminized position as the object of a judging gaze. But Weber also details how the shows' narrative and rhetorical strategies actively work to mitigate this positioning and to maintain a binary conceptualization of gender—such as allowing men to actively resist the ministrations of their makeover "gurus." "Neoliberalism," like "consumerism," can be conceptualized as an almost anthropomorphic force, a suprahuman agent that overcomes and replaces what often seem like more "authentic" forces—a politics free from consumer culture, for example, or a noncommodified form of selfhood.

It is an article of faith in much work on neoliberal logics, particularly as manifested in popular culture, that neoliberalism marks a decline, if not the destruction, of something more authentic and authentically political. Within this work, the commodified self or consumer-mediated forms of expression and political activism are, by definition, false or fake, and the argument need not be made for why or how this is so. Scholars use the modifiers "commodified" and "consumer" as a shorthand for "bad" or "deluded"—in much the same way as mid-twentieth-century critics of consumer culture demonized the "masses" as passive dupes. Neoliberalism is consumer culture on steroids—the market "infecting" all aspects of human life and activity—and the new habit of explaining everything wrong with the world through reference to neoliberalism has produced a new master narrative whose authority rivals the authority of the old master narrative about mass culture, mass man, and the decline of authenticity. Within these master narratives, forms of cultural dissent and activism are evaluated as real or false, effective or co-opting, depending on their relation to commodities and to consumer practices.

Nowhere is this more evident than in recent work on postfeminism in the mass media and popular culture, where the governing assumption is that "commodity feminism"—marked by the appropriation of "real" feminism by a popular, consumerist culture that aims to understand female empowerment as the result of consumer and lifestyle choices—is inauthentic and politically ineffective. "Postfeminist culture," one account claims, "works in part to incorporate, assume, or naturalize aspects of feminism; crucially, it also works to commodify feminism via the figure of the woman as empowered consumer" (Tasker and Negra 2). While there is ample evidence that a popular feminism that embraces consumer culture can be seen in many places—the "chick lit" genre to which the *Shopaholic* books belong is one example—there is a whiff of the kind of "Kill Your TV" elitism evident in some of these critiques. In addition, accounts of postfeminism as commodity feminism draw on the pervasively self-evident claim that the "real" is always endangered by consumer mediation; often, just repeating the terms *consumption, commodified,* and *consumerist* substitutes for evidence-based arguments because, of course, once you grant that consumer culture does not offer "real" empowerment, it is no longer necessary to open up consumerism (or, for that matter, empowerment) to critical analysis.

Further, analyses of postfeminism encounter some of the problems posed by feminist engagement with postmodernism: If, as Linda Hutcheon asked many years ago, postmodern feminist practices both install and subvert male dominance, how can we tell the difference? In their introduction to the volume *Interrogating Postfeminism,* Yvonne Tasker and Diane Negra struggle over the question of whether we can always tell the difference between "feminist *politics*" and "postfeminist *culture,*" an opposition that they uphold even while warming against an "either-or" approach to the texts of popular culture. Although they grant that the "images and icons of postfeminism *are* compelling" and "the women and girls who (literally) buy into this visual and narrational repertoire are not merely dupes" (21; emphases in the original), that phrase "(literally) buy into" undercuts the attempt to treat postfeminism as a real form of feminism. To say that "as an idiom, postfeminism popularizes (as much as it caricatures) a feminism it simultaneously evokes and rejects" (21) is to raise, but also to avoid answering, the question of agency. Does "postfeminism" take over agency from the women and girls who find commodity feminism empowering? Do these women and girls themselves evoke and reject feminism because postfeminism tells them to do so? From what position can feminist media critics evaluate whether women and girls are the "dupes" of a postfeminist, neoliberal order? And can we do so without further institutionalizing a series of oppositions between masculine and feminine, authentic and inauthentic, political and commodified?

I raise these questions here not to chide the many interesting treatments of postfeminism in popular culture, but to insist that, despite the progressive or feminist intentions of these critiques of commodity feminism, it is easy to fall into the habit of assuming as always already established the idea that consumerism or commodification *necessarily* endangers political resistance. This habit, as I will argue throughout this book, carries residual traces of a historically consistent association of consumer culture and the consumer subject with the feminine and of commodifying or consumer practices with feminization. To be clear, one of the effects of anti-consumerist discourse, even of the feminist kind, is to further entrench a deeply gendered system of meaning from which the denigration of the feminine cannot be disentangled. In an effort to respond to the ways in which consumer culture has purportedly eroded individual autonomy and authenticity by valuing the material over the abstract, anti-consumerist discourses turn to a structure of gender as a stabilizing force. Because anti-consumerist discourses rarely define in any concrete terms what has been lost through consumerism, the concepts of "authenticity" and "individual autonomy" get their meaning primarily through reference to other systems of meaning, particularly systems of gendered meaning.

One of the surprising things I have discovered as I worked on this project is that critiques of consumerism are unusually *invested* critiques. When Dwight MacDonald criticized what he saw as the corruption of culture produced when literature is dominated by commercial aspirations, he seemed so angry, so insulted, so personally offended. The same can be said for Goldberger's essay fifty years later. What is it about consumer culture that provokes such a seemingly unreasonable response? When writers lament the loss of authenticity they imagine as the result of commercialization and of the dissolution of cultural hierarchy, what exactly are they lamenting? Where does this emotion come from? The hostility, anger, protest, sarcasm, self-righteousness, and haughtiness marking this set of discourses seem to point to a deep reservoir of resentment from which so many anti-consumerist critiques draw their energy and force. That resentment might be explicitly directed against the economic structures and practices of corporations and the dominance of consumer logics, but the very excessiveness of the responses suggests a more personal investment in positioning oneself against consumer culture. It is for this reason that I use the term *anti*-consumerism to describe the discourses I am attending to; it is a posture that draws strength and emotional force from being *against* something. That "something" too often turns out to be the feminine, women, and the "masses." The anti-consumerism I analyze here is best understood as an emotional masculine protest against all those forces, practices, and products that are perceived to threaten authenticity, autonomy, and individuality. Protests against feminization are saturated with a righteous indignation at the broken promise of an "authenticity guaranteed."

Because I am interested in how a particular anti-consumerist narrative dominates American thinking about consumer culture, I draw more heavily on critical reception of the texts the argument is built on than is perhaps usual in a book of this nature. When making the argument for the existence and influence of a master narrative, it is necessary to show how that dominant story makes other stories illegible. In some instances, I argue that critical response to a particular text, such as *Fight Club,* for example, follows pretty closely the text's own position on consumer culture. In other instances, as in my reading of critical reception of DeLillo's *White Noise,* I suggest that in reproducing a dominant narrative about postmodern consumer culture, critics actually miss some important things going on in that novel. My strategy is to read against the grain, to unearth alternative narratives and alternative interpretations—not to prove that other readings are "wrong," but to demonstrate that our allegiance to the master narrative about consumer culture makes it difficult, if not impossible, to see other possibilities. In addition, like Williams's insistence that the commodification thesis be subjected to evidentiary scrutiny, I put pressure on critical reception of these texts (as well as the texts themselves) to see whether there is adequate evidence to support the commonsense and apparently self-evident proposition that consumer culture feminizes American citizens and American culture, that consumer culture distances us from authenticity, that it is possible and even necessary to distinguish between genuine emotions, experiences, and values and false emotions, experiences, and values. Everyone, from the Left and the Right, feels comfortable rejecting consumerism; even certain apologists for capitalism can reap a moral dividend from differentiating "crass consumerism" from free-market capitalism, as, for example, William Irwin does in a book with the head-scratching title *Free Market Existentialist: Capitalism without Consumerism.*

I begin, in the first chapter, by situating the project in relation to the "feminization thesis" that dominates much American anti-consumerist discourse. I argue that anti-consumerist critique betrays an elitist desire to differentiate between heroic rebels against consumer culture and passive conformists to it. The chapter also lays out the logic through which "authenticity" is imagined to be threatened by consumer culture. My focus is on arguments about popular culture that mobilize "authenticity" as a way to differentiate between higher and lower forms of culture and between savvy and naive producers and consumers of those forms. Arguments about how consumer culture "co-opts" artistic forms and robs them of their political or aesthetic value are plagued by confusions over what constitutes agency in the relations among producers, consumers, and the industries that intervene between them. Like the feminization thesis, what we might call the authenticity thesis—as it emerges in the later decades of the twentieth century, particularly in relation to countercultural practices—relies on a set of unexamined assumptions and, somewhat oddly, retains the mid-century critique of mass culture as its frame. The quest for authenticity in popular culture also expands into the literary field, and I end the chapter by analyzing how fantasies of authenticity play out in the nonfiction writings of two literary figures who have become somewhat notorious as critics of consumer culture, Jonathan Franzen and David Foster Wallace.

The surprising persistence of the mid-century critique of mass culture and "mass man" well past the 1950s calls out for a return to that critique, and in the second chapter I focus on the popular and immensely influential critiques of the damage done to an authentic (masculine) individualism by the rise of the "organization" and suburbia and the mandate to conform to the group inhabiting those spaces. I begin by analyzing how William Whyte's *Organization Man* and David Riesman's *The Lonely Crowd* naturalize competitive individualism and the gender ideology it perpetuates in their efforts to describe new "types" of American citizens and new norms of American behavior. These texts launch a masculine protest against the "feminizing" forces of consumerism, the bureaucratic workplace, new business models and practices, and the rise of suburbia. Further, these highly popular and influential books set the terms for a cultural critique that is still dominant. In the process, they naturalize an equation of masculinity with national identity and demonize as feminine or feminizing any social practices that threaten the imagined freedom of the liberal individual. I then turn to two iconic mid-century texts, J. D. Salinger's *The Catcher in the Rye* and Jack Kerouac's *On the Road*. I read Salinger's text as participating in the masculine protest against the perceived loss of authenticity, individuality, and autonomy; like the critiques in Whyte and Riesman, Holden Caulfield's laments target the "feminizations" required by conformity to the group and an acceptance of the commodified self. These themes are repeated in Kerouac's *On the Road,* which reveals an investment in reclaiming a paradoxically traditional masculine autonomy and authenticity in resistance to the forces of conformity and normativity. Here, "authenticity" names a fantasy of masculine freedom from any and all feminizing social constraints. But despite the fact that the text has very little to say about consumerism, critics of the novel have assimilated it to the anti-consumerist narrative. The canonization of the novel as an anti-consumerist classic demonstrates the dominance of this master narrative and the temptation to read any form of rebellion as rebellion against consumerism.

Anxieties over the waning of authenticity were resurgent in the 1980s, and in the next chapter I analyze the critique of mass media and consumerism launched under the banner of "postmodernism." Using Don DeLillo's *White Noise* and critical response to it as my main case study in this chapter, I argue that the version of postmodernism read in this prolific novelist's work has been used to support a "master narrative" of crisis that itself reproduces some of the same oppositions that were supposed to have gone the way of the delegitimated master narratives: active-passive, intellectual-bodily, high culture–mass culture, abstract-material. This mode of reading postmodernism, consumerism, and DeLillo betrays a nostalgia for a fantasized modernism marked by a clear separation of literature from mass culture, aesthetics from consumer practices, reading from shopping, and masculinity from the feminizing forces that threaten autonomy, authenticity, and meaning. Here, as in the following chapters, shopping and the female (or feminized) shopper bear a host of anxieties around the perceived loss of authenticity and individualism through the increasing dominance of consumerism in American life.

Nowhere is the moral dimension of anti-consumerism so evident than in the scores of narratives that take as self-evident the "fact" that shopping is a "false" form of sociality and shoppers the passive dupes of the consumer system. In order to counter these narratives that are entrenched within literary criticism and in American cultural criticism more broadly, I use histories of shopping as material practice to reopen the question of what constitutes consumer citizenship. After complicating the standard reading of DeLillo (and of postmodernism), I turn to a writer widely thought to be an heir of the DeLillo tradition of postmodernism, now understood as something like "post-postmodernism": Jonathan Franzen. Franzen positions himself against a false and feminizing consumer culture, but does so ambivalently, anxious to avoid the appearance of elitism. In doing so, he unwittingly exposes the blind spots in a version of cultural critique that, while appearing to espouse democratic principles and American multi-culturalism, actually makes the case for shoring up the boundary between authentic culture and mass culture and between authentic masculine selves and those feminine selves benighted by their participation in consumer culture.

Shopping also functions as a prime source of inauthenticity in the texts I read in chapter 4, two films from the 1990s that popularized the so-called crisis in masculinity. These films draw heavily on mid-century mass-culture critique and insist that consumer culture feminizes men and America. Raising the alarm against feminization, these films are less concerned with offering a serious critique of contemporary social and economic systems and more interested in reproducing a mythic narrative about the antagonism between a feminized society and an always endangered masculine individual. Using the wildly controversial film *Fight Club* and the much-admired *American Beauty* as case studies, I analyze how these late-twentieth-century representations of cultural crisis repackage an ahistorical narrative whose explanatory power is severely compromised by its gender and class politics. *Fight Club*'s articulation of its anti-capitalist rebellion as a fight against feminization not only relies on and perpetuates a stable transhistorical idea of gender difference but also imagines contemporary social realities as serving the needs of women at the expense of men. Shopping and shoppers are the villains in an anti-consumerist narrative that nostalgically looks back to a fantasized pre-modern moment before masculine individualism, autonomy, and authenticity were endangered by consumer culture and the women it imagines to be in league with it. *American Beauty* also represents a masculine authenticity endangered by women and the feminizing forces of consumer culture, but it more fully dehistoricizes the contemporary moment through aesthetic means and is primarily interested in the personal rather than the social or political.

Anti-consumerist discourse tends to flounder on the question of agency, particularly political but also artistic agency. When shoppers are read as the passive dupes of a system who, unwittingly, perpetuate that system and enact the damage it does to individuality and authenticity, the question of intentionality or will is often left unspoken. The idea that shopping could itself be a form of agency has typically been understood, if at all, as further evidence of the decline of the authentic in contemporary culture. But the rise of "ethical" consumption along with the emergence of new moral and psychological explanations of how consumerism shapes the self offer possibly new ways of understanding the relations among producers, consumers, corporations—as well as new ways of understanding compliance and resistance.

In the fifth chapter, I analyze texts that offer both old and new ways of thinking about these questions: Naomi Klein's *No Logo,* Judith Levine's *Not*

Buying It: My Year without Shopping, and Sophie Kinsella's *Shopaholic* series. Against the backdrop of new forms of what I'm calling "consumerist anti-consumerism," I investigate how these three texts negotiate questions of agency, authenticity, compliance, and resistance. Klein's book, despite its good intentions, ends up reproducing the feminization thesis by swearing allegiance to an account of agency rooted in what feminist theorists have identified as a "masculine" concept of the subject. She also betrays a familiar nostalgia for a modernist construction of the artist poised in rebellion against consumer culture and the masses. The moralism and elitism implicit in Klein's book are an explicit focus of Levine's, and my reading of it foregrounds the differences between a masculinist rebellion against consumer culture and a more complex resistance to it. Levine also meditates on the idea of guilty pleasure—not, as Klein does, to produce guilt in those who seek consumer pleasures but to challenge the moralism behind the very idea of guilty pleasure. The *Shopaholic* series, by British "chick lit" author Sophie Kinsella, offers a somewhat surprising defense of the female pleasures of shopping.[3] *Shopaholic* short-circuits the logic of "addiction" that places shopping within a moral narrative about the proper management of female desire. While Kinsella's novels might seem to support the feminization thesis—by focusing on a woman who embodies the worst fears of the anti-consumerist critics I analyze throughout the book—they actually imagine a way out of this moralistic discourse and unabashedly explore the pleasures of consumption as a positive expression of female agency rather than a threat to individualism and authenticity.

The fact that *No Logo* reproduces, albeit in updated form, a posture on consumer culture that has been dominant since mid-century suggests the stubborn hold this anti-consumerism exerts over cultural critique. The wide range of discourses that celebrate a masculine rebellion against the feminizing effects of large systems has worked to limit the forms that countercultural critique can take. Feminist attempts to shift the terms of New Left critique away from a focus on masculinity and authenticity are a case in point. As David Rossinow argues in *The Politics of Authenticity,* feminists aiming to influence the terms of countercultural critique in the sixties came up against "the whole tradition of existentialist politics that had developed throughout the cold war period. The longing for an authentic masculinity was one of that tradition's pillars. Men who pursued authenticity in the realm of politics had, explicitly and repeatedly, equated a strenuous sense of self and a vigorous citizenship with masculinity, just as they equated alienation with emasculation" (16). There is a circular logic here, through which authenticity guarantees masculinity and masculinity guarantees authenticity. Countercultural rebellion of this type, thus, defines the "political" as a genuine expression of the "vigorous self" and imagines any threat to that self as emasculating, feminizing, and inauthentically political. Rossinow concludes that "because not enough radical men wanted to join a left not built on the pursuit of masculinity . . . . feminists discovered one of the limits of the American culture of dissent" (18). While he is more interested in analyzing the existentialist character of the rebellion that did happen, I want to highlight the importance of the rebellion that did *not* happen. The "limits of the American culture of dissent" are the limits of gender—or, rather, the inability of countercultural critique to get beyond a narrative about feminization or emasculation. The tradition of masculine protest has produced a national mode of dissent that is impoverished, perhaps most strikingly by its inability to shift its own terms and to imagine new narratives of dissent and countercultural critique.

Anti-consumerist critique need not necessarily enact a cycle of masculine loss and redemption by reproducing a narrative about serial feminizations followed by remasculinizations, and toward the end of the book some alternatives to this narrative will emerge. However, I have found that it's extremely difficult for those who aim to position themselves against consumerism to resist the temptation of claiming for themselves and their political positions a moral superiority that, in my view, ties in pretty neatly with the gendered logics I spend the majority of the book analyzing. For my part, I want to resist positing something like an *authentic* anti-consumerism, one that avoids the logic of feminization and the many unexamined assumptions that underwrite that logic—including the idea that there is an authentic versus faux way to articulate a critique of consumerism and the idea that what is mostly endangered by consumerism is the existence of a true self. As I will argue in the next chapter, concepts of individual and cultural authenticity depend for their meaning on a set of gendered oppositions that it is high time we interrogate. When we diagnose contemporary conditions—calling them neoliberal or postfeminist—we need to be careful not to reproduce these oppositions and the assumptions on which they are based. It is time to question those assumptions and put pressure on the commonsense truth that consumer culture robs "us" of our autonomy, agency, and authenticity, concepts that cannot be separated from masculinity.

CHAPTER 1

FANTASIES OF AUTHENTICITY

Masculinity, Feminization, and
Anti-Consumerist Critique

The cultural elitism that marks the "Kill Your TV" version of anti-consumerism appeals to both men and women, and women, like men, can position themselves as rebels against mass culture and consumerism. But anti-consumerist critique often relies on and perpetuates a gendered discourse about value, identity, and meaning that favors the masculine over the feminine and, more importantly, naturalizes the binary structure of gender itself. Because anti-consumerist critique rests on the assumption that consumer culture is inauthentic and de-individualizing, it must also identify and locate the authentic and the individual. And it is through a symbolics of gender that that identification and location are secured. In this chapter, I consider the "feminization thesis" that has long governed American studies accounts of the dangers consumer culture poses to individualism. Anti-consumerist narratives reserve agency for the producers whose autonomy and authenticity are threatened by a consumerist ethos. Like the notion that consumer culture "feminizes" men and the nation, the notion that consumer culture threatens "authenticity" is everywhere stated, but nowhere argued. Anti-consumerist discourses draw on seemingly self-evident truths in order to make moral arguments about good and bad modes of cultural production and reception; they also reveal problematic assumptions about what kinds of cultural production and reception qualify as authentically "political." No matter what mode of production is the subject of the critique, however, the consumer is, by fiat, deprived of agency. But consumer*ism* is often represented as a collective, sometimes agential, force aiming to influence the reception of cultural products and to potentially undermine hierarchies of taste. Audiences, often coded as feminine, threaten to exert an illegitimate power to determine the value of the artistic or cultural text.

CONSUMER CULTURE AND THE LOGIC OF FEMINIZATION

Narratives about the feminizing effects of consumer culture have a long history in American culture, with both material and symbolic bases. The idea that women are the primary consumers of goods and services has been enshrined in the American imaginary since the birth of advertising.[1] But while the link between women and consumerism might stem from historical, material causes, it has also long worked to naturalize a system of meaning that is more properly ideological: persistent reenactments of the drama of feminization function to reinforce a structure of gender difference. The idea that consumers are helplessly lured into making unnecessary purchases reinforces the symbolic femininity of the consumer. Passive, deprived of individual autonomy, and powerless to resist the seductions of luxury and indulgence, the consumer is the epitome of the "feminine" self against which the masculine self erects its defenses. Those who have worried about the feminizations of consumer culture, and have elaborated the feminization thesis, have focused on how that culture affects men, who come to stand in for the American nation as a whole. Men, in this narrative, are always and only producers, and the authenticity secured by production is always potentially threatened by the entrance of those products into the consumer sphere. Further, men's participation in the consumer sphere endangers constructions of the masculine individual as independent, autonomous, and self-determining: the worry is that men who buy and sell products in the marketplace might themselves become commodities.

Women, on the other hand, are always and only consumers and, thus, occupy the position of threat rather than threatened. Feminist work on women and consumerism has taken a different path from the feminization thesis and has focused on the complex and often contradictory ways that consumerism has functioned as the source of both women's power and women's disempowerment. The rise of consumer culture can be seen to liberate women from the home, and thus could be read as offering a public stage for the exercise of female will, desire, and agency. At the same time, however, that same consumer system manipulates women into literally buying into their own subordination (through the marketing of various products designed to improve female bodies, minds, and lives) and ensures that women, themselves, are commodities to be purchased by men. Domestic ideology attempts to suture over these contradictions by making consumption coterminous with domesticity; witness the iconicity of scores of advertisements featuring aproned (and, later, business-suited) women smiling or grimacing over their kitchen appliances.

But the link between consumerism, women, and domesticity is neither natural nor inevitable; indeed, as the work of numerous scholars makes clear, the masculine consumer has lived a shadow life alongside the feminine consumer. The historian Mark Swiencicki, writing about pre-Depression masculine forms of consumption, notes that the idea of the "consumer as feminine [has] become so entrenched ideologically that little need was felt to fully examine men's role as consumers" and challenges scholars of gender and consumerism to interrogate the "'fact' that women [are] society's main consumers" (794). For every era of American history, scholars have unearthed discourses promoting male consumption and constructing the masculine consumer. While it should come as no surprise that commercial discourses, such as advertising, catalogs, and popular magazines, would understand that women alone could not sustain a consumer system that is as much a part of the public sphere as the private, it is significant that such discourses often explicitly work to differentiate the male consumer from the female and to make men's consumption itself look more like production. Writers intent on "masculinizing" the consumer often did so by "inadvertently tapping into producer categories" (Donohue 41). To differentiate male from female consumers, marketers, advertisers, and magazine editors devised modes of representation that stressed the different motives and meanings of masculine consumption.

For example, while women might be represented as shoppers, men are more often represented either as clients seeking services or as collectors who exercise aesthetic judgment and investment savvy. Joining clubs, getting haircuts, spending money on dinners and sporting events, men have always enjoyed a vigorous regime of consumption, its differing forms having more to do with class than with gender (Swiencicki 774). Because "consumption" tends to get conflated with "shopping" in the literature on gender and consumerism, other, more male-centered, forms of consumption remain hidden,[2] with the female shopper occupying center stage as the icon of the consumer economy. The ideological work performed by the construction of consumerism as feminine and feminizing requires the figure of the female shopper and the evacuation of men from scenes of shopping. When men consume, as they inevitably do, pressure is put on this gendered ideology, and it is fascinating to watch how those who promote and engage in male consumption evade the taint of feminization that attaches to shopping.

One of the key modes of this tricky logic can be discerned in the efforts to portray certain forms of male consumption as *active* operations through which men transform, through physical or cultural labor, the various commodities they acquire. Although writing about another country, Leora Auslander's study of men's collecting in nineteenth-century France offers one particularly intriguing example of how "certain forms of consumption were characterized to make them male and compatible with definitions of masculine individuation and citizenship. . . . Appropriate consumption for bourgeois men was deemed to be highly individual and often authenticity-based, a creative, self-producing, order-making activity—one best enacted in collecting" (85–86). Collecting, and its more elevated cousin connoisseurship, is made into a "manly" form of consumption, as the male connoisseur or collector actively exercises an aesthetic sense to determine the value of things. Differentiated from the shopper who more passively accepts the mass-produced objects that threaten standardization and the loss of individuality, the masculine collector and connoisseur seeks authenticity, exercises creativity, and makes order out of the world of goods. Collecting, unlike merely shopping or buying, is an agential act and, thus, does not threaten the autonomy or authenticity of the masculine self.

Men's magazines have also negotiated the treacherous minefield of men's consumption, and numerous scholars have detailed the ways in which consumption, even domestic consumption, was made safe for men at particular historical moments. When advertisers undertook to entice men to consume particular goods and services, they had to dissolve the gendered meanings of consumerism they, themselves, had helped to engineer in an effort to capture the female consumer. Kenon Breazeale's analysis of *Esquire*'s efforts in the 1930s and '40s to attract the male consumer and to construct him as a virile, desiring, and safely heterosexual target for the magazine's ads provides one example. "Somehow," writes Breazeale, "*Esquire* had to displace all the woman-identified associations so firmly lodged at the center of America's commodified domestic environment" and did so, in part, by the staff writers' "knit[ting] misogynistic cultural threads familiar for decades into a wide-ranging set of assertions about the gendered meanings of good and bad taste" (229–30). The magazine had to engage in a "simultaneous exploitation and denial of the feminine," an effort that, according to Breazeale, resulted in a "kind of hysteria" (232). More disturbingly, perhaps, as Tom Pendergast argues in his analysis of *True,* a magazine published around the same time, worries about the dominance of advertising in men's magazines produced a misogynist backlash through which a "string of complaints against women . . . eventuated in a remarkable antiwoman campaign" (234).[3] What these examples suggest is that issues of gender difference are at the heart of discourses about consumption and that consumer culture has long been a primary arena in which femininity gets differentiated from masculinity.

Even in its heyday, in the late nineteenth century as in the mid-twentieth century, separate-spheres ideology, with its gendered constructions of production and consumption, showed signs of strain in the face of the complexity of economic arrangements. Jealously guarding the masculine independence of the productive public sphere, anti-consumerist discourses must come to terms with the anxieties over a putative feminine dominance of the domestic, consumer-mediated realm as well as the necessity of male consumption to the health of a capitalist economy. Nowhere are the rhetorical gymnastics needed to make consumption safe for men more in evidence than in the discourse around the "bachelor apartment," the "bachelor pad," or the "man cave." Like the editors of *True,* who aimed to make male consumption another form of male dominance, magazines and other media intent on enticing men to consume in order to enhance and masculinize their domestic spaces also must perform some heavy lifting in evading the dangers of feminization.

Not surprisingly, but somewhat paradoxically, men's magazines have drawn on the very gendered production-consumption dichotomy that masculine consumption would seem to disrupt. Like the collector, the subject of the men's magazines' address had to be imagined as an active participant in consumer culture, and his consumption needed to be understood as productive. Katherine Snyder, in work on the bachelor apartment at the turn of the twentieth century, notes how popular discourse about domestic masculinity imagined interior decoration as a *manly* effort in actively producing a domestic space from raw material (268). The "bachelor pad" really comes into its own in the mid-twentieth century when *Playboy* undertakes to reassure men that they can be shoppers, decorators, and domestic agents and still remain fully masculine. As Steven Cohan has observed, "The bachelor pad was not a den of iniquity but a site of consumerism. Historically, the bachelor apartment marked the single man's marginal position within domestic ideology . . . but it also indicated his recuperation as a consumer whose masculinity could be redeemed—even glamorized—by the things that he bought to accessorize his virility" (*Masked Men* 266).

Playboy offered an alternative to a domestic and domesticated masculinity by urging men to express their power and desire through the consumption and display of consumer goods.[4] Implicit in this construction of the male consumer is the linkage between consumerism and sexuality; far from feminizing men, *Playboy*-style consumption actually promises to rehabilitate a masculinity endangered by the "soft" and female-dominated family home. "*Playboy*'s most radical effect on fifties American culture," writes Cohan, "may well have been to encourage married men not to leave their families in defiance of the breadwinner ethic of responsibility, but to go shopping, to purchase all those products associated with the single man's pleasures. The magazine addressed its readers in such a way as to conflate their sexuality, their membership in the professional class, and their tastes as consumers" (*Masked Men* 270). Such a realignment of masculinity away from the breadwinner-producer pole to the lifestyle-consumer pole was bound to produce a great deal of tension in conventional gender ideologies; this "clash of gender codes" is everywhere evident in the pages of *Playboy,* where competing discourses of masculinity struggle over the contemporary meanings of manhood. As Bill Osgerby suggests in his analysis of the magazine, one way that *Playboy*

defused male anxieties both about women being the "queens" of domestic spaces and about men entering those feminized spaces was to "'colo-
nize' the traditionally 'feminine' spaces of commodity consumption on
behalf of men" (129). This formulation provides one lens through which
to view the growth of "lifestyle" culture aimed at men, in which the desire to take over the feminine, anxieties over feminization, and a barely
concealed misogyny are all on display. Tania Modleski suggests that the
envy of women "is in fact concomitant with a fear of feminization, even
though existing in logical contradiction to it, so that male identification
with woman is hedged about with varieties of 'masculine protest'" (78).

For example, current iterations of the masculinized domestic space,
known as the "man cave," are a veritable stew of contradictory ideas about
gender, domesticity, and consumer culture. A recent title in the annals of
the bachelor pad, *The Man Cave Book,* offers an overwhelming gallery of
man caves (nearly eighty) and a discourse that veers toward the hysterical
as it tries to ward off threats of feminization even while quite literally colonizing domestic spaces formerly dominated by women. A cross between
a how-to manual on producing masculine domestic spaces and a paean
to essential sexual differences between men and women, *The Man Cave
Book* features photographs of a wide variety of spaces, interviews with the
men who have constructed them, and an editorial style best described as
retro-sexist. The man cave is explicitly imagined as a space free of women
and women's influence: this is where men can have the things that their
wives will not allow in the rest of the house, where ratty old couches
are welcome, but anything that "can be described as a 'love seat'" should
"be doused with kerosene and lit with a match" (Yost and Wilser 11). It is
also an anti-consumerist space whose architects and inhabitants collect,
scavenge, and "plunder" (26). The following advice to the reader perfectly
exemplifies the book's style and its careful efforts to save heterosexual
masculinity from the taint of the feminine: "Think of yourself as a museum curator. Like a museum, you collect valuable pieces of art, you suggest a donation from your guests (usually in the form of a six-pack), you
treat your collection with respect, and you stop at nothing to improve and
grow. Unlike a museum curator, you've never been stuck in a locker" (23).[5]

Despite efforts to place the male consumer at the center of political
and economic processes at varying moments in history, the links between

consumption and femininity have managed to survive any attempts to "masculinize" consumption for political purposes. While there may be some fluidity in the categories, the opposition between producer and consumer does, in fact, seem to keep surfacing as a primary means of gendering, with consumer culture constructed as feminizing *in order to* safeguard some concept of masculinity as independent of the market and the forces of commodification. Historian Kathleen Donohue concludes that the consumer is valued or devalued *not* because that consumer is masculine or feminine; rather, the consumer is masculine or feminine *because* he or she is valued or devalued. The gendered meanings of consumption are not predetermined by any essential link between gender and consumption or production; instead, "when the consumer was supposed to play a pivotal political role, establishing it as a male identity went a long way toward justifying such a role. And, by the same token, feminizing the consumer helped to justify its marginalization" (40). The work on men and consumption suggests that the feminization thesis is less about helping us understand the place of consumerism in American culture than it is about keeping in place a binary gender order that can be played out in the production-versus-consumption trope as just one discursive mode among many invested in reproducing sexual difference. In addition, discourses invested in supporting the differentiation between the masculine producer and the feminine consumer are also engaged in policing the meaning of individual autonomy and political agency.

Throughout so many historical accounts of gender and consumerism, we can uncover the assumption that production is the site of political and artistic agency, while consumption remains a non-agential act. This logic is so prevalent in histories of American consumer culture that it has become something of a self-evident truth, and it goes beyond the banal construction of production as active and consumption as passive. What is at stake in the feminization thesis is securing the masculinity of the agential self, but, ironically, this security depends on the existence of systemic threats. The "feminine"—embodied by women and by putatively feminizing social systems—is the necessary foil that enables the construction of a rebellious, authentically political masculine agent. Anti-consumerist rhetoric depends on a clear boundary between production and consumption, but anti-consumerist discourses express an anxiety about the blurring of that boundary. To assuage this anxiety, these discourses often work to demarcate the difference between modes of production and consumption that secure agency and modes of production and consumption that endanger it. In this effort, "popular" culture—a consumer-oriented mode of production tied with the feminine—is opposed to "authentic" culture. How to keep audiences from treating serious culture the way they treat popular culture—that is, *consuming* it—is a major problem for those who aim to police the boundaries between production and consumption.

As an example of this logic, we can turn to perhaps the most famous articulation of the "feminization thesis," found in Ann Douglas's *The Feminization of American Culture,* which argues the existence of a "masculine" America threatened, in the mid-nineteenth century, by the forces of a "feminine" sentimentalism in popular literature and religion. This model depends on a number of assumptions, including the assumption that an identifiably "masculine" culture and society existed before sentimentalism and the market for it entered to dilute, displace, or even destroy it, and the assumption that "feminine" modes are disqualified from political agency or even political consciousness. Further, what threatens a fully masculinized conception of America within sentimentalism is the substitution of the artificial and the performative for the *real.* Douglas poses a "genuine" sensibility against the pursuit of publicity:

Sentimentalism, unlike modes of genuine sensibility, never exists except in tandem with failed political consciousness. A relatively recent phenomenon whose appearance is linked with capitalist development, sentimentalism seeks and offers the distraction of sheer publicity. Sentimentalism is a cluster of ostensibly private feelings which always attains public and conspicuous expression. Privacy functions in the rituals of sentimentalism only for the sake of titillation, as a convention to be violated. Involved as it is with the exhibition and commercialization of the self, sentimentalism cannot exist without an audience. It has no content but its own exposure, and it invests exposure with a kind of final significance. (307)

Sentimentalism threatens the authenticity normally secured through freedom from commercialization; it is a product of capitalism and, in its feminizing, publicity-seeking form, works in league with capitalism. In her construction, Douglas stresses sentimentalism's surface ("ostensibly private," "conspicuous"), and we are meant to read its lack of depth; sentimentalism is all about "titillation" and performance for an "audience," "exhibitionism," and "exposure." Sentimentalism masks the *real* and, in particular, substitutes surfaces for depths; it understands the self as performative instead of essential. Worse, that self is not independent or autonomous but instead depends on an audience that, thus, has the power to determine authenticity and value. Worth noting here is also the opposition between effective and "*failed* political consciousness" and the logic that opposes the political to the commercial. Why the political is, a priori, damaged by the commercial is never completely specified; as we will see, the impulse to cordon the political away from the marketplace betrays a nostalgia for an imagined pre-consumerist paradise, a desire to short-circuit certain forms of social critique, and an anxiety about the blurring of gender and other boundaries.

In the introduction to a special issue of the feminist journal *differences* devoted to rethinking the "feminization thesis," Philip Gould argues that Douglas's work further institutionalized an already existing post-war "master narrative" within American studies, a narrative that quite clearly emerged not from within the nineteenth-century texts it was crafted to explain but from the twentieth-century liberal vision that had ruled American studies for decades. The feminization thesis "depended on the dual associations of mass culture with cultural totalitarianism and sentimentality with naïve ideology. Liberal politics, in other words, naturalized a masculine vision of 'American' culture that was perpetually endangered by feminization" (iv); the postwar critic, continues Gould, "feminizes sentimentality to the point of creating a cultural metaphor—indeed, a cultural history—of declension, where an originally masculine *American* political culture has lost its way. Put another way, this is a secular and exclusively masculine jeremiad of postwar American culture" (iv; emphasis in the original). Consumerism plays a major part in that cultural history of declension, and scholars have enthusiastically endorsed the feminization thesis they have found in the texts they analyze. In a certain sense, the attraction of the feminization thesis is *not* the thrill of seeing men and the nation continuously under threat (although one suspects this is operative here, too) but the perpetuation of an entire meaning system that insists on the importance of retaining an us-versus-them, self-versus-other, masculine-versus-feminine logic.

What I would like to suggest, then, is that the *content* of the feminization thesis is far less important than its *function* as a legitimating narrative for an American gender system whose binary logic is put into service as a mode of critique even when the ostensible topic of critique has nothing to do with gender. Discourses, both elite and popular, concerned with the threat of "feminization" function to remind us that femininity is not-masculinity and thus to continuously renaturalize the gender divide. "Masculinity" functions structurally in narratives about cultural decline, rendering the meaning or content of that "masculinity" irrelevant. As long as the logic of the feminization thesis holds sway, it doesn't matter whether "masculinity" means strength, social utility, aggression, moral character, violence, or whatever you like, in the mid-nineteenth century or the early twenty-first. What matters is that "masculinity" signifies the always threatened cultural norm, of meaning and value, and that American culture remains in a perpetual cycle of crisis and resolution. Narratives about "feminization" are governed by a logic that assumes that *any* movement to control men and masculinity, to limit the free expression of "authenticity" and "autonomy," necessarily robs men and masculinity of their power and, by extension, threatens the culture that men are entrusted with ruling. We continue to use the language of feminization not because it best describes how consumer or mass culture functions to create gendered subjects but because it is one particularly powerful way to ensure that gendered subjects continue to be produced at all.

CONSUMER CULTURE, AUTHENTICITY, AND THE GENDER POLITICS OF REBELLION

Anti-consumerist critique tends to rely on often vague terms with which consumerism is compared and found lacking, the most common of which is *authenticity*. Virtually every critique of consumerism I will consider in this book takes as self-evident the "fact" that consumerism endangers authenticity by distancing the consumer, the citizen, and the nation from genuine values. Discussions of authenticity—and, most frequently, the quest for authenticity—suffer from a circular logic: Authenticity is endangered by consumer culture because consumer culture endangers authenticity.[6] And consumerism alienates us from the authentic self because the authentic self is alienated within consumer culture. Authenticity features in anti-consumerist critique as an a priori good that is always under threat, and while a great deal of energy is devoted to detailing that threat, the actual meaning of authenticity remains maddeningly vague. As numerous writers who have undertaken to pin down the meanings of authenticity have found, authenticity is known only by what it is *not.* Jacob Golomb points to how existentialism's classic elaboration of the importance of individual authenticity reveals an "insistence that authenticity is something we are aware of when 'we flee it.'" Authenticity is not a concept with identifiable meaning or substance but is instead a self-evident value that becomes visible only in its absence: "Its presence is discerned in its absence, in the passionate search for it, in inauthenticity and in various acts of 'bad faith' (*mauvais foi*)" (7).[7] The logic here is not unlike the binary logic that has governed both thinking about gender (the feminine is the not-masculine) and about consumerism (consumption is not-production).

The familiarity of this logic works against any new interrogation of what authenticity actually means or of its relationship to consumerism. It is also worth noting that the privileged term in the binary—*authenticity, masculinity, production*—is not subject to the same kind of scrutiny and analysis that marks discourses about the other term; just as, until very recently, masculinity remained opaque while femininity was endlessly analyzed, authenticity enjoys a self-evident value and meaning that belies the fact that authenticity must be continually negotiated and constructed. At the heart of invocations of authenticity is a barely suppressed contradiction: that which is most real and genuine (authenticity) is simultaneously actively and persistently *constructed.* As we will see shortly, authenticity is also relentlessly *marketed* by the very consumer culture that purportedly destroys it.

The quest for authenticity, as most observers note, begins with a romantic desire to express a "true" self not constrained by social convention. From Rousseau to existentialism, the desire to locate a genuine or authentic self free from the requirements of conformity and the demands of the marketplace is, arguably, *the* narrative that underwrites not only constructions of rebellious subjectivity but liberal individualism itself.[8]

The posture of the romantic individual battling the forces of conformity can be traced throughout many discourses and produces an essentially adversarial relationship between the individual and society or the self and social formations. In American terms, this relationship relies on a gendered opposition between the heroic masculine rebel and the feminized and feminizing society against which he struggles. We recognize this narrative in what Nina Baym long ago called "melodramas of beset manhood," in language that, surprisingly, still resonates with cultural representations today. When Huck lights out for the territory, he leaves behind the "civilizing" forces of modernity and seeks out a more "primitive" because pre-modern space for the expression of his true self. While we might be tempted to laugh off this well-worn narrative—boys will be boys—the form of radical individualism it engenders continues to haunt American culture, both in its social formations and in the *critique* of those formations. The quest for an authentic self free from convention, from social determination, is a fantasy that survived into the late twentieth century and one that continues in the twenty-first to inhibit the forms that social critique can take. Marshall Berman points out that the search for authenticity "began with a negative interpretation of the world, but initiated no positive attempt to change it. In this form, as an ethic of disengaged conformity and internal liberation, it passed into the mainstream of Western culture" (xxii). In other words, "the search for authenticity, nearly everywhere we find it in modern times, is bound up with a radical rejection of things as they are" (xix). The obsession with authenticity historically marks a turning inward and away from social engagement.

What Berman points to here is the problem of the radical individualist who, when freed from the rigors of conformity, can secure his authenticity only by turning his back on the social. The "social" means different things in different historical contexts, but in the late twentieth and early twenty-first centuries worries about authenticity increasingly play out in the cultural realm and, in particular, against the backdrop of mass or popular culture. Fantasies of authenticity are evident with increasing frequency within popular culture (and within consumer culture more broadly) and reflect the same desire to differentiate the elite from the mass and the artistic from the commercial, as is evident in the desire to differentiate the popular *from* the authentic. In some versions of this fantasy, recourse to gender allows producers and critics to articulate the difference between the authentic (linked with the masculine) and the inauthentic (linked with the feminine). The authentic cultural producer is figured as a male rebel who battles the forces of "co-optation" and feminization. In other versions, rebellion is not explicitly gendered as masculine, but the underlying construction of individual agency readable in narratives about co-optation and appropriation of the authentic by commercial or corporate forces reproduces the logic of active producer versus passive consumer that, in my view, inevitably raises the specter of gender.

One place that the explicitly gendered fantasy of authenticity can be found is in the discourse around rock and roll and other forms of popular music.[9] Ideas about authentic versus commercial rock music echo modernist constructions of the difference between true art and mass-produced goods.[10] Where the discourse around the authenticity of the self imagines a pure self uncorrupted by the social and free from its determinations, the discourse around the authenticity of cultural expression in rock and roll installs a hierarchy of value that categorizes not only types of popular music but also the audiences for those types. Leerom Medovoi notes that high modernism and rock culture have in common a "masculinist mode of cultural articulation," one that relies on the presence of a feminine difference to secure its authenticity. Rock music, especially in its early days, "shared the misogynistic narrative politics of male modernism in its construction of a villainous feminine Other (mass culture/society) against which it rebels. Like modernism, early (and some later) rock provided a male preserve of masculine heroes whose story is the struggle for authenticity against the ever-present danger of selling out to the feminizing horror of pop" ("Mapping the Rebel Image" 157–58).

The "feminizing horror of pop" construct imagines not only a beleaguered masculine artist struggling against a feminizing marketplace but also a feminine audience intent on consuming, rather than appreciating, the artist and his music. As Keir Keightley suggests, one strategy that music critics utilize to keep in place a gendered hierarchy of musical genres, and to secure the freedom of masculine rock from commercial corruption, is to gender pop as feminine. Rock's "displacement of the 'bad'—the negative and corrupt features of mass society—into pop serves to shore up rock's apparent authenticity and autonomy. However, it also obscures rock's own status as mass-mediated commodity culture" (128). This sleight-of-hand is accomplished, in part, by drawing attention away from the consumption of rock and toward its production. In this way, rock remains linked with (artistic) production, while pop is only ever linked with (mass) consumption (129). The logic here always threatens to unravel, however, as can be seen in an oxymoronic concept that appears in a surprising number of treatments of authenticity: "authentic inauthenticity" (Weisethaunet and Lindberg 473).[11]

It is, of course, highly ironic that "authenticity" has so fully been embraced by the very consumer culture often imagined to endanger it. Such irony is the hallmark of a popular version of postmodernism that lauds the breakdown of cultural boundaries between high and low and challenges the distinction between the real and the simulated. As we will see in chapter 3, this account of postmodernism competes with an account of postmodernism as *decline,* and it is this latter account that inspires some writers to understand postmodernism as ushering in a lamentable flattening of the difference between the authentic and the inauthentic (as well as the difference between the artistic and consumerist). Perhaps not surprisingly, "postmodernism" has been invoked in popular discourses that aim to explain the contemporary landscape of the real and the fake; more surprising, perhaps, is the enthusiastic embrace of postmodernism by theorists of marketing who aim to read philosophical trends for their impact on consumer behavior.

James Gilmore and B. Joseph Pine II, experts on marketing, look to postmodern theorizing to help explain "what consumers really want." Arguing that what consumers really want is "authenticity," Gilmore and Pine offer advice on how to market authenticity in an economy where mass production and simulation rule the day. Gilmore and Pine argue that advertisers and marketers can and should enter the breach created by "the rise of postmodern thought," "our eroding confidence in our major social institutions," and the "emergence of the Experience Economy" to provide consumers with the authenticity they find lacking in everyday life (10–13).[12] These two management consultants whose aim is to help marketers and the corporations they serve improve their consumer profiles share with anti-consumerist, anti-corporate crusaders a common vocabulary tying the waning of authenticity to the rise of postmodernism.

In analyzing the contradictions endemic to a consumer culture that markets mass-produced authenticity, these theorists of the market also demonstrate the naïveté of the opposition between corporate culture and countercultural critique. This last point has been driven home repeatedly in a spate of books and articles that challenge the dominant narrative about how consumer culture has "co-opted" or "appropriated" countercultural critique—and, thus, rendered it inauthentic. This narrative is based on the same seemingly self-evident claim that underwrites the feminization thesis; that is, that consumer culture, the marketplace, and commodification necessarily destroy authenticity and value. This narrative is so deeply entrenched in our thinking about mainstream and counterculture that it does not even have to be argued. In *Nation of Rebels: Why Counterculture Became Consumer Culture,* Joseph Heath and Andrew Potter humorously debunk the foundational notion of a countercultural rebellion speaking out against consumerist conformity and instead argue that the countercultural stance has not been co-opted by consumer culture so much as it has, in fact, *driven* consumer culture since the 1960s. Because "anti-consumerism has become one of the most important cultural forces in millennial North American life," it's difficult to sustain the idea of anti-consumerism as countercultural (98). The 1950s critique of "mass society," which still remains dominant according to Heath and Potter, has erred by identifying consumerism with conformity. Social critics—including academics and popular writers of all political persuasions—have, as a result, "fail[ed] to notice that it is rebellion, not conformity, that has for decades been the driving force of the marketplace" (99).

Heath and Potter chide mid-century anti-consumerist critics and their heirs for oversimplifying the relationship between mainstream and counterculture—and, more to my point here, for ignoring the complicity if not collaboration between a counterculture that is invested in imagining itself "outside" of the dominant order and a corporate culture invested in transforming that dominant order by making outsiders the primary subjects of its address. Anne Elizabeth Moore's *Unmarketable: Brandalism, Copyfighting, Mocketing, and the Erosion of Integrity* energetically enters this fray and provides an interesting example of efforts to salvage "alternative" culture from corporate co-optation. Moore focuses on what she calls a network of "underground" cultural producers who position themselves against the "mainstream" in general and corporate control of culture in particular. These underground producers include zinesters, punk rockers, and various DIYers who, according to Moore, "reclaim the joy inherent in making something by hand" rather than buying it in a heavily marketed, artificially packaged form (11). As one former member of a punk rock group defines it, punk differs from mainstream music because it has "integrity . . . taking an active part in your life rather than being a consumer."[13]

"Integrity" functions in *Unmarketable* like "authenticity" functions in so many treatments of the destruction of art and culture by corporate interests. In Moore's book, it means nothing so much as *not corporate*. But Moore realizes that the binary thinking that poses the underground against the mainstream—and, more particularly, poses authenticity against "selling out"—is too simplistic to account for the complex dynamics she uncovers in her analysis of DIYers' engagements with corporate culture. She confesses that "addressing core issues of integrity directly has always been exceedingly difficult without restating worn-out tropes: bitching about whether or not your favorite band sold out by signing to a major label, reminiscing about the first time you noticed that chain stores had co-opted your fashion sense, or what exactly a barcode on the cover of a zine denoted" (13).

Moore represents a new generation of anti-consumerist critics whose ire about the appropriation and exploitation of counterculture by commercial culture is not couched in the rhetoric of feminization. But despite the fact that Moore does not utilize a gendered rhetoric to distinguish between authentic culture and commercial culture, her analysis relies on the same assumptions that mark articulations of the feminization thesis. As I noted above, the structure of arguments about the ways in which commercial culture endangers the authentic (artistic) self reproduces a binary logic that gets its force from analogy to gender: like the rock critics who invoke the figure of the masculine artist battling against the corrupting forces of a feminizing pop, Moore's anti-consumerist rebels position themselves within a system of meaning that gauges the value of cultural production in moral terms. These moral terms are rooted in the binary thinking that inevitably points back to the fundamental gendered opposition that structures and grounds arguments about how a homogenizing consumer culture threatens artistic integrity. Can the logic that poses mass culture against authentic culture be articulated without invoking the gender binary? Perhaps, but traces of that gender binary, traces of its history, still haunt the anti-consumerist discourse that aims to delineate just what qualifies as authentic culture, modes of authentic cultural production, and modes, as well, of cultural reception. The kind of argument Moore makes draws at least some of its force from the tradition Andreas Huyssen identifies, in which the "nightmare of being devoured by mass culture through co-option, commodification, and the 'wrong' kind of success is the constant fear of the modernist artist, who tries to stake out his territory by fortifying the boundaries between genuine art and inauthentic mass culture" (53).

Unmarketable is a funny and smart book, but it is also a frustrating book because, try as she does to escape the binary logic, Moore ends up constructing the "corporate entity" as the "sole agent of co-optation" and the independent cultural producer as an unwilling participant in that co-optation. Brushing aside complications, Moore concludes, again and again, that *any* participation in corporate culture and, particularly, the marketing machine of consumer culture, necessarily and always "subverts" the integrity of the underground product—the zine, the CD, the graffiti. Moore's argument, like Heath and Potter's, is that the marketers at large corporations like Nike, Starbucks, Toyota, and Lucasfilms have figured out how to cash in on the "hip" qualities of the underground and so reach a demographic that would *seem* to be the very demographic unavailable to them. But, further, what Moore uncovers—and what troubles her so deeply—is the fact that her buddies who produce independent record labels and non-corporate zines are actually getting sucked into doing work for these corporations. She wants them to stand firm against corporate co-optation and judges them harshly for failing to keep "integrity" intact and alternative cultural production pure.

Acknowledging that such "selling out" is often the only way that struggling underground producers can hope to get their work out to the world (and have the luxury of eating and paying for housing), Moore nevertheless worries that her friends—the independent music producers, the zinesters—are trading in their "integrity" by, for example, participating in a zine workshop sponsored by Starbucks or being paid by Tylenol to devise "edgy" content about pain. When one of her friends, Christen Carter (a "major figure" in the DIY movement), admits that she knew Toyota had paid her to "deliver her people" as consumers via the Toyota YarisWorks DIY: Drive It Yourself campaign, Moore is surprised and appalled that this friend knew what she was doing, was willingly participating in a marketing campaign that targeted the underground that Moore wants to think is immune to such strategies. Carter was not troubled by her so-called selling out and told Moore that "she didn't feel she'd given up anything significant, particularly not her claims to authenticity" (199). Because for Moore DIY is by definition "radical," and corporate products by definition inauthentic, she cannot understand Carter's blasé attitude. But why is Carter "selling out" rather than simply "selling"? How much is "integrity" worth, and who decides? When Moore uses this example to conclude that "the problem isn't a lack of commitment to integrity in punk and DIY culture; it's that structures have been put in place to deliberately erode that integrity" (202), she reinstalls the us-versus-them logic that she has tried to avoid throughout the book and, further, produces an account of co-optation that imagines shadowy systemic forces willfully setting out to destroy independent, non-corporate culture.

Moore's book is driven by a desire to control the meaning of her undergrounds, to short-circuit attempts on the part of corporate entities to lay claim to that meaning and, thus, the logic goes, to destroy it. If Nike can claim a stake in skateboard culture, Toyota in DIY, Tylenol in punk, what makes those realms different, pure, oppositional? Moore constructs the relation of corporate to underground culture as a closed economy that can sustain only a certain amount of edginess; when corporate entities enter the DIY arena, that is, they necessarily (and illegitimately) take a share of a limited resource. She writes, "At the same exact moment the authenticity, sincerity, honor, and personal vision of autonomously produced media and cultural products are being emulated for the purposes of increasing sales of corporate goods and services we begin to feel that our need for these crucial noncommodities has been satisfied. Our desire for integrity has been slaked. Meanwhile . . . genuinely independent media and cultural products—made out of passion and not in pursuit of profits—are unable to compete" (210–11).

But is this logic persuasive? If the "integrity" that independent producers believe their audiences want can be so easily "slaked" by what Moore sees as the faux integrity marketed by Toyota and Tylenol, how *real* is that desire in the first place? Are those audiences merely the dupes of the corporate system and the co-opted formerly independent producers their unknowing collaborators? Don't the stories Moore tells actually complicate this narrative? Moore is too invested in the conventional narrative about corporate plundering of the counterculture that she is almost forced to neatly tie up all the loose ends that her actual analysis has so intriguingly exposed. As persuasive as Moore's analysis of corporate tactics and underground complicity in them is, it's difficult to know what she wants her readers to take away from her book—except a sense of moral superiority over those who are, in fact, satisfied with the fake and cannot distinguish the "real thing."

In the final chapter, "Taking Dissent Off the Market," Moore expresses her worry that despite her own efforts to "identify an effective language of dissent," the "new mash media arises anyway, a hybrid culture created from the corporate adoption of the trappings of independent culture" (215). She proposes the model of the "stain" as a way to think about how these independent producers might infiltrate and subvert the corporate model. But the example she offers of this process raises more questions than it answers: "HeWhoCorrupts, Incorporated, a megacorporate entertainment empire run out of the Chicagoland basements and bedrooms of CEO Ryan Durkin and label manager Andy Slania" (216–17). What Moore sees in HeWhoCorrupts is an independent operation that flaunts its own appropriation of corporate logic: the CEOs admit that profit is their only motive. The "label's blatant moneygrubbing, scorn for audience, and ever-ready willingness to strip off their business drag" by performing naked on the stage "isn't exactly a parody of a top-five media conglomerate. It is also authentic. HeWhoCorrupts, Inc., is a struggling label in a rough environment, competing directly with companies like Sony for survival" (217). What secures HeWhoCorrupt's "authenticity" appears to be nothing more than the fact that it is *genuinely* struggling to compete in a corporatized music business. Such struggles, in Moore's view, transform HeWhoCorrupts from complicit to authentic; for Moore, this small difference rests on the band's success in controlling the conditions of their own production and reception. And what does that production look like? Moore argues that the band is as "difficult to digest as the model they emulate. Their hypermasculine posturing, while intended to be read as (ahem) nakedly profit-minded, is offensive in every possible way. On purpose" (218). Is it an accident that the one example of the genuinely "unmarketable," the subversive "stain" on corporate culture, is the hypermasculine antics of an offensive "bunch of white guys" (217)? Ultimately, Moore's entire argument rests on the question of who controls the mode of production—not of CDs or zines or punk fashions but of *meaning*. Because HeWhoCorrupts, Inc., is doing what they do "on purpose," they qualify as exemplars of integrity, whereas Carter and others do not.

Moore's book raises the question of agency that plagues much anti-consumerist critique: Who or what orchestrates the commodification of everything? Is the identification of intention in corporations or consumers an adequate method for understanding how and why consumers participate in the systems of consumption? Why does it matter that HeWhoCorrupts do it "on purpose"? Is purpose or intention or will necessary to *real* anti-consumerism?

Douglas B. Holt's *How Brands Become Icons*, although a book on marketing rather than a critique of consumerism, offers some intriguing answers to the question of agency. Like Gilmore and Pine, Holt also theorizes the importance of "authenticity" in the science of marketing and makes good use of the vocabulary and methods of cultural studies to outline the "principles of cultural branding." Holt theorizes that iconic brands are born when consumers start to become aware of contradictions in the "national ideology," producing the need for new "myths." Although he does not explicitly frame his argument in gendered terms, he is, in fact, tracking how new forms of masculinity arise in response to shifts in the "national ideology": "Far and away the most important myths concern how citizens are linked to the nation-building project: how Americans, as individuals, see themselves as part of the team to build the nation's economic and political power. These myths are usually constructed around ideals of individual success and manhood—what it takes to be a man" (57). In fact, all of his examples of how cultural branding works foreground processes through which ad executives and corporations have tapped into cultural anxieties about masculinity to create iconic brands that help men negotiate changing gender norms and find new forms of "authenticity" as old forms become outmoded. Because of his conflation of "nation-building" with "manhood," this "pro-consumerist" manifesto shares a logic with the anti-consumerist feminization thesis.

Although oddly unself-conscious about its gendered project, *How Brands Become Icons* analyzes how advertising, marketing, and consumer culture more broadly are in the business of managing recurrent crises in masculinity. Such an analysis helps us to see the illogic of claims that consumer culture is antithetical to masculinity and that rebellions against consumer culture involve a clear separation between corporate culture and counterculture. For example, Holt analyzes the same set of discourses that will be the subject of chapter 2: critiques of the Organization Man and the culture of conformity in the 1950s. Holt argues that the myth of the rugged individual was threatened by the rise of the Organization Man, and American men felt a contradiction between what they believed to be the foundation of masculine identity and the new push toward conformity: "Men found these ideals coercive and emasculating" (41), and needed a new source of national myth. They found it, Holt argues, in the "hillbilly" myth, created through a collaboration of Hollywood, television, consumer culture, advertising, and marketing. Like all of the myths Holt identifies as arising to resolve contradictions in national ideology (which, for him, means masculinity), this one involved tapping into "populist worlds" as a resource for renewing dominant constructions of masculinity. Populist worlds are outside the mainstream and, thus, provide a model of "resistance" to that mainstream. What Holt is tracking here is how "ordinary," primarily middle-class white men have looked to alternative cultures to renew themselves—and they have been helped in this process by the "creatives" in the corporate world who facilitate the creation of new myths when the old ones stop working.

The language in which Holt describes this process perfectly encapsulates the quests for authenticity that mark so many discourses intent on rebelling against consumer culture. Populist worlds are "potent cultural sites because the public perceives that populist world ideologies are authentic" (58). This authenticity springs from the following characteristics: The "ethos" of the populist world is imagined to be "a collective and voluntary product" of those who participate it in; it "has not been imposed upon them" from the outside. The activities of the populist world "are perceived as intrinsically valuable to the participants. They are not motivated by commercial or political interest." Finally, populist worlds are located outside the "centers of commerce and politics" and, thus, provide the consumers of these myths—who might exist within those centers—"with an imaginary connection to [that] world. The authenticity of these populist worlds gives the myth credibility" (58–59). Holt describes virtually the same dynamic that Moore laments in her book, whose title, *Unmarketable,* starts to sound ironic. The difference here is that Holt is not interested in making moral judgments or in adjudicating questions of agency, intention, and blame. He's interested in shedding light on a complex process of meaning making that illuminates, in turn, the processes through which consumer culture participates (along with many other actors and forms) in the ongoing project of constructing a national ideology. For Holt, ads, marketing schemes, films, and other forms of popular culture *and* consumers all work together to "coauthor an identity myth" (161) that allows men to resolve the contradictions between traditional American myths (of the frontier, rugged individualism, and the like) and the reality of changing economic and social conditions that challenge those traditional myths.

Two further points are worth stressing here. First, Holt presents the creation of "populous worlds," "myth markets," and iconic brands as a collaborative process that involves consumers experiencing social contradictions, marketers interpreting those contradictions, and advertisers figuring out how to fulfill the needs of consumers by linking their products to the populist world. Anti-consumerist discourses would have us believe that this is a process best understood as "brainwashing," on the one hand, with consumers being sold an identity and authenticity through manipulative means; and on the other hand, a process of "co-optation" or appropriation, with "real" members of these populist worlds finding their values and beliefs stolen from them. But Holt's analysis paints a picture that is far more complex and cooperative than that—in part because his goal is not to criticize and expose these tactics but to describe what he sees as a historically legible process through which iconic brands (Mountain Dew, Volkswagen, Budweiser, Harley Davidson) help to express the zeitgeist, the national ideology. Second, for Holt, that national ideology is always and only an ideology of masculinity, and what is at stake in the creation of these iconic brands is a constant renegotiation of masculinity.

While we could perhaps imagine a set of iconic brands and myths that would help women negotiate changing conceptualizations of femininity, I think it's fair to say that when it comes to changing myths of national identity and ideology, women have historically taken a backseat, our concerns understood as of little interest to the dominant myths.

If we think about consumer culture as targeting men, as Holt does, we can perhaps see that far from being a "feminine" realm, consumer culture is invested in aiding men in negotiating the contradictions of their gender and identity. Rather than endangering masculinity, then, consumer culture becomes a partner in the construction of it; advertising and marketing need not be understood as the discourses of con men and hucksters who aim to strip men of their "real" identities and substitute fake values for authentic values. Instead, the business of cultural branding becomes one discourse among many involved in the ongoing construction of the national ideology, populist myths, and masculinity—discourses that include, in Holt's examples, the mid-century critiques of the Organization Man and late 1980s attacks on "political correctness," to name two. Of course, the very idea that men might need help in this endeavor is part of what raises the alarm about the "feminizations" of consumer culture in the first place; as we will see with particular force in chapter 4, the power of masculinity is secured, in part, by the fantasy that it is *not* constructed but natural, timeless, essential, and authentic.

Holt's work, along with the work of Gilmore and Pine, suggests that "authenticity" has long been a value that is painstakingly constructed, over and over again, by the very forces understood to endanger it. Authenticity has become a valuable commodity, and marketers, advertisers, and corporations have learned how to profit from it. But the reason that authenticity "sells," according to Andrew Potter's *The Authenticity Hoax*, is that the contemporary craze for "artisanal" everything is just the latest version of a romantic narrative that holds that expressions of the true self and apprehension of authentic experiences are hampered by the forces of modernity. Potter also notes the "biblical texture" and ahistorical character of this narrative, as it retells again and again the story of a fall from a preconsumerist paradise (11).

Like the "feminization thesis," this narrative of the fall from grace structures a wide range of social critique invested in diagnosing how the present represents a decline from the past. The nostalgia that fuels this narrative covers over, but does not come to terms with, an ideological conflict between the forces of progress and the forces of reaction. As Potter puts it, we "are caught in the grip of an ideology about what it means to be an authentic self, to lead an authentic life, and to have authentic experiences. At its core is a form of individualism that privileges self-fulfillment and self-discovery, and while there is something clearly worthwhile in this, the dark side is the inherently antisocial, nonconformist, and competitive dimension to this quest" (14). As I will argue in my reading of William Whyte's *The Organization Man,* an ideology centered on the worship of the individual, the denigration of the collective, and the belief that the one relies on the other has the effect of positioning the individual *against* society in a narrative that can only imagine social formations as endangering the self, as destroying the self's authenticity. Potter introduces the idea of "conspicuous authenticity" and suggests that anti-consumerism sets up a competition for who is the coolest rebel, complete with a "Manichean" structure that he argues "allow[s] us to situate everyone on one side or the other of a great divide" between the rebels and the conformists. This agenda, first set in the 1950s by Norman Mailer, produces "cool" as "the universal stance of individualism" (123–24).[14] The reference to Mailer points again to the odd fact that the specter of the fifties haunts anti-consumerist critique into the twenty-first century. That the mid-century critique of mass society, mass man, and mass consumerism gets virtually reproduced verbatim in so many late-century analyses and representations points to a nostalgia that has several dimensions: while its primary, mostly explicit object is a fantasized, pre-consumerist time and space, it also, less explicitly, expresses a desire to turn back the clock to a moment before the middle-class white man's status as normative American was challenged.

Anxieties about the fate of "the individual" in consumer culture are also always anxieties about who gets to represent that individual and about what social forces might be working to strip him of his power and privilege. That mid-century anti-consumerist posture, as we will see in the next chapter, is a mode of differentiating cool, authentic rebels from square, phony conformists. But Potter demonstrates that the pull of the "authenticity hoax" has, if anything, become stronger at the end of the twentieth and beginning of the twenty-first century. He offers the example of the fall of "organic" and the rise of "local" food to make his point that authenticity seeking remains a "positional" operation that "derives its value from the force of invidious comparison. You can only be an authentic person as long as most of the people around you are not." Authenticity, Potter concludes, "is a positional good with a built-in self-radicalizing dynamic" (133), and it is often an elitist one; it goes without saying that the "ratcheting up" of authenticity prevents any but the wealthiest individuals from attaining this status.

The relationship between "authenticity" and consumer culture is, thus, a complex one. Against the idea that authenticity can be found only *in opposition to* consumer culture, many recent cultural observers have noted the fact that nowhere is authenticity more clearly a good than in the very consumer culture that supposedly endangers that authenticity. And lest we invoke a "real" authenticity versus a "fake" authenticity—as some already have—let me hasten to point out that the qualification of authenticity with "real" or "fake" simply exposes the fiction at the heart of the quest for authenticity, what Potter calls the "authenticity hoax." Sarah Banet-Weiser plays on the conceit that authenticity can be found only outside the marketplace of consumer culture by appending the trademark symbol to the concept that is supposed to be the antithesis of the trademark: *Authentic*™. Her book challenges the "binary understanding of culture as authentic versus commercial" (43) and argues that what progressives who insist that commercial culture destroys an erstwhile noncommercial authenticity miss is the *ambivalence* of brand culture. Neither simply a good nor a bad thing, consumer culture is a complex cultural condition in which familiar oppositions between authenticity and inauthenticity, politics (or identity or religion or art) and consumerism no longer hold. Resisting the narrative of decline or loss that fuels the moral rhetoric of anti-consumerism, Banet-Weiser argues that the opposition between "the consumer" and "the citizen" is a "nostalgic trope." In language that points to the gendered meanings of anti-consumerist positions, she notes that "consumption is often positioned as detrimental to citizenship, in that it is largely seen as motivated by emotion, impulse, and irrationality, whereas politics is ostensibly about rational thinking and reasonable deliberation" (133).

As I will argue throughout this book, anti-consumerist discourses are best understood as making *moral* arguments that aim to distinguish between the "good" and "bad" forms of culture, selves, and values. These arguments are seductive because they enable the rescue of (masculine) individualism and authenticity in a world where such values, we are told, are constantly under threat. Further, the logic depends on a less than fully theorized idea of "production" as the opposite of consumption, an opposition that is always gendered. When intellectuals and cultural critics bemoan the *passive* consumption demanded of mass culture, or point to the ways in which consumption is "motivated by emotion, impulse, and irrationality," they are simultaneously claiming for their own critical and aesthetic practices an active, *productive* power.

Nowhere is this more evident than in two figures who have been heralded as the heirs of the American novel in a post-postmodern era: David Foster Wallace and Jonathan Franzen. Both of these writers have written extensively on the relationship between literature and mass culture, and their writings reflect all of the major assumptions that I have pointed to in this chapter. They both position "serious" fiction writing and reading against consumer culture, particularly television, and both see "authenticity" as endangered by the rise of that culture. Wallace and Franzen are both highly ambivalent about elitism, and both are self-conscious about their own location as straight white middle-class men. This is perhaps not entirely surprising; as I argued in *Marked Men,* the end of the twentieth century produced a great deal of angst over the fate of the white male writer in an America marked by multi-culturalism, identity politics, and a liberationist zeitgeist. But these two more recent spokespersons for the white male writer disguise their own anxiety about their relevance as a critique of the state of literacy in American culture (Franzen) and of the nation's psychological health (Wallace). In both cases, these writers imagine themselves as beleaguered Jeremiahs whose warnings fall on deaf ears. Both Franzen and Wallace skirt issues of class and gender in their writings, loath to appear elitist and anxious to avoid the equation of high culture with masculinity and low or mass culture with femininity. However, it proves impossible for either of them to articulate their critique without resorting to the rote thinking that characterizes the anti-consumerist critique that is my subject here.

ENDANGERED WRITERS AND RADICAL INDIVIDUALISTS

The masculine protest articulated against the feminization and the commercialization of American literature in the nineteenth century has proved itself to be a resilient cultural motif for writers who aim to diagnose the condition of American literature and to lament the decline of an autonomous artistic sphere. Jonathan Franzen has spilled a great deal of ink over the dilemma of the white male "literary" author in the late twentieth and early twenty-first centuries, and watching him negotiate among contradictory claims (for himself and for American culture) is a fascinating study. As one reviewer of Franzen's fourth novel, *Freedom,* points out, here is a writer with a "persistent habit of looking for the zeit in his own geist" (Franklin), a writer, that is, who persistently connects his own malaise to the condition of the national culture. His essays whipsaw back and forth between diagnoses of what ails American culture and what ails him, Jonathan Franzen, as he tries to find a place within that culture. Franzen proves that the logic of feminization by which nineteenth-century "male authors often oscillated between a desire for commercial success and a need to define themselves as independent creators resistant to a feminizing marketplace" (P. Gilmore 13) still afflicted male authors in the late twentieth century. That oscillation is on display with particular clarity in the essays in which Franzen performs ambivalence: Franzen wants to disavow elitism but cannot quite surrender his belief in the importance of an elite, autonomous, and essentially masculine cultural sphere.

Franzen begins one of his essays, entitled "The Reader in Exile," by telling a literal "Kill Your TV" story. He writes about getting rid of a Sony Trinitron given to him by a friend and uses this story to set up his special status as a critic of consumer culture rather than a passive recipient of it. Franzen trots out the usual banalities in this essay about the reader "in exile," including the specter of "an excess of passive reception" (*How to Be Alone* 165) and the failure of a society to "inoculate its children against the worst ravages of electronic media" (166). As happens in many of Franzen's essays, serious attention to cultural issues rapidly gives way to musings on the self, as Franzen little by little constructs a picture of himself as a Serious Writer[15] threatened with obsolescence by a public that does not share his belief in the importance of the writer's vocation. After explaining why he decided to give his television away, Franzen goes on to make a claim for his uniqueness and his rebellious position vis-à-vis (what he takes to be) the culture he is forced to live in:

> I was born in 1959, on the cusp of a great generational divide, and for me it's a toss-up which is scarier: living without electronic access to my country's culture, or trying to survive in that culture without the self-definition I get from regular immersion in literature. I understand my life in the context of Raskolnikov and Quentin Compson, not David Letterman or Jerry Seinfeld. But the life I understand by way of books feels increasingly lonely. It has little to do with the mediascape that constitutes so many other people's present. (164–65)

This passage suggests that the writer and reader of "literature" faces marginalization (or worse) in the "mediascape" that substitutes for a more authentic culture. There is something a little bit arrogant in Franzen's claim that he understands his life "in the context of Raskolnikov and Quentin Compson," but he tempers that arrogance by foregrounding the emotional costs of rejecting what so many others accept: he is "scared" and he is "lonely." At the same time, the swerve from social critique (his country's culture is dominated by the mediascape) to personal complaint (he is hurt by this) stems from Franzen's sense of lost privilege—*he*, not David Letterman or Jerry Seinfeld, should be representing his "country's culture" because *he* embodies the high literary tradition that is threatened by the rise of the popular. Authenticity here is connected to high tragedy (and male pain) through the figures Franzen chooses to identify with; inauthenticity is connected to comedy through the figures he chooses to identify against. Disguising his personal lament as social commentary, Franzen exemplifies the logic through which narratives about social and cultural decline become laments about the decentering of individual white men.

Franzen styles himself as a radical individualist who abandons his belief in the purportedly unpopular idea that art can function in socially useful ways and decides to devote himself to writing "about the things closest to me, to lose myself in the characters and locales I loved" (*How to Be Alone* 95). As an artistic credo, there's nothing wrong with this; many a good novelist has taken a similar tack. But Franzen cannot let things rest here because he sees that his "relevance" in a "technoconsumerist" and "multicultural" age is potentially compromised by his abandonment of social critique or even social engagement. For Franzen, abandoning the "radical critique" that he formerly thought was his duty as a writer to express means seeking out something like "authenticity." But to put things in these terms is to ignore the essential ambivalence of Franzen's essay and its somewhat hysterical outbursts, such as the following: "The American writer today faces a cultural totalitarianism analogous to the political totalitarianism with which two generations of Eastern bloc writers had to contend. To ignore it is to court nostalgia. To engage with it, however, is to risk writing fiction that makes the same point over and over: technological consumerism is an infernal machine, technological consumerism is an infernal machine . . ." (69; ellipsis in the original). Ignoring the self-pitying logic by which a privileged and financially successful white American writer imagines himself the victim of a "totalitarian" state, I want to point out the poverty of the either-or choice that Franzen articulates here. *Why* are these the only two options? Why must we choose between nostalgia for a pre-consumerist moment and the despair of being dominated by that consumerism? In fact, aren't these two sides of the same coin? What does Franzen get from putting things in these terms? And why does this outburst follow on the heels of, and in the very same paragraph as, his discussion of identity politics (what he incorrectly calls "regionalism")? Is it technological consumerism that seeks to deprive "us" of the relevance of "serious art," or is the complaint really more about the decentering of a certain *type* of, and *attitude* toward, "serious art," one characterized by the elitism that has underwritten the image of the "great American novelist" as white, male, and completely independent of the marketplace?

Because Franzen oscillates among so many different positions in the essay, we can't really find clear answers to these questions. Franzen flirts with some retrograde ideas about the relative value and importance of gender and race in the marketplace but avoids owning them or considering the implications of the stances he seems to be taking. Discussing the disappointing response to his first novel, Franzen uses a metaphor that is, perhaps, more telling than he means it to be and, thus, points toward an unacknowledged sense of envy (and anger) that the white male writer has been displaced:

> The literary America in which I found myself after I published *The Twenty-Seventh City* bore a strong resemblance to the St. Louis I'd grown up in: a once-great city that had been gutted and drained by white flight and superhighways. Ringing the depressed urban core of serious fiction were prosperous new suburbs of mass entertainments. Much of the inner city's remaining vitality was concentrated in the black, Hispanic, Asian, gay, and women's communities that had taken over the structures vacated by fleeing straight white males. (*How to Be Alone* 62)

Now, I do not believe that Franzen means exactly what his metaphor says here; throughout the essay, and in others covering roughly the same topics, he pays lip service to the ways in which the expansion of the literary field has made American literature richer than when it was dominated by a few white males. However, the fact remains that imaging the devastation to "literary America" as caused by the twin evils of hyper-consumerism and multi-culturalism borders, to say the least, on the kind of cranky conservatism that marks such works as Allan Bloom's *The Closing of the American Mind*.

Such suspicions find some confirmation in another essay in the volume, "Scavenging," in which Franzen crafts a fantasy of authenticity and indulges in a retrograde nostalgia for a pre-technological age. Fancying himself a lone rebel against techno-consumerism, he explains why he hangs on to his rotary phone when the rest of the world has opted for the touch-tone: "Touch-Tones repel me. I don't like their sterile rings, their plethora of features, their belatedness of design, the whole complacency of their hegemony. I prefer the reproachful heaviness of my rotary, just as I prefer the seventies clunkiness of my stereo components for the insult it delivers to the regiments of tasteful black boxes billeted in every house across the land" (*How to Be Alone* 199). Telling this story in the age of cell phones allows Franzen to claim his old-fashioned preferences as a badge of honor and mark of resistance. His palpable desire to distinguish himself from the masses in "every house across the land," however, is self-consciously quaint, as if he is at one and the same time articulating a point of view and inoculating himself against criticism for the absurdity of that point of view. This is more evidence of his characteristic, and I would say his *strategic,* ambivalence, his crafty self-presentation as torn between warring impulses. While he does (*really*) imagine himself as part of a beleaguered minority, he is also aware that his claims to uniqueness rest on pretty shaky ground. Touch-tone hegemony? I can't help but think of the moment in *The Corrections* when the narrator exposes the superficiality of Chip's response to "techno-consumerism" by pointing out that "Chip hated cell phones mainly because he didn't have one" (102). Franzen seems to acknowledge the inefficacy of a rotary phone as an emblem of resistance while simultaneously wanting to claim for himself an embattled radical position as a resister of all thing consumerist and, so the logic goes, a defender of literature.

Franzen's worries about the position and status of literature in American culture get expressed through his frequent allusions to the fact that women constitute the major share of the audience for all kinds of fiction; for example, he argues that "the 'general' audience our national literature once possessed was always predominantly female, and that sometime around 1973 women finally got tired of getting their news of the world via (frequently misogynist) male perspectives, and that was the end of the 'general' audience" ("I'll Be Doing More" 37). The idea that women readers exercise an inordinate amount of power over the literary field has been cause for distress on the part of gatekeepers, academics, and writers for many years. That distress was fully on display in Franzen's response to being selected as an Oprah author; as he told Terry Gross on NPR's *Fresh Air,* "I had some hope of actually reaching a male audience, and I've heard more than one reader in signing lines now in book stores that said, 'If I hadn't heard you, I would have been put off by the fact that it is an Oprah pick. I figure those books are for women and I would never touch it.' Those are male readers speaking."[16] Like the rock musicians who worry that their status as authentic artists is threatened by the consumption of their music by the wrong kind of audience, and like the modernist artist who worries, in Huyssen's terms, about the "wrong kind of success,"

Franzen here expresses a desire not only to cordon the masculine literary away from the feminine mass but also to control who reads his books and how they are read.

I dwell at such length on Franzen's meditations because it seems to me that he embodies a new form of anti-consumerist critique that understands its own terms as deeply problematic. Such is also the case with David Foster Wallace, who, in the essay on television and culture, "E Unibus Plurum," tries to have his cake and eat it, too. Wallace's essays do a much better job than Franzen's of making an argument and supporting it with logic and evidence, but, like Franzen, Wallace indulges far too much in a rhetoric of complaint to devote his attention to anything like a solution to the problems he identifies, or to work his way out of a dead-end circuit toward something like a new take on the problem of the writer in the age of television. Interestingly, Wallace positions himself *against* the very leftish *New York Times* critique of mass consumer culture that I identified in the introduction. He does so in order to distinguish his critique from what he sees as the paranoia of the "wearily contemptuous" (*Supposedly Fun Thing* 29) attitude toward television articulated by both the *New York Times* and academic criticism.

Making the excellent point that "so much of the pleasure [his] generation takes from television lies in making fun of it" because "younger Americans grew up as much with people's disdain for TV as we did with TV itself" (27), Wallace aims to think his way out of the typical "Kill Your TV" attitude and into a more radical critique of the *real* problem with television. For Wallace, the real problem with TV is that it has cornered the market on the very same form of irony that also characterizes what he sees as "postmodern" fiction, so that the younger generation of American writers—all, in Wallace's estimation, white and male—are left simply to reproduce the cultural zeitgeist governed by televisual logic instead of offering a usable critique of, or alternative to, it. Like Franzen, Wallace tries to have it both ways: he criticizes television by criticizing the critics of television, managing to articulate the typical "Kill Your TV" attitude even while claiming to be contemptuous of it. If this does not make Wallace "postmodern," I don't know what does: his attitude in this essay is a perfect example of what Linda Hutcheon, in *The Politics of Postmodernism*, famously called its characteristic "complicitous critique": installing *and* subverting authoritative pronouncements and master narratives about culture, history, and identity.

Wallace, however, is invested in positioning himself *against* postmodernism and the heirs of postmodernism, the "New Imagists." Because he wants to keep high and low culture separate, he is particularly bothered by the fact that American fiction of the last five or so decades has exalted in breaking down the barriers between high and low. Wallace rightly sees the traffic between consumer culture and literature as traveling in both directions, with borrowings and appropriations moving from the high to the low and vice versa, but he never explicitly states why this two-way traffic is a bad thing because he thinks the answer is self-evident. Cultural hierarchy—the division between high and low—is sacred to Wallace, and the language he uses to distinguish between what fiction *should* do that television *can't* do reproduces the binaries that are my subject in this book. Television creates "pseudo-communities" (57) rather than "genuine" ones; TV is "addictive," a "Special Treat [that] begins to substitute for something nourishing and needed" (38–39); television has the "power to jettison connection and castrate protest" (35); television, Wallace complains, has a "hold on my generation's cojones" (41). The fact that Wallace uses both the language of authenticity and the language of masculinity to paint this picture of what's wrong with television—and, more to the point, how television has stripped authentic literature of its "genuine socio-artistic agenda" (51)—suggests that his reasoning depends less on the discovery of new insights into how television and literature function in relation to each other and more on the rote repetition of the same mass culture critique that has dominated American responses to consumer culture since the middle of the twentieth century.

Like Franzen's almost self-destructive and contradictory responses to his selection as an Oprah author, Wallace's essay somewhat hysterically oscillates between self-promotion and self-denigration. And for both of these "hip" writers, it is around the specter of elitism that this ambivalence pivots. Franzen says, "I resist, finally, the notion of literature as a noble higher calling, because elitism does not sit well with my American nature" (*How to Be Alone* 74). But this claim is unconvincing, given the obvious ways in which his elitism surfaced around his very vocal whining about how the Oprah seal on *The Corrections* would attract the "wrong kind" of readers. Franzen does, in fact, believe that literature is a noble higher calling, a calling threatened by "technoconsumerism." Even the arch-conservative, unapologetically elitist book critic Joseph Epstein notes that in his *Harper's* essay "Franzen pulls out every rubber chicken, toy trumpet, and whoopee cushion of literary snobbery of the past 40 years"—even after averring, Franzen, that is, oh so sincerely, that "'both Oprah and I want the same thing and believe the same thing, that the distinction between high and low is meaningless'" (Epstein 34). Wallace, for his part, cherishes his elitism but can do so only as long as it's mixed with a good dose of self-consciousness and the "right" kind of irony—that is, sincere irony, as oxymoronic as that may sound, as opposed to televisual irony of the "smirking" variety. This comes through, perhaps, most fully in his essay "Authority and American Usage," where he wears as a badge of honor his membership in the class of "SNOOTS," "just about the last remaining kind of truly elitist nerd" (*Consider the Lobster* 70).

Both Franzen and Wallace are on the trail of authenticity, attempting to track it down in a world they deem hopelessly compromised by the rise of consumer culture and peopled by a variety of "tribes" (Franzen's term) who are all more or less willing to surrender their autonomy and uniqueness to be just like everyone else. In an interesting analysis of "cultures of authenticity," Abigail Cheever suggests that what worried social critics about the 1950s was homogeneity, not conformity, and that a focus on conformity allowed these critics to save the concept of individualism even as they detailed the de-individualizing forces of consensus culture. The reason that these social critics "discuss conformity rather than uniformity is because they are so committed to the ideal of individuality that the only way they can account for individuals who look, act, and talk the same is to imagine they are compelled" (13). Further, "Authenticity in the postwar period was understood to separate the individual from her social context," and although Cheever uses the feminine pronoun here, her example is of a female character, Holly Golightly, who serves as the negative example of the authentic and who, "in perfect alignment with her social world, cannot count as fully real" (15). As Timothy Melley's analysis of "agency panic" in the same era suggests, anxieties over masculinity were never very far below the surface in accounts of threats to individualism.

While Cheever argues that, by the late twentieth century, authenticity shifts to become a sign of belonging rather than uniqueness, I have found that thinking about authenticity still draws on mid-century constructions of individualism and uniqueness. What comes through in the writings of Franzen and Wallace is precisely this tension between individualism and what we might call post-individualism—the *post* referring not to the demise of individualism but rather to the revamping of it.

My argument in the chapters that follow will suggest that social forces are coded as "feminizing" not because women are phony, self-indulgent, dependent, or will-less but because American ideologies of individualism have a deep and stubborn attachment to the idea that only the normative, unmarked citizen has a claim to individualism; and the corollary idea that the individual can emerge only in contradistinction either to those citizens marked by gender and other differences or to a "society" that is radically at odds with his needs. In important ways, the very act of protest against feminization becomes the guarantee of remasculinization and, in turn, the resuscitation of a stable gender order. The rhetoric of feminization and the masculine protest it produces thus function as a primary technology of gender. Claims about the feminization produced by consumer culture, or men's and women's participation in it, need not be substantiated, since the narrative about the feminization of the (masculine) individual by (feminine) social forces is a seductive fiction that has the force of ideology—that is, it is not understood as ideological because it has been naturalized as "reality." It is my goal to denaturalize this reality and the gendered logic that produces it.

CHAPTER 2

AUTHENTIC INDIVIDUALS AND ORGANIZATION MEN

Masculine Protest in the 1950s

During the middle decades of the twentieth century, a great deal of intellectual energy was spent diagnosing the ills of American culture hidden behind the facade of affluence and contentment. Scores of books and articles documented a shift in the "American character" resulting, according to a range of commentators, from the subordination of the individual to an increasing number of large organizations or systems. In particular, critics warned that the fall of traditional models of economic production, linked with the rise of consumerism as both an economic system and an ideology, could deliver a death sentence to cherished American ideals of rugged individualism and self-determination. The overarching thematic of the social critics writing at mid-century articulated fears that large social structures—the corporation, the bureaucracy, consumerism—were controlling the individual by forcing him to submit his initiative to their power, rendering him passive, weak, and feminized. Jeremiads about the "organization man," the "man in the gray flannel suit," the "other-directed individual," and the conformity of suburbia were rife with the rhetoric of feminization, articulating a masculine protest against the perceived dangers to the self and to authenticity. Popular books like William Whyte's *The Organization Man* and David Riesman's *The Lonely Crowd* set the terms for public debate about postwar changes in economic, political, and social systems. Fueled by new business and organizational practices—including rising bureaucratization, the popularity and influence of market research, and the new "sciences" of management and personality testing—these books warned that traditional versions of masculine individualism were in decline and that the authentic, creative, self-determining man was being displaced by a feminized, commodified self. C. Wright Mills most directly invokes the core anxiety provoked by the spread of consumerism when he notes that white-collar workers "sell not only their time and energy but their personalities as well" (xvii). Such comments testify to a widespread suspicion that gender difference is eroding as men begin to look, act, and behave more like women are supposed to and as women start to benefit from their symbolic power as the embodiment of a consumer ethos.

These books tapped into a vein of cultural anxiety that continues to haunt critiques of American culture because they articulated, in impressively totalizing terms, an urgent account of the costs of larger social and cultural shifts. As we will see, the figure of the "organization man" and the cultural dominant of "other direction" have fueled anti-consumer critiques into the late twentieth century and beyond. Here, I will use *The Organization Man* and *The Lonely Crowd* as companion pieces representing a masculine protest against the feminization of American men, and argue that the rhetoric of anti-consumerism enables both writers to position themselves as heroic fighters against the new normal of mid-century consumer culture. Both Whyte and Riesman claim to be disinterested observers, reporting on but not judging the shifts they witness, but their language betrays an emotional investment as they construct a narrative about the decline of rugged American-style individualism. The story they tell about the rise of the organization man and of the other-directed personality depends on a version of the feminization thesis that identifies consumer culture and its falsifying operations as assaulting a more authentic model of individualism and of the self. Whyte, Riesman, and other mid-century social critics have been lionized as "countercultural" voices in an age of conformity and consensus, their gender, racial, and class privilege notwithstanding. Rather than arguing for a rejection of consumer culture or offering a critique of capitalism, however, Whyte and Riesman focus on the guilty individual who fails to actively fight against those forces that seek to rob him of his independence, autonomy, and authenticity. As I noted in the introduction, the dominant form of anti-consumerist critique in the postwar era is a discourse about the *self* and the self's success or failure in rebelling against the feminizations of large social systems.

The mid-century anti-consumerist critique, with its construction of an authentic individualism endangered by the de-individualizing and feminizing forces of consumer culture, provides the background for two iconic narratives of masculine protest, Salinger's *The Catcher in the Rye* and Kerouac's *On the Road*. *Catcher* bears witness to the gender trouble caused by rapid changes in the political, economic, and psychological state of American normativity, changes that threatened the stability of gender difference by unmooring masculinity from its traditional supports and blurring the distinction between masculine and feminine. The novel articulates a fantasy of authenticity by representing as "phony" every norm, form, and convention that aims to curtail the full and free expression of masculine autonomy and artistic authenticity. *On the Road* can be seen as the heir of *The Catcher in the Rye* in its further articulation of masculine protest against the mid-century cultural dominant. But despite the fact that *On the Road* has been canonized as the quintessential refusal of a consumerist ethos, I will argue that the novel actually says very little about consumer culture, instead articulating a more general complaint against *any* system—oddly, including white privilege—that threatens to put *any* limits on masculine freedom and authenticity. In all of these texts, the desire to find a lost "authenticity" works to construct the figure of the alienated white middle-class man as the tragic embodiment, and feminized victim, of contemporary cultural norms.

ORGANIZATION MEN AND SUBURBAN CONSUMERS

In February 1958, *Look* magazine published two articles raising the alarm about the current state of an American masculinity threatened by shifting relations of production and consumption, as well as shifting norms of gender. "The American Male: Why Does He Work So Hard?" and "The American Male: Why Is He Afraid to Be Different?" made it clear that the rise of the "organization" and "groupthink" constituted a direct assault on men and on ideals of masculinity. Arthur Schlesinger, writing in *Esquire,* a bit later in 1958, boldly announced "the crisis of American masculinity," which he described thus: "Today men are more and more conscious of maleness not as a fact but as a problem. The ways by which American men affirm their masculinity are uncertain and obscure. There are multiplying signs, indeed, that something has gone badly wrong with the American male's conception of himself" (237). Such comments register the belief that while large social shifts might be traceable to the world of work and its requirements, it is the effect of these changes on individual men and on concepts of masculinity that causes the most distress. That women might also be affected by such changes does not seem to worry these social critics.

More interesting than the expected exclusion of women's concerns from the sociological analysis is the way in which these studies rely on a metaphorics of gender to make their case that the American character is in decline. Whyte's *The Organization Man,* in many ways, encapsulates the historical moment as a crisis in masculinity. The book is an impassioned plea for a return to competitive individualism, and although Whyte never identifies competitive individualism with masculinity, he couches his critique in terms that invoke an opposition between a strong America characterized by self-made manhood and rugged individualism and a weak America characterized by the individual's subordination to a social system. When Whyte summarizes the organization man's condition as one of overwhelming passivity, his use of the generic *people* to mask the specific *men* fails to disguise the gendered dynamic at work here: "Once people liked to think, at least, that they were in control of their destinies, but few of the younger organization people cherish such notions. Most see themselves as objects more acted upon than acting—and their future, therefore, determined as much by the system as by themselves" (437).

The book clearly comes out of a Cold War climate, in which "collectivism" equates with anti-Americanism via the communist threat. Whyte has some fun with the suggestion that these organization men and their wives are gleefully adopting something akin to socialism in their enthusiasm for the collective. Indeed, at one point in the book, an organization man, addressing the creation of community within one of the suburbs that have sprung up around large corporations, quips, "'We laughed at first at how the Marxist society had finally arrived," complete with collective responsibility for child care—in the form of babysitting "banks"—and a bartering system that would appear to be at odds with advanced capitalism (316). Whyte notes that, except for the monastic orders and the family itself, there is probably no other social institution in the United States in which there is such a communal sharing of property, noting that "to hoard possessions is frowned upon; books, silverware, and tea services are constantly rotated, and the children feel free to use one another's bikes and toys without asking" (316). Lest his readers begin to admire this turn of affairs, Whyte is quick to lampoon this growing impulse toward collectivity, and he does so in the terms that dominate this highly influential study: the problem with the collectivism spawned by organization culture—what he dubs the "Social Ethic"—is that it goes against the grain of American individualism, which is based on private property, competition, and the subordination of the larger social good to the individual.

Throughout *The Organization Man,* Whyte is hard-pressed to identify just what is *wrong* with what, at times, appears to be a welcome social alternative to a competitive individualism that produces social inequalities. Indeed, he is often at pains to point out that the Protestant Ethic—the opposite of the Social Ethic—can be taken too far and that an extreme individualism can produce the "unrestrained self-interest" that marks the thinking of the "right wing": "Even more than those who preach the Social Ethic slough over the individual's rights against society, the right sloughs over the individual's obligations to society," he admits (and this is why the right "has remained a comparatively negative force in American thought") (443). Yet this moment comes too late and does little to qualify the book's rock-solid faith in the a priori value of competitive individualism. In any event, Whyte need not have worried that white middle-class American men would ever surrender their entitlement to determine the fate of individualism. It is worth noting that, in the late 1980s and early 1990s, a spate of books and articles was taking stock of the fate of the organization man in a culture that had more or less abandoned anything remotely resembling the "Social Ethic." The titles of two of these books, *The New Individualists: The Generation after the Organization Man* and *The Death of the Organization Man,* say it all.

Whyte objects to the idea of the "organized self" and the "organized life," suggesting that what gets lost in the transition from the Protestant to the Social Ethic is something like freedom from structure, or at least freedom to act spontaneously and autonomously. Throughout *The*

Organization Man, Whyte relies on a narrative of decline, lamenting what has been lost in the zeal to "organize" everything. Like earlier jeremiads against the rise of the marketplace or the "feminization of America," Whyte's book relies on a foundational notion of authenticity, once secure and now lost, and so his book is pervaded by nostalgia. Early on, Whyte disavows this nostalgia, claims that his goal is not to "censure the fact of organization society," and argues that "in contrasting the old ideology with the new I mean no contrast of paradise with paradise lost, an idyllic eighteenth century with a dehumanized twentieth" (12). Yet this is precisely the picture that emerges in the book, and this is so, at least in part, because Whyte relies on a language saturated with the codes of gender hierarchy, in which "passive" equates to "feminine" and in which the normatively masculine "individual" must actively fight to "wrench his destiny into his own hands" (15) and not submit to the forces that impede his autonomy.

It is hard to overstate Whyte's antipathy to the Social Ethic, for, in his account, this new ideology invades every aspect of American life. The greatest threat to individualism Whyte discerns in the rise of this ideology, however, is the organization man's willing, indeed gleeful, surrender to the social forces that render him psychologically weak, his ego "sublimated" (54), and his value determined by his willingness to adapt to the group. Whyte bemoans the lack of resistance to the organization and looks in vain for brave rebels who will buck the system—he even includes an appendix titled "How to Cheat on Personality Tests" to foster resistance. Rather than arguing that the Social Ethic has destroyed individualism, Whyte instead paints a picture of how the organization ethos perverts individualism, robs it of its "ruggedness"—in other words, *feminizes* it. The men who submit to the strictures of organization life are not surrendering their individualism so much as acquiescing to its appropriation. What emerges in the book is an image of an inauthentic or faux individualism that has replaced the real individualism of earlier eras. The era of men striving to conquer, to express genuine creativity, to pursue adventurous projects of all kinds has given way to an era in which men strive only to adjust to the group, to adapt their desires to the desires of the many, and to suppress their ambitions. The problem that Whyte outlines here is that "society" has become the "hero" of the American narrative, displacing the rugged individual who formerly occupied that position. But rather than construct a "melodrama of beset manhood," to borrow from Nina Baym, Whyte instead traces something worse: the failure of society and its organization men to discern the fact that manhood is beset at all.

The Organization Man spends a great deal of time analyzing how the organization man is formed—from college, through training programs, in science, and in literature—before turning to "The New Suburbia: The Organization Man at Home." In this section of the book, Whyte links the business model he has been critiquing to the domestic arena and the forms of consumption practiced by the organization man and his wife. For Whyte, suburban life centers on consumption, and that centrality works to dull any rebellious impulses the organization man might feel. While Whyte's informants might express their satisfaction with the Social Ethic enacted in the suburbs, Whyte is having none of it, and his informants uniformly appear to be in the grips of a major delusion. The narrative persona Whyte creates in the book—that of an impartial and balanced observer of organization behavior—cannot quite hide the alarm sounded through the language in which he describes seemingly innocuous practices, as we can see in the following comments: the organization man who finds his roots in the new suburbs "has plunged into a hotbed of Participation. With sixty-six adult organizations and a population turnover that makes each one of them *insatiable* for new members, Park Forest probably *swallows up* more civic energy per hundred people than any other community in the country" (317; emphasis added). This language evokes rampant twentieth-century fears of machinelike systems and an engulfing mass culture that threatens to consume everything in its wake.

That the language here also expresses a fear of a *feminine* force has been amply demonstrated by Janice Radway in her study of the ideological contest over cultural value embodied by highbrow responses to the rise of the Book-of-the-Month Club in the 1930s and 1940s. That Whyte mentions the "Great Books Course" as a key mode of enculturation into the "Social Ethic" (317) suggests that the battle over class, gender, and cultural hierarchy Radway locates earlier in the century continues unabated. Indeed, some of Whyte's language suggests that the debates over literary value, fears of standardization and the demise of individual agency, and anxieties over women's changing political and social status are alive and well in the 1950s, not buried in the past. Radway argues that the book-club wars, while focused primarily on the literary field, had a larger relevance in a world characterized by "widespread fears about the coming of machines and the fate of individual agency in a world growing more bureaucratic and regimented at every turn. The discussions were also informed by a profound gender anxiety." This anxiety takes the form of a "deep distaste for the purported feminization of culture and the emasculation of otherwise assertive artists and aggressively discriminating readers" (*Feeling for Books* 189).

Just as the Book-of-the-Month Club threatened to democratize American culture and to dissolve the boundaries between the highbrow and the middlebrow, so Whyte's diagnosis of organization culture suggests that such boundaries are further breached as traditional class distinctions start to dissolve. Somewhat surprisingly, one of the key features of the new suburbia that Whyte notes is its "classlessness" (its whiteness does not compel his attention). While we might think that the suburbs are homogeneous spaces defined by class segregation, Whyte understands the suburbs as a "great melting pot," where all workers and families are leveled into one homogenous mass. As a 2016 *New Yorker* retrospective on *The Organization Man* suggests, the suburbs Whyte imagines are an egalitarian space, one that offends his patrician sensibilities. Noting that Whyte is a "member in good standing of the Wasp elite," writer Gary Sernovitz points out that the book "portrays young men—and Whyte's business world was all men (and all white)—without cynicism toward a system that was growing more egalitarian. 'In the managerial ideology,' Whyte writes, 'it is not the leaders of industry that are idealized—if anything, they are scolded—but the lieutenants.'" Whyte believes that these young men should be cynical about the organization if not openly in revolt against it. Against the yes men of the contemporary organization, Whyte nostalgically poses his own training in the Vick School of Management, a "gladiators' school," which valued "strife," "combat," and the "survival of the fittest" (127–29). Concluding that "we were giants in those days," Whyte confides to his readers, "I suppose I should be ashamed, but I must confess I'm really not" (132). Although Whyte does admit that the "democratic" principles of the new organization men might be justified because "the old style individualist was often far more of a bar to individualism in other people," he cannot countenance how the organization man must "sublimate his ego" for the good of the group (54).

"Democracy" and the erosion of class distinction in the suburbs are read as signs that the Social Ethic levels the field to the point that there are no winners or losers, only members of the group. In his discussion of the suburbs, as in the earlier discussions of the business world and the relations between "executives" and the lower-tier white-collar workers, Whyte reveals an elitist regret that class boundaries appear to be dissolving. The expansion of the middle class might be good news for those who occupy lower socioeconomic positions; however, from the perspective of the patrician Whyte, the disappearance of something like a natural aristocracy is cause for alarm. Not owning up to this alarm, and sticking to his "objective" reporting, Whyte instead warns that the kind of upward mobility represented by the organization should be resisted because it is less than fully authentic: "The fruits of social revolution," he laments, "are always more desirable in anticipation than fact, and the pink lamp shade in the picture window can be a sore disappointment to those who dreamed that the emancipation of the worker would take a more spiritual turn" (341–42). As Shelley Nickles suggests, Whyte's comments here reflect a disdain both for the lower classes whose new purchasing power "signaled the infiltration of working-class values into mainstream culture" and for the women who were entrusted with consumer choices: "The pink lamp shade represented a new majority of American women who drove design standards in the marketplace and created new suburban domestic lifestyles without regard for the values of cultural arbiters" (Nickles 590). Indeed, Whyte makes explicit the feminization of taste when he notes that, in the new organization world, it is women who are the guardians of taste and that "suburban housewives are quick to take injury" at "what they fancy are slights to their taste level" (Whyte 349).

The suburbs threaten to overturn the traditional taste hierarchies on which the American class system is based, and in this endeavor suburban husbands and wives are aided by consumer culture. "The good-life standard is being revised upwardly so rapidly that planners of suburban shopping centers have had a hard time keeping up with it," writes Whyte (349). Whyte does not object to consumerism per se; what he objects to is the organization man's adoption of a particular type of consumerism.

He differentiates between a good, individualist consumption and a bad, collectivist consumption; while the former might be spun as a productive offshoot of the Protestant Ethic, the latter further entrenches the individual in the webs of the de-individualizing (and emasculating) organization culture. This comes through most forcefully in Whyte's discussion of "inconspicuous consumption," which he glosses as "keeping down with the Joneses." In a nod to David Riesman, he notes that "even those sophisticated enough to talk, albeit a trifle nervously, about 'other-directed' consumption of their group see a valid reason for it" (346)—that reason, of course, being to safeguard the collective character of suburbia by eschewing conspicuous, status-seeking consumption and display. Whyte reads suburban consumption as de-individualizing and feminizing, the organization man and his wife not exercising consumer choice, but rather allowing the group ethos to determine what they buy and how they display it.

What these suburban consumers express is *not* a desire to be at the top of the heap, to succeed as savvy consumers, but, on the contrary, anxiety about appearing out of step with the group. It is almost as if suburbia has perverted the competitive spirit Whyte identifies in the pre-organization era, when "'rugged' individualism" was "the business of business" (20): rather than competing to win, these organization men, driven at home by their wives and at work by bureaucrats, compete to lose. Whyte homes in on how the drive to "keep down with the Joneses" is a female-dominated process and a feminizing one, affecting even the "most resolute individualists" who get sucked into a group-oriented mode of consumption:

> In the early stages, when only a few of the housewives in a block have, say, an automatic dryer, the word-of-mouth praise of its indispensability is restricted. But, then, as time goes on and the adjacent housewives follow suit, in a mounting ratio others are exposed to more and more talk about its benefits. Soon the nonpossession of the item becomes an almost unsocial act—an unspoken aspersion of the others' judgment or taste. At this point only the most resolute individualists can hold out, for just as the group punishes its members for buying prematurely, so it punishes them for not buying. (347)

What Whyte describes here is the use of consumer goods as an index of conformity or rebellion, and it is clear that, according to Whyte, conformity is necessary in order to appease the group. But, interestingly, Whyte does not imagine some Machiavellian force behind this luxury-becoming-necessity cycle, conspiring to make these suburbanites buy more and more; to the contrary, Whyte sees "merchandisers," salesmen, and even advertisers as "comparatively passive" (348) in this process, more or less meekly following the herd of consumers (particularly "house-wives") who are in control of it.

Where the critique of mass culture articulated by the Frankfurt school imagined a "culture industry" that ensnared individuals and robbed them of their autonomy, Whyte's critique acquits all industries of manipulation and imagines the individual as happily orchestrating his own ensnare-ment because "in self-entrapment is security" (357). This is also the case in his discussion of what he calls "budgetism," a highly "organized" type of financial management that reflects a "person's desire to regularize his finances by having them removed from his own control and disciplined by external forces" (362). Organization men have their taxes withheld for them; they have their retirement savings automatically deducted; they open "Christmas Club" savings accounts to ensure that they save; they make heavy use of revolving credit; they take out loans and happily pay high interest charges. "Bankers," Whyte tells us, "have not yet recognized how inclusive is the urge for the organized life" (362–63), and "even the most hardened credit men" in department stores are "flabbergasted" by the craze for revolving credit (361). As dismissive as he is of the impulses behind revolving credit, Whyte cannot resist the temptation to throw an-other jab at feminine consumption, constructing women as shoppers who need to be controlled; revolving credit does deliver the benefit of being a "disciplining factor for the wife. The old coupon-book plans that preceded revolving credit had many of the same features, but the coupon book was 'hot money,' and, more often than not, the wife spent every bit of it on the trip between the credit department and the store's exit. The regular monthly limit provided with revolving credit has a different psychological effect, and the wife, to the delight of the husband, can confidently pre-plan her impulse buying to the penny" (362).

The idea of "disciplining" the wife clearly appeals to Whyte, despite his sarcastic account of the organization man's own desire for "external disci-pline," suggesting that one of the worrisome things about the organized life is that *men* are willingly accepting, even welcoming, the strictures and structures that have always been necessary to the management of female desire. Worse, although Whyte does not say this directly, the reader gets the strong impression that the "housewives" are pulling the strings in the realm of consumption, and the men are going along with this feminine manipulation in order to maintain their place in the group. For Whyte, this signals a double loss of autonomy for the organization man, who is, thus, governed by his wife and her management of their place in the sub-urban collective *and* by the corporation that controls his creativity and his production at work. Whyte places the blame for acquiescing to these controls squarely on the shoulders of the individuals who fail to resist; he has no interest in critiquing the motives and methods of corporations, banks, or capitalism.

Like Whyte, David Riesman balks at blaming "society" for what ails contemporary men, arguing that the "ritualistic pressures" leading men toward conformity "spring not from the . . . institutions of America but from the increasingly other-directed character of its people" (240). *The Lonely Crowd* also differentiates between "inner-directed" (masculine) and "other-directed" (feminine) forms of consumption, making use of a strategy, as we saw in the previous chapter, that enables writers to keep the baby of consumerism while throwing out the bathwater of the fem-inine. Instead of posing consumption against production, this strategy makes it possible to see consumerism as a system that is itself structured by gender difference, with more or less masculine, more or less individu-alist, more or less "inner-directed" forms of consumption. Like Whyte, Riesman frames his account in relation to Veblen's classic model of con-spicuous consumption and, also like Whyte, tracks how the postwar con-text reveals significant changes in Americans' relation to consumption. Whereas the "inner-directed" man either sought the power over others gained by his display of conspicuous consumption or sought, on his own initiative, to pursue both "high" and "low" leisure activities as an escape from this self-driven work life, the "other-directed" man participates in consumer culture as part of his larger "adjustment to the group" (149).

In order to flesh out his argument about the "other-directed round of life—the night shift," Riesman uses the consumption of food and of sex as his two case studies. Where the inner-directed man put on display his knowledge about the best cuts of meats, standards of nutrition, and basic techniques of food preparation, the other-directed man "puts on display his taste and not directly his wealth, respectability, cubic capacity, or caloric soundness" (142). "Taste," in this context, becomes an index not of an individual's deeply felt, sincere likes and dislikes but rather an individual's desire to *appear* to have the proper likes and dislikes, as sanctioned by the group. The "conservative" and no-nonsense *Boston School of Cooking* has given way to the "chatty and atmospheric" *The Joy of Cooking,* "for the other-directed person cannot lean on such objective standards of success as those which guided the inner-directed person: he may be haunted by a feeling that he misses the joy in food or drink *which he is supposed to feel*" (143–44; emphasis added). Such joy is insincere and inauthentic because it springs not from the individual himself, or from a "tradition" that is tried and true, but from "fashion," which is, by definition, superficial and inauthentic. Riesman is on pretty shaky ground here, the argument resting on some fine distinctions between "taste" and "knowledge." However, as he moves on to sex, things get a bit more clear and, of course, also more interesting.

The discussion of the "consumption" of love and sex drips with sarcasm, as Riesman uses the language of consumption to indicate that contemporary sex, like everything else, is experienced as a consumer relation. The discussion is also riven by an unacknowledged gender tension. On the one hand, Riesman grants that women, who are "no longer objects for the acquisitive consumer but are peer-groupers themselves," have "become pioneers, with men, on the frontier of sex." On the other hand, the growing sexual agency of women causes problems for the other-directed man. "The relatively unemancipated wife and socially inferior mistress [!] of the inner-directed man could not seriously challenge the quality of his sexual performance," but as women "become knowing consumers [of sex], the anxieties of men lest they fail to satisfy the women also grows." Riesman sees this new sexual bargain as "another test that attracts men who, in their character, want to be judged by others"—suggesting that the other-directed man, perhaps masochistically, willingly puts himself in a position to be judged and found wanting by these newly sexualized creatures who are now able to "respond in a way that only courtesans were supposed to respond in an earlier age" (148).

Riesman's discussion of both inner-directed and other-directed sex is, perhaps not surprisingly, completely male oriented, despite his willingness to grant women a sexual agency, albeit a threatening one. The reference to "mistresses" and "courtesans" resonates back to his earlier discussion of the inner-directed man's use of consumption as an escape from the pressures of his own success-driven strivings at work and from the "feminine influence" that pushes him to escape "upward with the arts." This man, embodied for Riesman by the nineteenth-century businessman, "combated becoming merely a passive consumer by protecting, as a rebel in shirt sleeves, his escape downward to the lower arts of drink mixing and drink holding, poker, fancy women, and fancy mummery" (122). Such manly forms of rebellious consumerism have disappeared along with the dominance of inner direction as the American characterological model, and while Riesman claims not to be arguing that inner direction is *better* than other direction, his book is, in fact, saturated with the "understandable nostalgia" he disclaims (159). His portrait of the other-directed man does, inescapably, point toward the "shallowness and superficiality" of this "type" (159).

In addition to his other-directed consumption habits, Riesman's new type also produces *himself* as a commodity and, thus, is further distanced from individuality, autonomy, and authenticity. In Riesman's account, the other-directed man formed in the shift from a production to a consumption economy has no core self or character in the tradition of American individualism; he "tends to become merely his succession of roles and encounters and hence to doubt who he is or what he is" (139). Where the inner-directed man used escape to bolster his self, the other-directed man has nothing real to escape *from:* "He may say, when he takes a vacation or stretches a weekend, 'I owe it to myself'—but the self in question is viewed like a car or house whose upkeep must be carefully maintained for resale purposes. The other-directed person has no clear core of self to escape from; no clear line between production and consumption; between adjusting to the group and serving private interests; between work and play" (157). Riesman here paints a picture of boundaries and binaries at risk, and the primary boundary threatened by other-directed personalities and institutions is between the autonomous, self-knowing masculine self and the dependent, numbed, and empty "roles" produced through other direction.

For both Whyte and Riesman, what is inexplicable is the apparent willingness of men to surrender their autonomy and authenticity: Why, they both wonder, are these men not resisting? To echo the *Look* magazine question with which we began this section, what is wrong with men? What Riesman is describing here is not only a shift in the characterological dominant in postwar American culture, which he insists is a result of "the abundance of America in the phase of incipient population decline" (143), but also a shift in understandings of the self, what constitutes a self, whether that self is autonomous, or whether that self is, necessarily, formed by its insertion into numerous systems of meaning. The emphasis on "roles" that mask or even replace an essential self begins, in mid-century, to erode faith in the inviolable "core" that makes an individual an individual, authentic and autonomous. Although the concept of "roles" does not necessarily imply falseness, mid-century efforts to characterize shifts in American individualism inevitably pose a true "core" self against the "roles" that self is forced to perform. As we will see in both *The Catcher in the Rye* and *On the Road*, anxieties over the violability of a "core self" coexist with anxieties over masculinity.

PHONIES, FALSIES, AND FLITS

In a 1997 essay on the "social history" of *The Catcher in the Rye*, historian Stephen J. Whitfield argues that "little that is fresh can still be proposed about so closely analyzed a text" (581). Whitfield looks to the history of the book's censorship and defenses against censorship as the only fertile ground remaining for the historian or critic.[1] Whitfield's own essay demonstrates how this "utterly apolitical" novel has been used by critics and apologists alike to further their own political, moral, and social agendas; making the novel into a symptom of what's wrong with "American character," or reading it as whatever flavor of political allegory is currently *en vogue*, critics have, in Whitfield's estimation, unwittingly created a public record on the shifting mores of postwar American culture. Vulnerable to right-wing moralism and left-wing political opportunism alike, Whitfield's *Catcher* becomes the blank slate on which postwar anxieties and obsessions are inscribed. Yet one important wind of twentieth-century cultural criticism escapes Whitfield's notice. Mentioning in passing that the book cannot be made guilty of promoting the identity politics that critics on the Right claim to have splintered American culture, Whitfield is certain that the book "promotes no class consciousness, racial consciousness, or ethnic consciousness of any sort. . . . Nor does [the] novel evoke the special plight of young women and girls" (589). Perhaps because the novel focuses on an unmarked young man—white, putatively straight, and of the dominant class—*Catcher* is deemed to be uninterested in racial, ethnic, class, or gender ideologies. Whitfield is not alone in discounting the relevance of gender to the novel. Unlike Sylvia Plath's *The Bell Jar,* which is often read as a female version of *Catcher,* detailing a specifically female experience, Salinger's novel has not been read as an anatomy of a specifically male experience; rather, *Catcher* has been read, and canonized, as a novel about adolescent angst, unmodified by gender.[2]

Salinger's novel, in fact, is as much about gender as is *The Bell Jar,* both novels articulating how sensitive young protagonists negotiate the gender norms of their time and place and risk the punishments for failing to perform gender in a culturally intelligible manner. But it also registers a broader protest, not only against conformity and "phoniness" but also against a series of perceived slights to, even attacks on, masculinity. As my opening section argued, protest against conformity, against "groupthink," against "other direction" and the "organized life" are also and always a *masculine* protest against a society perceived to threaten individualism, autonomy, and authenticity. While some critics of *Catcher* have already pointed to the novel's relationship to contemporaneous sociological discourses concerned with diagnosing the condition of the "American character" at mid-century, the relevance of these discourses to the novel's engagement with gender has escaped notice—in part because neither *Catcher* nor the sociological critique has been read as having *anything* to say about gender because they have little to say about women. Here, I will argue that Holden becomes a spokesperson, not for adolescent discontent or rebellion but for a form of masculine protest that was itself fast becoming part of the postwar consensus.

Like Riesman and Whyte, Salinger's protagonist bemoans the "prostitutions" required for full male membership in American culture. As Leerom Medovoi notes, "phoniness" in *Catcher* is not limited to those who enjoy class privilege, as some readings of the novel suggest; instead, the term is applicable to any individual who produces himself as a commodity to be sold. Phonies are those "whose self-promotion for the consumption of others is an index of their inauthenticity" ("Democracy, Capitalism, and American Literature" 277). While Holden deems women, as well as men, to be "phonies," phoniness in women is more or less expected, with their "damn falsies pointing all over the place" (3) and their devotion to fashion and celebrities. Significantly, it is the writer, the teacher, and others who make their living by words who most often provoke Holden's ire at phoniness. Holden's brother D. B., we're told at the outset, is "out in Hollywood . . . being a prostitute" (2), while his father is a corporate lawyer who finances Broadway shows. Advertisers and others who twist words to manipulate reality come in for Holden's contempt.

The subjection of the writer to the demands of the marketplace has historically been cause for concern in American culture. As amply demonstrated in a wide range of cultural and literary histories, American male writers have long positioned themselves as heroic individuals seeking to tell the truth in a commercial culture where the values of celebrity and popularity trump the values of authenticity and originality. As Paul Gilmore argues convincingly in the aptly titled *The Genuine Article,* the great American writers of the late nineteenth and early twentieth centuries felt themselves to be fighting against the corruptions of the feminine marketplace. Being a "manly writer meant resisting commercial demands. Because their profession and the literary market were largely imagined in feminine terms and because many of the most successful authors were women, male authors often oscillated between a desire for commercial success and a need to define themselves as independent creators resistant to a feminizing marketplace" (13). The figure of the prostitute is useful in articulating this anxiety, for what better way to bring home the purported collusion between commercialization and feminization than to describe the male writer as a prostitute? Against D. B.'s prostituted talent, Salinger positions two forms of anti-commercial and, thus, authentic writing: the writing on Allie's baseball glove and Phoebe's novels featuring Hazle Weatherfield.[3] Much has been made of the novel's privileging of these two youthful Caulfield siblings as figures for the childhood innocence that Holden desperately aims to hold on to, but their significance as representatives of an anti-commercial, anti-consumerist ethos is equally important. In Holden's imagination, Allie and Phoebe occupy a pre-lapsarian, nonconsumer paradise uncorrupted by "phonies" who allow the movies, advertising, and corporate values to define and commodify their identities.

Holden's extreme emotional investment in depicting mass culture as endangering the values of originality, creativity, and authenticity connects Salinger's novel to a more general mass-culture critique being mounted by mid-century intellectuals. Dwight MacDonald's famous *Partisan Review* essay "Masscult and Midcult" reads as an addendum to Holden Caulfield's excoriation of the "phony" culture he finds everywhere around him. Each example of "phoniness" in the novel relates to a performer's effort to please an audience rather than to express a personal belief, aesthetic, or truth—or, as Whyte and Riesman might say, the subordination of individual "genius" or creativity to the demands of the homogenizing group. Speeches made at the various prep schools Holden attends, movies and shows, Ernie's piano playing—each performance is corrupted by the audience's desire. Responding to Ernie's artistic compromises, Holden swears allegiance to an ethic of creative genius, in which the artist retains his integrity only by maintaining his independence from an audience: "If I were a piano player or an actor or something and all those dopes thought I was terrific, I'd hate it. I wouldn't even want them to *clap* for me. People always clap for the wrong things. If I were a piano player, I'd play it in the goddam closet" (84). For MacDonald, there is no doubt that the problem with "masscult" and "midcult" is that "mere popularity" determines merit in the marketplace of consumer culture. The result is "impersonality," "lack of standards," and "total subjection to the spectator" (7). "Today, in the United States," he writes, "the demands of the audience, which has changed from a small body of connoisseurs into a large body of ignoramuses, have become the chief criteria of success" (18).

While neither Salinger nor MacDonald employs an overtly gendered rhetoric to critique mass culture, gender nevertheless is implicit in these laments for the lost days of solitary genius and independence of mind. Code words for "feminine" culture abound in MacDonald's critique, in which "the cheapest, flimsiest kind of melodrama," "bathetic sentimentality," and "the most vulgar kind of theatricality" compete with "the most acute psychological analysis and social observation," "superb comedy," and "great descriptive prose" (7). The language here recalls Ann Douglas's discussion of sentimentalism in *The Feminization of American*

Culture: "Involved as it is with the exhibition and commercialization of the self, sentimentalism cannot exist without an audience. It has no content but its own exposure, and it invests exposure with a kind of final significance" (307). Melodrama, sentimentality, and theatricality are linked with the feminine in an aesthetic system that, as Andreas Huyssen and others have argued, ties true creativity to the masculine. The modern male artist, "the suffering loner who stands in irreconcilable opposition to modern democracy and its inauthentic culture" (Huyssen 51), must battle against the "phoniness" that defines mass culture and distances it from the authentic, masculine expression of true artistic genius. As I noted in my discussion of the modernist and masculine ethos of rock-and-roll music, one anxiety fueling the rejection of mass or consumer culture is that the male artist must submit his work and himself to an audience, and then that audience (often imagined as feminine) might have the power to determine value.

The pull of this romantic ideology of the lonely genius is so strong that it appears even where we might least expect to find it: in Whyte's analysis of the business culture of the organization. Like MacDonald, who claims that a "mass society, like a crowd, is inchoate and uncreative" (9), Whyte excoriates the new Social Ethic for destroying the possibility and power of individual genius. The "false collectivization" driving the new emphasis on creative groups, rather than creative individuals, is based on a mistaken belief that groups "think" and "create." Whyte argues that group advocates, now dominant in the sciences and humanities, "are engaged in a wholesale effort to tame the arts of discovery—and those by nature suited for it. In part this effort is propelled by the natural distaste of the uncreative man for the creative," but it is also part of the self-justifying strategy through which the individual must necessarily be subordinated to the group (57). The solitary genius—the artist writing in his isolated garret, the scientist alone in his lab—is endangered by the collectivization of creativity. As Whyte would have it, the delegitimization of an ideology of competitive individualism in "the fight against genius" means the death of creativity itself. Once again, Whyte's language betrays his disdain for the Social Ethic and his nostalgia for a society in which a meritocracy is underwritten by gender and class hierarchies. The effort to "tame" the creativity of the genius amounts to an emasculation.

MacDonald's worry that audiences are usurping the power of the creator is shared by Salinger, but the audience, too, is threatened with a feminization. The lack of discrimination and the confusion of standards rob the truly discerning reader, viewer, or listener—such as Holden Caulfield, for example—of the power and authority to make authentic critical judgments. That *Catcher* was chosen as a Book-of-the-Month Club main selection—and that it was mass-marketed in paperback with a sensationalist cover—suggests that the mass-culture critique in the United States was so normalized as to be commodifiable. Holden's rebellion against mass culture, like his rebellion against conformity, places him *not* in a select group of outsiders or rebels but squarely within the dominant intellectual mode of his era. The masculine protest against feminization articulated by Whyte, MacDonald, and others is at mid-century a primary mode of identity formation, in addition to a primary mode for reproducing gender.

Holden's fears of becoming just another organization man (like his father) and of getting sucked into consumer culture (like D. B.) are balanced against fears of what it would mean to opt out of successful masculinity as it is currently defined. Barbara Ehrenreich has shown that men who chose not to pursue the dream of domestic masculinity in the fifties were suspected to be insufficiently heterosexual. Anxieties over a general feminization of American character connect in *Catcher,* as in the broader Cold War discourse, with more overt fears of same-sex desire and the "homosexualization of America." As Robert Corber has argued, the release of the Kinsey report on male sexuality in 1948 fed an already rampant hysteria about gay men and lesbians as national security risks (*In the Name* 61–65). Kinsey's statistics, showing that a full one-third of the adult male population reported some homosexual experience, effectively blurred the line between hetero and homo, normal and deviant, and raised the troubling question of how to tell the difference between the two. Just as red hunters worried that communists could infiltrate the United States masked as "ordinary Americans," anti-communist forces seized on the indistinguishability between gay and straight as the occasion to ferret out deviants.[4]

Given this context, it seems reasonable to conclude, as Alan Nadel does, that Salinger's novel links sexual and political deviance, positioning Holden as an anxiety-ridden subject unable to tell "the truth" from lies, seeking out phoniness everywhere. Certainly, Holden sees "flits" around every corner, and his overwrought reaction to Mr. Antolini's supposed advances indicates a high degree of anxiety over sexual orientation; indeed, Holden's comment that he would opt to play the piano "in the closet" starts to look like nothing so much as a coded reference to same-sex desire. The novel exhibits a fascinated interest in sexual deviance and the sexual underworld: for example, Holden voyeuristically spies on a transvestite and on "water games" between a heterosexual couple. Not only does he claim to be "traveling incognito" (60), but he also seems obsessed with the question of other men's sexual orientation: the "Navy guy" he meets in a bar "is one of those guys who think they're being a pansy if they don't break around forty of your fingers when they shake hands with you" (86–87); he identifies a "very Joe Yale-looking guy, in a gray flannel suit and one of those flitty-looking Tattersall vests," and avers that "all those Ivy League bastards look alike" (85). The overstatement in "forty of your fingers" indicates a degree of hysteria and the idea that all those "bastards look alike" and look like flits evidences a certain amount of paranoia.

Holden wants to identify flits by their consumption of particular items of clothing, but his reference to the uniform of a particular class of white men suggests not that all men of this class are flits but rather that the wearing of a uniform per se is evidence of a failure to express a properly masculine individuality. At the same time, the idea that flits *don't* wear an easily identified uniform instills a good deal of homosexual panic. Old Luce, whom Holden looks up to as a mentor, had earlier instigated this panic when he "said half of the married guys in the world were flits and didn't even know it. He said you could turn into one practically overnight, if you had all the traits and all. He used to scare the hell out of us. I kept waiting to turn into a flit or something. The funny thing about old Luce, I used to think he was sort of flitty himself" (143). The impossibility of distinguishing between gay and straight leads to a generalized sexual panic, with Holden unsuccessfully seeking a code to read the truth of sexuality, much as he creates a code to define the difference between phony and authentic.

Holden's seemingly reluctant attraction to "flits" and an urban bohemian lifestyle suggests an interest in an alternative to the "phoniness" required by respectable adulthood. As it turns out, "flits" seem both less feminized and less phony than the respectable men who earn Holden's sharpest contempt. In the fifties, homosexuality was widely understood as "immaturity," a failure to accept the burdens and rewards of mature manhood, but, as Ehrenreich suggests, it might also offer an alternative to entrapment in the family and domesticity. Given Holden's resistance to the "adulteries" of that mature manhood, it is possible to see his attraction to "flits" as a potential escape from the phoniness embodied by lawyers, businessmen, and other "organization men." *Catcher* also tries out the possibility that marriage and domesticity might offer an escape from phoniness into authenticity when Holden fantasizes running off to the woods with Sally Hayes. But bringing a woman along in an attempt to escape from what Corber calls the postwar gender "settlement" is doomed to fail, for as Holden quickly understands, Sally represents the road to the very thing he yearns to escape from: "working in some office, making a lot of dough, and riding to work in cabs and Madison Avenue buses, and reading newspapers, and playing bridge all the time, and going to the movies and seeing a lot of stupid shorts and coming attractions and newsreels" (133). Given Holden's resistance to the very idea of domesticity and breadwinning, his response to Sally makes perfect sense; what doesn't make sense, and what points to a sexual ambivalence if not sexual panic, is Holden's confession, earlier, that "I felt like marrying her the minute I saw her. I'm crazy. I didn't even *like* her much, and yet all of a sudden I felt like I was in love with her and wanted to marry her" (124). Holden doesn't actually "feel" in love with Sally; he both is seduced by a mass-produced version of heterosexual romance and mature masculinity and resents that seduction. His ambivalence about gender is further evidenced by the fact that he habitually performs a Hollywood-produced masculinity (104, for example) while voicing a violent opposition to Hollywood. Like his response to other women, here Holden exhibits an extreme ambivalence that borders on the hysterical and predicts Holden's later panicked response to Mr. Antolini.

As tempting as it might be to conclude that all of this talk of flits evidences Holden's uncertainty over his own sexual orientation,[5] I would like to suggest that what's at issue here is not sexual, but gender, identity. Holden's ambivalence about sexuality is part of a larger uncertainty about, and protest against, the erosion of secure, binary gender difference. Holden's desire to evade the compromises of adulthood can be read as a desire to escape the pull of gender in a culture where even the staunchest embodiments of mature masculinity—the corporate lawyer, the creative artist—are subject to the confusions of feminization. Gender is unstable in this world in which men are constantly faced with the threat of feminization. Masculinity is no longer grounded in a producer ethos—or, as Whyte would phrase it, the Protestant Ethic. Just as Phoebe and Allie are positioned as authentic writers against the prostitutions of a D. B., these two figures also point toward the possibility of freedom from the gender conventions that Holden struggles with. Quasi-androgynous, Allie and Phoebe represent not only Holden's lost childhood but also a lost social and cultural order where authenticity has not yet given way to phoniness. Outside the symbolic circuit of gender, Allie and Phoebe are not subject to the "feminization" that Holden fears or the "masculinization" he ambivalently accepts. Masculinization, in this context, means acceptance of mass-produced norms of mature manhood, modeled by Holden's corporate-attorney father and the various businessmen who govern the prep schools he has attended. Ironically, this masculinization also means feminization: mindless adaptation to a social order that denies the individual (man) power to determine his own fate.

Like the postwar discourse engaged in diagnosing disturbing changes to "the American character," The Catcher in the Rye hides its anxieties about gender difference beneath a narrative about conformity, consensus, and phoniness. When speaking of "American character," these social critics are in actuality speaking about a tradition of American masculinity based in an economy of production and on the naturalization of a model of competitive individualism that cannot stand the stresses of new business models, new modes of consumption, and new sciences to explain human desires and behaviors. Lizbeth Cohen notes that while the social critics of the fifties were bemoaning the standardization and mechanization of a consumer culture that homogenizes individuals into one mass, advertisers and others were already moving ahead to create what might turn out to be a greater threat to notions of masculine individualism, authenticity, and autonomy. Market segmentation—the strategy of identifying consumers by their race, class, and gender—was to lead to a commodification of identity that Whyte and his fellow critics could only imagine.[6] The Catcher in the Rye seems to acknowledge that phoniness is here to stay, and this accounts for a good portion of its pleasurable tone of melancholy and nostalgia, a tone created by the novel's protest against an inevitable series of shifts and changes. Holden's lament is, as I have argued, part of a larger tradition of masculine protest: protest against threats to masculinity and protest as an expression, however compromised, of masculine power and authority. Such masculine protest against an always rising tide of feminization functions to reinforce gender difference even as it appears to be offering evidence of its destabilization. That protest has the effect not of creating *new* forms of masculinity but of creating a nostalgic desire for the old forms, even as those forms become increasingly impossible to maintain.

REBEL MALES AND WHITE SORROWS

It is more or less a critical commonplace that the Beats were rebelling against the conformity required by postwar American culture, symbolized by the man in the gray flannel suit, his perfectly appointed and utterly materialistic suburban lifestyle, and his meaningless pursuit of consumer pleasures. Brainwashed by advertisers and buying wholeheartedly into the ethos of a corporate culture that favors groupthink and collective responsibility over individual thought, creativity, and originality, this American—white, male, and middle class—is the figure against which the Beats positioned themselves and their rebellion. This mythologized construction of postwar American culture, rarely challenged, demonizes consumer culture, and, by extension, the "femininity" associated with it, and positions the white male rebel as a heroic figure who speaks for the "authenticity" from which the man in the gray flannel suit has been alienated. According to Barbara Ehrenreich, "The short-lived apotheosis of the male rebellion, the Beat, rejected both job and marriage. In the Beat, the two strands of male protest—one directed against the white-collar work world and the other against the suburbanized family life that work was supposed to support—come together into the first all-out critique of American consumer culture" (52). Similarly, Allan Johnston claims Beat rebellion "involved a desire to escape from socioeconomic conditions that . . . subordinated the person to a world of consumer objects, while also suggesting a broader critique of sociocultural developments that were generating an increasingly totalitarian, commodity-driven world" (107). Warren Bareiss, commenting on Kerouac's representation of the "commodity-driven world," says that "for the Beats, suburbia, shopping malls, advertising, limited access highways, fast food, and other developments indicative of the postwar explosion in production and consumption were prisons of the mind and spirit" (13).[7]

The Beats occupy a privileged position in narratives of postwar culture, representing for many a clear "countercultural" assault on consumer culture and its normativities. One episode in a longer historical narrative about feminization, Beat culture has been mythologized as a "cultural brand" that enabled men to evade the "emasculations" of conformity (Holt 41). Kerouac's *On the Road* has become, in American popular culture and American mythology, the iconic representation of rebel males rejecting consumer society and the compromises required of men who agree to participate in it. As the comments cited above suggest, a master narrative about the Beats' rejection of consumer culture has been institutionalized, with *On the Road*'s male characters embodying the very image of rebel males mounting a countercultural resistance against the "commodity-driven" world and, of course, its assaults on masculinity. Yet Kerouac's text spends no time detailing the problems of consumer culture. The forces against which Sal rebels are left vague—just as vague, it turns out, as the "authenticity" he seeks in supposedly rejecting consumer culture and its domesticating traps. Countless critical treatments of the text create the expectation that *On the Road* offers some specific analysis—or at least descriptions—of the elements of consumer culture against which Kerouac might be rebelling. But as it turns out, *On the Road* is silent on the questions of shopping malls and fast food, which raises this question: Why insist that *On the Road* targets consumer culture as the thing against which Sal is rebelling, even when the novel pays very little attention to shopping or commodities? What makes even feminist critics see the Beats as articulating "the first all-out critique of consumer culture"?

On the Road does sometimes draw on an anti-consumerist logic as part of its effort to reinstall white men as fully empowered, authentic individuals in a world where "society" threatens to curtail masculine movement, freedom, and autonomy, but it does not offer anything like a coherent critique of consumerism. Readings of *On the Road* as an assault on *consumer* culture work to justify and even to monumentalize what in my view is a more general and inchoate "rebellion" against all those forces that aim to deprive men of their autonomy and agency. The masculine protest articulated in the novel is a protest against *any* perceived threat to masculine individualism and authenticity—rather than a specific protest against any socioeconomic condition or against the capitalist system. The master narrative of postwar culture I am tracking in this chapter is elastic enough to gather any perceived threat under its structure. Whether the threat is suburbia, bureaucracy, consumerism, or the organization, this master narrative works to legitimate male rebellion against the feminizing forces that aim to place limits on a fantasy of freedom from constraint. For Kerouac, *any* social system, or, indeed, any set of socially imposed roles or expectations, necessarily threatens the freedom and purity of masculine self-expression. The coding of Beat rebellion as anti-consumerist (rather than more vaguely anti-establishment) supports the deeply entrenched feminization thesis and perpetuates the signifying chain that links women, consumer culture, and inauthenticity.

Many readers of *On the Road* have delighted in exposing Kerouac's bad faith, catching him out for supposedly rejecting commodity culture while busily commodifying the women and people of color he meets on his journeys. In doing so, they subject him to the kind of anti-consumerist litmus test that has become common in social criticism, whose goal is to determine which rebellions are authentically political and which are not.[8] Allan Johnston, for example, notes that both Dean and Sal practice forms of consumer behavior in their relations to others, "consistently reducing the direct, personal relations the characters think they pursue into 'I-It' commodity relations" (119). Rather than chide Kerouac for failing to be sufficiently anti-consumerist, for failing to pass the litmus test, I want to put pressure on the reading of this text as a countercultural anthem critiquing consumerism (or, indeed, any social system) and to suggest how this reading obscures and, implicitly, justifies its more problematic investments.

A road trip across the United States in the postwar moment would seem to provide the perfect vehicle, as it were, for an exploration of American consumer culture. Indeed, Vladimir Nabokov had done just that in *Lolita*, published just two years before *On the Road*. Humbert Humbert both ecstatically and condescendingly describes, in great detail, the roadside motels, diners, souvenir shops that dot the American landscape. Nabokov has fun with the kitschy names of the motels, "all those Sunset Motels, U-Beam Cottages, Hillcrest Courts, Pine View Courts, Mountain View Courts, Skyline Courts, Park Plaza Courts, Green Acres, Mac's Courts" (146). Humbert Humbert foregrounds Lo's "disgustingly conventional" tastes in music, food, and reading material, concluding that "she it was to whom ads were dedicated: the ideal consumer, the subject of and object of every foul poster" (148).[9] In contrast, Kerouac's road trip is strangely devoid of such descriptions. The one exception is Sal's rather ecstatic embrace of a certain very "American" commodity, apple pie. In the space of three pages, Sal tells us that he ate "apple pie and ice cream in a roadside stand" (13); "I ate another apple pie and ice cream; that's practically all I ate all the way across the country, I knew it was nutritious and it was delicious, of course" (14); "I ate apple pie and ice cream—it was getting better as I got deeper into Iowa, the pie bigger, the ice cream richer" (15). Here, Sal sounds more like a market researcher than he does a rebel against consumerism, once again raising the question of how the novel has earned the reputation it has.

On the Road, then, offers little evidence to support the idea that the novel articulates anything like a critique of consumerism. Sal seeks nothing but personal freedom and individual self-fulfillment, and if consuming ice cream and apple pie gets him there, so be it. It is worth noting as well that Sal is constantly commenting on his accommodations, the houses and apartments where he stays, registering the differences between "the really swank apartment" (40) in Denver and the "shack" in Mill City (63). In Denver Sal also has the opportunity to impersonate a "cultured" man by attending the opera, an opportunity he welcomes for its boost to his masculinity: "Only a few days ago I'd come into Denver like a bum; now I was all racked up sharp in a suit, with a beautiful well-dressed blonde on my arm, bowing to dignitaries and chatting in the lobby under chandeliers" (52). That this is the same character who, later, fantasizes about being a "man of the earth" by working alongside migrant workers in California suggests that, for Sal as perhaps for Kerouac, it's all about the freedom to play a part, to remake the self as one sees fit. The self that's made is less important than the freedom to make it, and social differences of class or race can be put on and taken off like a sharp suit. It is worth noting that Kerouac develops a more accepting view of "roles" and their relation to authenticity than do the mid-century social critics with which I began this chapter or Salinger's Holden Caulfield. To recall, Riesman worries that the authentic self disappears as the other-directed man "tends to become merely his succession of roles and encounters and hence to doubt who he is or what he is" (139), and Holden sees the taking on and taking off of roles as evidence of phoniness. Kerouac, in contrast, seems to welcome the freedom that comes from unmooring the self from the demand for consistency. Rather than rejecting "roles" because they endanger authenticity and threaten commodification, Kerouac embraces them because they promise an escape from social responsibility. This is another reason I find it hard to credit the view that *On the Road* offers a critique of consumerism. Indeed, I agree with Manuel Louis Martinez's point that *On the Road* romanticizes the "free market," and "Kerouac's facility for taking on liminal identities is based on his assumed right to trade, to exchange, to try before he buys" (91). Unlike Martinez, however, I see this as evidence that the novel is not actually interested in critiquing consumer culture rather than evidence that it fails in doing so.

The one place where a straightforward critique of consumerism peeks through is in the character of Bull Lee, who is based on William S. Burroughs. Kerouac frames Bull as a drug-addled eccentric who was "magnificent" in the morning but whose energy flagged because "he took so much junk into his system he could only weather the greater proportion of the day" sitting in his chair (150). Hopped up on junk, Bull rushes from topic to topic, making it hard to credit as sincere or serious his tirade against forced obsolescence, which veers into a conspiracy theory. Pointing out that "they" make shelves, houses, tires, tooth powder, and gum that either fall apart or actually harm the user, Bull concludes, "Same with clothes. They can make clothes that last forever. They prefer making cheap goods so's everybody'll have to go on working and punching timeclocks and organizing themselves in sullen unions and floundering around while the big grab goes on in Washington and Moscow" (149–50). Kerouac may intend for his readers to appreciate Bull the way Sal does, for being the "mad" cat that he is, inviting Sal and Dean to try his Reichian "orgone accumulator" (!)—"Put some juice on your bones. I always rush up and take off ninety miles an hour for the nearest whorehouse, hor-hor-hor!" (152). But it's difficult to buy into the critique he offers or the "liberation" he models. When Bull's "woman" Jane comments on Bull's discourse and the boys' plans for the afternoon, "'It sounds silly to me'" (153), I have to agree with her. If this is the high point of the novel's engagement with the culture it supposedly is rebelling against, it's hard to understand how the book has earned the reputation it has.

There's no doubt that the real "revolutionary" impact of *On the Road* stems from its prose, the ways that Kerouac energetically and idiosyncratically molds and shapes the language to express a certain sense of speed and excitement. This is the aspect of the novel that contemporary reviewers lauded, even as they echoed Jane's comment about the stories sounding "silly" or, worse, promoting delinquency and lawlessness.[10] The latter charge would amount to a badge of honor for Kerouac, but the suggestion that *On the Road* smacks a bit too much of adolescent male antics would not sit as well. One reviewer, writing for *Time*, suggests that, while Kerouac "commands attention as a kind of literary James Dean," the characters and their stories fail to rise to anything like an alternative to the culture the book seems to be imagining. In fact, the "frantic reunions" of the cast of buddies "are curiously reminiscent of lodge and business conventions, with the same shouts of fellowship, hard drinking, furtive attempts at sexual dalliance—and, after a few days, the same boredom" ("The Ganser Syndrome"). The male bonding that the novel centers on, complete with the "sharing" of women, *is* the story of *On the Road*, and Sal's ecstatic response to his buddies takes precedence over any other narrative or literary focus.

It goes without saying that *On the Road* cares not a bit about liberating women or even thinking about women as capable of enjoying the "purity" of an unfettered life or the search for "It." Women are mere objects to be used by men, and there are moments in this novel when the blatancy of its misogyny still has the power to shock. But women also symbolize the "society" against which these rebellious males define themselves; as Mary Paniccia Carden suggests, Kerouac's "traveling men not only resist the deadly grip of a feminized society but bond through manipulating women" (84). As I suggested above, however, the novel is more ambivalent about the appeals of domesticity and marriage than it has the reputation for being. This ambivalence is most fully demonstrated when Sal briefly abandons his travel adventures to create domesticity with the Chicana woman Teresa, whom Sal renames and Anglicizes as "Terry." This episode also exposes as a sham Sal's professed desires to occupy a marginal position in relation to bourgeois norms and white middle-class culture. This is the only domestic interlude Sal experiences in *On the Road*, in which refusal of the world of nine-to-five work is a badge of honor, a way for the male rebels to distinguish themselves from the alienated men "driving home from work, wearing railroad hats, baseball hats, all kinds of hats, just like after work in any town anywhere" (13). Conforming to "the story of America," where "everybody's doing what they think they're supposed to do" (68), such men are the victims of a culture that destroys masculine authenticity. What Sal rejects here is less consumer culture than it is a provider masculinity. It is only later that a Kerouac character articulates a (superficial) critique of that culture that "imprison[s]" men "in a system of work, produce, consume, work, produce, consume" (*Dharma Bums* 73).

While Sal seems sincere in his desire to experience the "authentic" world that Terry represents—he fantasizes that the white Okies in the camp "thought I was Mexican, of course; and in a way I am" (98)—I want to suggest that this episode exposes the absurdity of reading *On the Road* as a serious critique of mid-century consumer culture. In this sequence, Sal is as far from middle-class white consumer culture as he ever gets, living a subsistence life far removed from the "system of work, produce, consume, work, produce, consume." But rather than feel that he has, thus, found the "It" that he seeks—that is, a fulfillment outside of the terms of white middle-class normativity—Sal instead attempts to reproduce that normativity within this outsider space in what can only be read as a parody of bourgeois convention, marriage, and the protector-provider model of masculinity: "For the next fifteen days we were together for better or for worse," Sal explains (86). Sal envisions this interlude as precisely an escape from the world of "driving home from work" every day, wearing the proper "hat" of a profession, in order to buy the goods that enable the good life: "Every day I earned approximately a dollar and a half. It was just enough to buy groceries in the evening on the bicycle. The days rolled by. I forgot about the East and all about Dean and Carlo and the bloody road.

Johnny and I played all the time; he liked me to throw him up in the air and down in the bed. Terry sat mending clothes. I was a man of the earth, precisely as I had dreamed I would be" (97).

But while this life promises that Sal might realize the fantasy of authenticity he seeks, the reality of his situation starts to make that fantasy seem less than palatable. It takes Sal very little time at all to feel trapped by Terry and to balk *not* against a theoretical construct of provider masculinity but against the reality of the arduous labor it takes to embody it. Noting that Terry and her young son are far faster and more successful at picking cotton than he is, he starts to articulate an escape clause: "What kind of old man was I," he wonders, "that couldn't support his own ass, let alone theirs?" (96). While this admission might sound like an acknowledgment of failure, it actually functions in exactly the opposite way within the world of *On the Road*. Sal is playing at domesticity here, and he soon tires of the experience and yearns once again for the road and the freedom from domestic and financial burdens: "I could feel the pull of my own life calling me back. I shot my Aunt a penny postcard across the land and asked for another fifty" (98). Sal's reference to his "own life" confirms that this life with Terry—mimicking the suburban, domestic, consumerist norm of masculinity—will not deliver the fulfillment he seeks because the fantasy of authenticity cannot survive the reality of hard labor with little reward.

Sal's fantasy of authenticity takes a familiar form as he seems to want to reverse historical progress and go back to a time and a mode of masculinity that have been undermined by a variety of "modern" forces—including consumerism, but also including women's growing power in American culture. Going backward is also a theme in the mid-century social critics who look nostalgically back on a moment when men were not required to accede to women's sexual and other demands (Riesman) and when men were able to practice a swashbuckling kind of individualism (Whyte). Reading *On the Road*'s anthem to male liberation as rebellion against consumerism enables the mythmaking that characterizes so much anti-consumerist critique—and, not coincidentally, justifies hostility to women in the name of evading feminization. Citing Nina Baym's famous essay "Melodramas of Beset Manhood"—to which I have already had occasion to refer—Carden finds in *On the Road* an example of the "promise of authentic and unimpeded self-determination [that] remains a deeply resonant and highly influential foundational trope, which provokes both nostalgia and anxiety in American men living (what appear to be) more bounded lives" (79). This imaginative re-creation of a nineteenth-century dynamic can be seen as part of a larger push to reject "modernity" and its "compromises." As Rob Holton persuasively argues, the Beats' search for, and recourse to, an American "pastoral" betrays a nostalgic desire to reposition masculinity in an anti-modern time and space, to "return to an irreducible primal nature buried under stifling layers of cultural accretion" (94). As we will see with particular force in chapter 4, an anti-modernist impulse, fueled by fantasies of authenticity, is central to much anti-consumerist discourse. Here, that anti-modernism is connected to a fantasy of racial and class authenticity, with the poor and the racially marginalized coming to occupy a privileged position in this pastoral vision—a position that Sal attempts to appropriate for his own purposes.

Sal's domestic arrangements and lackadaisical participation in the grind of "work, produce, consume" amount to a performance of authenticity (as oxymoronic as that sounds). Sal also attempts to appropriate others' authenticity by aligning himself with racial others and poverty. *On the Road,* in this respect, reads like an early version of authenticity tourism, albeit a purportedly anti-commercial version. As Marilyn Halter argues in her *Shopping for Identity: The Marketing of Authenticity,* ethnic cultures have long been pursued as a fount of the "true," "untainted," and "authentic" to the point that "authenticity itself has become a commodity" (18). Many recent commentators on Kerouac's text have pointed to the problematic racial appropriations within it, most especially Sal's wish that he "could exchange worlds with the happy, true-hearted, ecstatic Negroes of America" (180). Martinez, for example, notes that Kerouac reduces material racial and class difference to "mere choice. As long as liminality is maintained as a consumerable product, it is kept safe. An illusory egalitarianism of white subjectivity is established at the cost of objectifying ethnic identity for consumption" (91).[11] What has received less attention is Sal's invocation of whiteness in these passages and how that whiteness comes to represent alienation. The effect of this construction is *not* to expose how the "possessive investment in whiteness"[12] secures privilege and power but rather to expose how "whiteness" *prevents* Sal and his buddies from fully occupying the paradoxically privileged position of people of color.

In its efforts to construct white middle-class men as the tragic embodiments of postwar alienation, and in seeking alternatives to that state
of affairs, *On the Road* goes so far as to claim that white privilege is just
another "system" aiming to curtail masculine freedom. Like consumerism or bureaucracy or the protector-provider ideal of masculinity, white
privilege keeps white men in little boxes and prevents them from experiencing authenticity. While such a construction of white privilege
could potentially be harnessed to an argument about how racism hurts
everyone by subjecting us to a structure that closes down the possibilities for freedom and autonomy, that is not what Kerouac is up to here.
Instead, he constructs white privilege as a system that harms *only* white
men and produces in them a desire to appropriate the "authenticity" of
others. This point comes home with somewhat shocking force when Sal
says, with absolutely no self-consciousness, "I wished I were a Denver
Mexican, or even a poor overworked Jap, anything but what I was so
drearily, a 'white man' disillusioned. All my life I'd had white ambitions;
that was why I'd abandoned a good woman like Terry in the San Joaquin
Valley" (180). Like the possessive investment in property that fuels the
consumer economy and the ideologies of consumption that afflict the
middle-class white man with alienation and lack of access to the authentic, the "It," the possessive investment in whiteness is here understood as
a product of a corrupt culture whose victims are not those marginalized
people whose race gives them no access to the value that accrues to whiteness. Instead, Kerouac suggests that it is white men who suffer because
the "dreariness" of the identity "white man" prohibits them from tapping
into the "joyous life that knows nothing of disappointment and 'white
sorrows' and all that" (181).[13]

But what exactly does Kerouac mean by the phrases "white ambitions"
and "white sorrows"? Is a white ambition the equivalent, or the opposite,
of a white sorrow? Do white ambitions produce white sorrows? I want
to suggest that these phrases mark a moment in *On the Road* when the
fantasy of white middle-class male victimization is exposed for what it
is. Unusually, Kerouac employs scare quotes here, indicating that "white
man" and "white sorrows" are both constructs that deserve our skepticism, but it's not entirely clear what he wants us to be skeptical of. On the
one hand, Kerouac might be problematizing the construct "white man" so

as to foreground the ways in which any racial and gender construction is a fiction that can be contested; on the other hand, he could be attempting to disavow the privilege that attaches to "white man." The same goes for the phrase "white sorrows." The fact that he does not enclose "white ambitions" in scare quotes suggests that he does not mean us to question this phrase, that he construes this phrase as a straightforward description of a set of desires that Sal has only pretended to disavow. These white ambitions might be what he has been running away from—the cycle of "work, produce, consume" that afflicts masculinity and feminizes men—and the fact that he attributes his abandonment of "a good woman like Terry" to them suggests that Sal is unwittingly acknowledging that what made him abandon her was *not* his disdain for normative American domesticity and the "domestication" of men that comes with it but his inability to imagine himself cohabiting with a woman of color and living a life of poverty. Collecting the money that his aunt sends him "saves [his] lazy butt again" (101), and Sal is able to escape not from the simulated normativity that he pursues with Terry but from the very real marginality that a life with her would mean. His "white ambitions" might separate him from the hipness he associates with racial others, but they also save his lazy butt from a life of poverty and want. The disavowed terms *white man* and *white sorrows,* thus, work as a perhaps unconscious recognition on Kerouac's part that Sal's arrogation of a victimized position is a white fantasy.

When Sal finally goes to Mexico, he finds not the "real" Mexico but something like a virtual Mexico—a white projection of what a space of otherness would look like. Sal reports that, "to our amazement, [Mexico] looked exactly like Mexico" (274). His retrospective regret for abandoning "a good woman like Terry" is here undermined by his unapologetic and outrageously ignorant construction of the women he encounters in Mexico City. Whereas in the San Joaquin Valley Sal worked beside Mexican migrant workers, here he throws money around a brothel, imagining the women whose labor he is purchasing as bit players in his own narrative. As Allan Johnston notes, here Sal changes from a "producer to a consumer" and "finds himself wealthy beyond all expectation, able to participate fully in the American dream" (119)—by, of course, "purchasing" Mexican women.[14] The sheer audacity of the sexism and racism expressed here and elsewhere in *On the Road* makes one wonder how Kerouac could possibly have imagined himself as a rebel against *anything*, so fully do his attitudes toward women and people of culture embody the status quo. Sal's disdain for his "New York friends [who] were in the negative, nightmare position of putting down society and giving their tired bookish or political or psychoanalytical reasons" (8) should make us hesitate before we attribute to *On the Road* the kind of critical, countercultural purchase on the 1950s that Barbara Ehrenreich, for one, believes it deserves. The fact that she describes the interlude with Terry as "a brief and loving stay with a young Chicana migrant worker" and chides a *Life* magazine profile of the Beats for misreading this as the self-interested and shallow experiment I have argued it is suggests a wish to recuperate Kerouac for a tradition of American counterculture, even while lamenting the unfortunate effects of this male rebellion on women. Ehrenreich represents the *Life* article as making this episode into a "soft-porn celebration of 'the delights of drinking with cheap Mexican tarts'" (63). What she does not mention is Kerouac's own language when, on first encountering Terry, Sal tries to disabuse her of the idea that he is a pimp. "O gruesome life, how I moaned and pleaded, and then I got mad and realized I was pleading with the dumb little Mexican wench and I told her so; and before I knew it I picked up her red pumps and hurled them at the bathroom door and told her to get out" (84–85).

The authenticity that Sal seeks is, thus, at best, a borrowed authenticity and, at worst, a racist fantasy of taking over the position of the other. Such a fantasy typically does *not* involve appropriating the place of the *feminine* other, although Sal does report, in passing, that "Dean once had a dream that he was having a baby and his belly was all bloated up" (177). *Authenticity*, as I've already suggested, is a term reserved for men and for the masculine, and it is a term that can be found in virtually every analysis of *On the Road*, despite the fact that Kerouac himself does not use the term. The idea that what Sal and his band of fellow travelers seek is some more authentic alternative to the conformist, consumerist, suburban mandates of postwar masculinity has become the "truth" of *On the Road*—and the "truth" about the cohort of writers whom Kerouac dubbed the "Beat generation." But the elaboration of this "authenticity" remains maddeningly vague, signified by a chain of interchangeable terms like *purity, It, the wow, the yes, the mad thing*. Kerouac ends by grounding this authenticity in racial and class marginality, earning him and his book the reputation for being the attempt of a privileged white man to claim for himself and his peers the "authenticity" that he imagines comes from being socially and politically outside the center, really occupying the margins. Many readers and critics have made the point that Sal (and Kerouac) is taking what amounts to a vacation from a more properly bourgeois and conventional life by appropriating the romanticized otherness he myopically sees in "Negroes," jazz musicians, hobos, and migrant workers. The charge that Sal and Dean are consuming this otherness *should* work to undermine the myth of *On the Road* as an anti-consumerist text, but it has more often been used as evidence that Kerouac's anti-consumerism is inauthentic.

When critics chide Kerouac and the Beats for claiming a "rebel" status while, simultaneously, cashing in on their celebrity, they are further entrenching the assumption that any connection to commercial or market logic necessarily endangers authenticity. Rather than question this logic, for example, Ehrenreich suggests that the history of the Beats' rise and fall can be understood precisely in these terms, arguing that "their rapid media transformation into 'beatniks,'" mere "imitators" of the real thing, came to replace the original Beats in the public eye (53). But this logic, intent on differentiating the non-commercial authentic from the commercial inauthentic, is, as I suggested in the previous chapter, faulty; as Mel van Elteren points out, "The Beat Generation as a whole enjoyed a peculiar relationship with its own hype as disseminated by the mainstream media. . . . The Beats were involved in creating and generating mass-mediated images about themselves and, in turn, responded to those depictions" (76). Warren Bareiss, in a fascinating article on the Kingston Trio, the Beats, and what he calls the "production of 'authenticity,'" underlines the myth that the "hipsters" who chose to entertain the public through music, performance, and writing were, somehow, *outside* the consumer culture that they appeared to be protesting against. The irony that the cultural rebel must market his rebellion through consumer means is the factor that, "more than any other, cut most deeply into the Beats'—and folk music purists'—self-construction. Taken to its logical conclusion, transparency regarding the commercial production of authenticity—in effect, artificial authenticity—undermined Beats' and folk purists' own pretensions regarding authenticity and identity construction, the latter notably including the Beats' tacit denial of their own typically economically privileged backgrounds" (26). Pointing out the absurdity in the notion of "artificial authenticity" brings us back to the points I made in the previous chapter about the fantasy of securing an authentic space outside of consumer culture.[15]

I want to end this chapter by returning to the organization man and briefly discussing an odd and interesting book called *The New Individualists: The Generation after the Organization Man*. In this book, management consultant Paul Leinberger and critical theorist Bruce Tucker provide a link between the mid-century organization man, who valued personality and pursued the Social Ethic, and the late-century postmodern subject, who registers a crisis in individualism. Leinberger and Tucker argue that the children of the organization men have abandoned the "social ethic" in pursuit of a "self ethic," which, somewhat paradoxically, is built on the premise that the authentic self at the core of American-style individualism is no longer viable. Contextualizing the life and career paths of these organization children in relation to the sixties rebellions, the rise of the "postmetropolitan suburbs," the development of a global economy, and the massive expansion of popular media through the seventies and eighties, Leinberger and Tucker theorize that what we are seeing in this new generation is a new social character they call the "artificial person." They argue that the "ideal of the authentic self is everywhere in retreat"—in part due to the development of "alternative and more inclusive conceptions of the self, especially those introduced into organizations by the influx of women," that "now challenge almost daily the more traditionally male conception of the unfettered self" (16). In a chapter titled "The End of Authenticity," the authors attribute the rise of the artificial person to the "seismic shift in Western thinking" known as "postmodernism" (285).[16] Leinberger and Tucker argue that, among other things, the "end of authenticity" presents a paradigm shift in intellectual, social, and characterological terms, and this shift heralds a crisis in our understandings of the self: "Either starting from the premise, or arriving at the conclusion, that any meaningful reality is structured like a language, each version of the paradigm in its fashion encourages us to see reality in a new way: as the convergence of self and culture in the play of signification. Thus, it is in the very artificial systems the self is supposed to flee that it finds its being, repugnant though such a thought may be to pursuers of the pure authentic self" (289–90). The postmodern subject will be the topic of the next chapter, where I will consider how postmodernism produces a new crisis in authenticity.

CHAPTER 3

SHOPPING FOR THE REAL

Anti-Consumerism and the Gender Politics of Postmodern Critique

Jonathan Franzen's *The Corrections* can be read as a post-organization novel, an exploration of what it means to be the son of a reluctant organization man. That Chip Lambert is a leftist academic resonates with the picture Leinberger and Tucker paint of organization offspring who reject and even vilify the organization for its squelching of individual creative expression. Chip articulates his critique of the organization by criticizing corporate culture, but while we might expect Franzen to cheer on Chip's attack on consumerism and corporatism, Franzen actually uses him to lampoon academic critiques of consumer culture. In an early scene in the novel, Chip, an assistant professor of "Textual Artifacts," scolds his students to "sit up straight like active critics rather than be passive consumers" (39). He instructs them in the classic tradition of anti-consumerist theorizing from the academic Left and is frustrated and annoyed when they pose their perceptions of everyday reality against his theoretical certitudes. In the final lesson of the semester, Chip shows his students an advertisement promoting the W___ Corporation's breast cancer awareness campaign and expects them to get in line behind his demystifying reading. But the students resist, and when Chip peevishly insists that they remember what they've learned from Baudrillard, his star student Melissa challenges his motives, calling the entire class "bullshit. It's one critic after another wringing their hands about the state of criticism" and the demise of radical critique in the postmodern era, all insisting that "people who think they're happy aren't 'really' happy" (44) because they are the dupes of mass consumer culture.

Shaken, Chip begins to question his certainty that he is fighting the good fight, doing the useful work of training his students to recognize the manipulations of a "sick" postmodern culture: "But if the supposed sickness wasn't a sickness at all—if the great Materialist Order of technology and consumer appetite and medical science really *was* improving the lives of the formerly oppressed; if it was only straight white males like Chip who had a problem with this order—then there was no longer even the most abstract utility to his criticism" (45).[1] Notwithstanding Franzen's own vexed relationship to mass culture (to which I will return later), his parody of a left-leaning cultural studies professor suggests that straight white men might be more invested in this mode of critique than others. When Melissa argues that the ad is "celebrating women in the work-place. . . . It's helping women feel like we own this technology, like it's not just a guy thing" (43), Chip's theoretical stance comes directly into conflict with a feminist emphasis on the material practices of everyday life. No cheerleader for consumer capitalism, Melissa nevertheless resists Chip's requirement that she reproduce a rote theoretical anti-consumerism.

In posing an abstract theoretical account of the postmodern against a more localized and *feminist* response to the realities of contemporary consumer culture, this classroom exchange gets at the dynamic I want to explore in this chapter. Focusing on Don DeLillo's *White Noise,* that quintessential postmodern text, and the critical response that has institutionalized it as such, I will argue that the anti-consumerist critique central to discussions of postmodernism reproduces, in problematic ways, both the gender order and the cultural elitism that structure so much anti-consumerist critique. Critics have long seen DeLillo as a master of anti-consumerist critique, but attention to gender (and class) in the novel has not been a part of the discussion—despite the obvious ways in which the novel connects with a gendered discourse about consumerism, particularly shopping.[2] Worse, as we will see, shopping, that most "feminine" of activities, becomes the emblem for all that is wrong with the postmodern, and the hostility toward consumer activities and consumers on the part of the mostly male critics of the novel suggests an emotionally invested masculine protest.

As we have seen in previous chapters, anti-consumerist critique is an unusually *interested* critique, invested in differentiating heroic rebels from deluded enthusiasts. Because the consumer culture enthusiasts in *White Noise* are men, not women, the hostility toward shopping and shoppers within the critical literature becomes more pronounced, the threat that consumer culture represents to masculinity more urgent. The almost universal disdain for the activities and forms of consumer culture that marks DeLillo criticism installs Chip Lambert's distinction between those who "sit up straight like active critics" and those who "passively consume" what these critics practice their active critique on. As is often the case, the distinction between active intellectual critique and passive material consumption is a gendered distinction. The critical commonplace relating postmodernism to consumerism in DeLillo criticism reproduces a master narrative of decline fueled by a fantasy of authenticity and betrays a nostalgia for a fantasized modernism marked by a clear separation of literature from mass culture, aesthetics from consumer practices, reading from shopping, and masculinity from the feminizing forces that threaten autonomy, authenticity, and meaning.[3] I will end the chapter by briefly returning to Franzen's *The Corrections* to consider how the reception of this novel replays the narrative about postmodernism as a crisis of (white) masculinity.

THE FEMINIZATIONS OF POSTMODERN CONSUMER CULTURE

As we have already seen, the idea that "mass culture" is modernism's feminized other is a common narrative within anti-consumerist critique. That narrative, to recall, is particularly prevalent in American culture and American cultural studies and seeks to figure any perceived triumph of consumerism as a defeat of authenticity, activity, and masculine autonomy. Critical response to *White Noise* has reproduced this narrative, as the novel's critics have almost unanimously characterized it as anatomizing a crisis in contemporary American culture. Broadly speaking, critics figure this crisis as a postmodern condition in which simulation has replaced originality, inauthenticity has replaced authenticity, and the subject has become fragmented by the operations of capitalism, consumerism, technology, and the exponential growth of the mass media. Drawing on theoretical work by Baudrillard, Jameson, and others, critics have argued that

DeLillo's project in *White Noise* is to represent an American culture so given over to consumerism and its various mediations (primarily television but also other forms of technology) that it is no longer possible to experience anything like an unmediated relationship to one's own reality, even and especially to one's own death. Seduced by the image, inhabiting a world dominated by simulacra, the novel's characters passively embody the crisis of postmodernity, futilely seeking meaning in supermarkets and malls.

Mark Conroy set the terms for this reading of *White Noise* in one of the first articles on the novel, when he argued that the novel explores a "crisis of authority" by detailing how traditional modes of cultural knowledge, experience, and transmission are all in decline. "Gladney's life has been in severe drift for many years, but his malaise may best be seen as a crisis of authority. His life is falling apart because it needs several registers of traditional authority in order to stay together. And all of them are coming under attack in the America of DeLillo's text: not from revolution, of course, but simply from those acids of modernity" (98). Conroy argues that the novel shows us what happens when these traditional modes of authentic authority and "cultural transmission" (religion, humanism, the nuclear family, and community) have been replaced by "phony" institutions (99), "fake" religion (101), "compromised and meretricious" humanism (102), an "errant" family narrative in which parents have abdicated their authority (98), and an "expression of civicism in its most perverse form" (100). The novel ends, for Conroy, with Jack "doubly victimized by modernity. . . . Only as that quintessentially passive figure, the consumer, does Gladney have the faint glimpse of immortality now allowed him" (108). As do most critics of the novel, Conroy reads the last scene in the supermarket as DeLillo putting the final nails in the coffin of an American culture and citizenship destroyed by the depredations of consumer culture and, as John Duvall has it, its "proto-fascist" purveyor, television (128).

In criticism of *White Noise,* claims that the "consumer" is *the* "quintessentially passive figure" and that consumerism has replaced authentic experience with "phony" experiences function as self-evident truisms, but, as I will argue here, they also function to represent the crisis of postmodern culture as a crisis of masculinity. Critics who read *White Noise* as exposing the problems of postmodern consumer culture carry on a tradition of cultural critique that insists that what's wrong with American culture is that it "feminizes" American citizens. As I noted in chapter 1, the post-war feminization thesis creates "a cultural metaphor—indeed, a cultural history—of declension, where an originally masculine *American* political culture has lost its way. Put another way, this is a secular and exclusively masculine jeremiad of postwar American culture" (Gould iv; emphasis in the original). While this cultural history of declension is perhaps most easily readable in mid-century accounts of the rise of the "organization man," the suburbs, the "other-directed" personality, and the "hidden per-suaders" who brainwash citizens into giving up their will, it continues to influence cultural critique and in fact grounds some versions of "post-modernism," in particular the work of those theorists whom DeLillo's critics are most likely to reference: Baudrillard and Jameson.[4]

The "postmodern" version of the anti-consumerist master narrative zeroes in on inauthenticity by noticing the dominance of simulacra in late capitalist culture and bemoaning the demise of the real. *White Noise,* of course, provides fertile ground for such an analysis, given its hilarious representation of "SIMUVAC," a government program that stages simu-lated disasters in order to prepare for actual disasters. What is hilarious about this representation is that the bureaucrats who spring into action when an actual disaster occurs—the Airborne Toxic Event—are using the real event to "rehearse the simulation." When Jack asks the SIMUVAC man how it's going, he replies, "The insertion curve isn't as smooth as we would like. There's a probability excess. Plus which we don't have our vic-tims laid out where we'd want them if this was an actual simulation. . . . You have to make allowances for the fact that everything we see tonight is real. There's a lot of polishing we still have to do. But that's what this exercise is all about" (139). DeLillo is clearly poking fun at bureaucratic nonsense and the ways in which technological systems seem to be an end in themselves, but he is also, in my view, acknowledging the interesting epistemological questions that emerge when the line between the real and the simulated is blurred. In addition, the novel's interest in scenes of shopping, and its exploration of how consumer culture might just provide new models for social interaction and identity formation, has led readers and critics to think that DeLillo is jumping on the anti-consumerist band-wagon and identifying grocery stores and shopping malls as the temples of a faux spirituality, offering only an illusion of meaning. The novel, too, in my view, resists this moralizing gesture, and, as I will argue, the critics who try to assimilate the novel to this version of postmodernism reproduce the rote anti-consumerist critique that is so self-evident as to require no demonstration at all. Failing to ground concepts of authenticity, and falling into the trap of circular thinking that reads consumption, alienation, and femininity as mutually constitutive, critical reception of *White Noise* produces a familiar narrative, despite its claims to read in postmodern representation something new.

The narrative of crisis or decline that governs so many readings of this novel is not the only possible account of postmodernism, and there are other accounts interested in the possibility that the delegitimation of traditional familial, religious, civic, and humanist narratives might not be a necessarily and entirely bad thing. As feminist theorists and critics writing at roughly the moment of *White Noise*'s publication suggested so forcefully, "postmodernism" might offer an alternative to the master narratives of Western history that cloaked the particularity of a masculine perspective with a sham universality. Feminists applauded the delegitimation of these master narratives, even as they worried about the motives and agendas of the mostly male theorists of the postmodern.[5] It is not necessary to rehearse these debates here; suffice it to say that the mode of postmodernism cited by the critics of *White Noise,* first, is not the only possible postmodernism and, second, has become its own master narrative of crisis that trots out some tried and true oppositions: active-passive, intellectual-bodily, high culture–mass culture, abstract-material. The mark of this postmodernism is a nostalgic anti-consumerism that values a modernist and masculinist notion of individual autonomy, authenticity, and meaning, while degrading as feminizing anything that compromises these values. It is worth noting here that in addition to feminist accounts of the potential positivities of postmodern culture, a feminist discourse aiming to read shopping and consumerism as empowering to women has also developed; these feminist discourses challenge the more masculinist accounts of postmodernism and of consumer culture, but they have not succeeded in displacing them.

Narratives of postmodernism that focus on the loss of the (modern) values of originality, authenticity, and individual autonomy—and the secure separation of high from low or mass culture that grounds these values—position the white middle-class male individual as the victim of what Conroy calls the "acids of modernity." As Andrew Hoberek has argued, the postmodernism theorized by Jameson mistakes the "experience of the postwar middle class in transition" for a more global cultural and political crisis and, thus, "requires us to understand postmodernism not as an external, reified phenomenon but rather as the universalized worldview of the new white-collar middle class" (*Twilight of the Middle Class* 117, 120). Although Hoberek does not identify it as such, this theoretical account of postmodernism carries on a tradition of social critique, begun in the 1950s, which reads the alienation of the white middle-class American *man* as the tragedy of postwar culture. It is this postmodernism that elevates consumerism to the status of malevolent force intent on depriving a formerly autonomous male agent of the power not only to produce authentic culture but also to tell the difference between the authentic and the inauthentic. In construing the postmodernized subject as that "quintessentially passive figure, the consumer," to recall Conroy once again, such versions of postmodernism insinuate that one of the most damaging effects of postmodern consumer culture is to dilute the power of gender difference, making men more like the women who are "naturally" aligned with consumerism.

As my emphasis on autonomy and individualism suggests, the crisis of postmodernism as it is imagined in the criticism of *White Noise* is an *existential* crisis rather than a social, economic, or political crisis. This construction of the novel's project focuses not on the economic realities of consumer culture but on the ways in which these various postmodern forces affect the *individual*. Postmodernism becomes a crisis of individualism, of the "real" self—and, more pointedly, of the death of the subject and its patriarchal moorings. For example, in his reading of *White Noise* as exemplifying the end of modernist "heroic narrative," Leonard Wilcox stresses what he takes to be the novel's representation of "modernist subjectivity in a state of siege" (348). While acknowledging that this state of siege is a "crisis in the deeply patriarchal structures of late capitalism, a world in which there is a troubling of the phallus, in which masculinity slips from its sure position" (358), Wilcox quickly generalizes from this crisis of masculinity to a cultural crisis tout court and, in doing so, aligns himself with critics who read *White Noise* as representing a Baudrillardian nightmare of postmodern loss and decline.

Wilcox's analysis raises the question of whether the crisis of postmodernism is only or primarily a crisis of masculinity, going so far as to suggest that Jack's confrontation with Willie Mink enacts a "confrontation with postmodern culture itself" (355), complete with an oedipalized struggle over the possession of Babette. But he stops short of considering the gender implications of his own analysis, concluding that the novel offers a "grimly satiric allegory of the crisis of the sign in the order of simulacrum, the dissolution of phallic power, and the exhaustion of heroic narratives of late modernity" (361). The slippage through which a crisis of masculinity becomes a crisis in the "heroic narratives of late modernity" returns the subject and his narratives (even if in crisis) to the normatively masculine. As many feminists writing about the relationship between feminism and postmodernism in the 1980s made clear, men and women have strikingly different relationships to the myth of the autonomous subject, and women are unlikely to mourn the death of a privilege they never have had (theoretical) access to in the first place.[6] Not interested in the question of whether the novel might do something other than *mourn* the loss of the patriarchal subject, Wilcox misses the opportunity to think about whether we might read the novel as parodying the very idea that postmodernism heralds the decentering of the masculine, phallic, autonomous self. The thrust of Wilcox's argument is that *White Noise* bears witness to a condition of general cultural decline coupled with, if not caused by, the crisis of an oedipalized "autonomous and authentic subjectivity" (349). Wilcox concludes, "A failure at heroism, Gladney shops at the supermarket" (364).

Although deploying the language of "authenticity" to describe what he believes *White Noise* mourns as lost through the transition from modernism to postmodernism, Wilcox does not *ground* the concept of authenticity, thus begging a number of questions: Is authenticity a quality that inheres in things or persons? Is it recognizable and, if so, by what signs? Can we know authenticity on its own or only in relation to the inauthentic? Often, authenticity is understood in opposition to irony, but it is also very often conceptualized in opposition to commercialization, as I noted in chapter 1. Critics of *White Noise* rely on unspecified notions of "authenticity," using this relative term as if it were an absolute or essential quality; not grounded in anything like a definition (or even a critical genealogy), "authenticity" stands in for a vaguely articulated set of values lost through the dominance of consumer culture in the novel's world. These readings assume that consumer culture is necessarily and always false, fake, and lesser than other, more "real," forms of culture. But *authenticity,* of course, is not a self-evident or ahistorical term, and in contemporary culture it is constantly being negotiated.

It is somewhat surprising that readers versed in postmodern theory would try to hang on to a concept of authenticity. It is as if the critical blinders come on when otherwise savvy critics are faced with the specter of inauthenticity. As we have already seen and will see again, anti-consumerist critique is an unusually invested critique, and the masculine protest against the feminizing (and inauthenticating) forces of consumer culture greets the perceived losses to masculine autonomy with a betrayed sense of a broken promise: "authenticity guaranteed." Despite the thorough commodification of "authenticity," as we saw in chapter 1, fantasies of authenticity persist and nowhere more stubbornly in the resistance to the postmodern attack on the existence of a "true" self. Mark Osteen, for example, articulates a fantasy of authenticity when he argues that "shopping produces a simulated self who is not an individual agent but an element of a system of capitalism. . . . [C]onsumption turns persons into packages radiating and receiving psychic data. We become spectacular commodities who consume everything we see, but most of all, ourselves" (171). The distinction between an "authentic inner self and the performative outer self" (Banet-Weiser 10) has been a fixture throughout the tradition of anti-consumerist critique to which I am tying *White Noise.* Although Osteen does not identify this problem of the simulated self with gender, the very notion of the "authentic self" threatened by large social systems is a fiction of masculinity particularly pervasive in a postmodern culture characterized by "agency panic."[7]

More than anything else, it is shopping that provokes this panic. Critics of *White Noise* have insisted that Jack's tendency to seek transcendence and existential value from shopping experiences simply demonstrates the distance *White Noise* tracks between an authentic modern sense of self and an inauthentic postmodern illusion of self. John N. Duvall, for example, mocks the sense of "power and control" Jack derives from shopping: "Jack replaces his inauthentic Hitler aura with the equally inauthentic aura of shopping, which he experiences, however, as authentic" (137). Thomas

Ferraro echoes William Whyte's *The Organization Man* when he judges that the novel "examines not so much the individuating force of consumer culture as its communalizing power. . . . [C]onsumerism produces what we might call an aura of connectedness among individuals: an illusion of kinship, transiently functional but without either sustaining or restraining power" (20).[8] Christoph Lindner, too, notes that "the 'fullness of being' derived from the experience of shopping is nothing more than an illusory effect, a transparent state of delusion, a false and fleeting sense of well-being" (160). If Jack is "deluded" into misreading shopping as "authentic," it is not clear where this "real" authenticity might reside. Such claims rely on the "common sense" that consumer culture, and the meanings found within it, is necessarily inauthentic because mass produced and packaged; consumer culture, in this reading, is an affront to the creative (masculine) individual who no longer has the power to discern the difference between the original and the copy, the true meaning of art and the false meanings of mass culture. This discourse of authenticity underwrites critiques of postmodern culture, betraying a retrogressive desire for some unspecified golden past before the age of simulations distanced us from the "real."[9] As Linda Hutcheon notes in her comments on Jameson's *Postmodernism; or, The Cultural Logic of Late Capitalism*, "It is precisely nostalgia for this kind of 'lost authenticity' . . . that has proved time and time again to be paralysing in terms of historical thinking" ("Irony" 203).

The logic through which shopping comes to represent the epitome of simulated, inauthentic experience is a gendered logic. In American culture, mockery of shopping and shoppers is a strategy through which gender differences are managed and cultural hierarchies based on class are stabilized. Indeed, the female shopper who inhabits the pages of many postwar critiques of American culture functions primarily to reinforce a binary construction of gender based on the opposition between masculine production and feminine consumption. She is perhaps most famously enshrined in Vance Packard's "Babes in Consumerland," where she is made to embody the dangers of a consumer culture that "scientifically" engineers consent. Describing the techniques through which market researchers study how women get sucked into making "impulse purchases," Packard wryly observes that the optimum goal is to put the "ladies" into a "hypnoidal trance" so strong that "they passed neighbors and old friends without noticing or greeting them," had a "glassy stare," and "were so entranced as they wandered the store plucking things off shelves at random that they would bump into boxes without seeing them" (92). Like zombies not even cognizant of their own will or identity, they passively embody the desires of the marketers and other professionals intent on ensnaring them in the consumer net. As Cecile Whiting comments, mid-century discourses about the female shopper represent her as "deceived by representation, los[ing] her grip on the real" (38). The worry fueling such discourses is that this femininity is contagious and that men, too, might find themselves subject to the "hypnoidal trance."

In a particularly blatant example of this mode of critique, Benjamin Barber diagnoses consumer capitalism as producing a crisis in masculinity: "The ethos animating postmodern consumer capitalism is one of joyless compulsiveness. The modern consumer is no free-willed sybarite, but a compulsory shopper driven to consumption because the future of capitalism depends on it. He is less the happy sensualist than the compulsive masturbator, a reluctant addict working at himself with little pleasure, encouraged in his labor by an ethic of infantilization that releases him to a self-indulgence he cannot altogether welcome" (51). The shopper envisioned here is a feminized man "infantilized" by American consumer culture. While Barber wants to assign agency to the economic system and to argue that the compulsory shopper cannot help but fulfill the terms "demanded" by consumer capitalism, at the same time he chides this shopper for his laziness, his self-indulgence, and his lack of will. Barber needs to imagine his shopper as male in order to create a sense of crisis here; no one worries that *female* shoppers might be "feminized" by consumer culture because the common sense of gender imagines women as always already feminized and men as always in danger of being feminized. Like Packard's "zombies," Barber's (male) shopper represents an affront to liberal individualism, acting not on his own volition but mindlessly following the dictates of his culture.

It is the figure of the entranced, feminized shopper that lurks behind readings of DeLillo's supermarket, although critics have seemed mostly uninterested in the possibility of DeLillo's engagement in a cultural history of shopping.[10] The surprisingly hostile condemnations of consumerism in *White Noise* are perhaps fueled by the fact that it is the *male* characters who shop so enthusiastically and it is an entirely *male* faculty in the Department of American Environments who devote their lives to studying cereal boxes and other forms of mass or commodity culture. Christoph Lindner raises the question of gender and shopping when he notes that Jack's "mall crawl" is provoked by the "emasculating" comments of his colleague Eric Massingale, who shows Jack that "even when surrounded by the aura of machismo emanating from the hardware store, he still looks harmless and insignificant (read *unmanly*) to his male colleague" (162; emphasis in the original). Given the prevalence of a discourse about shopping as a feminine experience, Lindner's suggestion that Jack seeks to "escape his feelings of inadequacy" by "los[ing] himself in a massive shopping binge" seems counterintuitive. In fact, the language Lindner uses echoes strongly with accounts of *women's* shopping "habits": Jack engages in "retail therapy," "reckless spending and impulse buying" (162), leaving the "masculine and masculinizing space" of the hardware store (161) to enter the mall, "alive with the delirium of shopping" (163). Lindner does not pause to consider the interesting idea that Jack might be said to pursue remasculinization through a *feminine* activity. For Lindner, shopping functions only as evidence of cultural decline, and Jack's enthusiastic participation in it signals the gender trouble that marks consumer culture.

The spectacle of male shopping, then, provokes the standard anticonsumerist accusations of inauthenticity and the suggestions of feminization. But might we look differently at these scenes of male shopping? Is it possible that DeLillo might be challenging, rather than ratifying, the cultural truths about gender and consumerism? DeLillo's representation of Jack shopping at the Mid-Village Mall does suggest pretty forcefully that he is pursuing communion with the *female* members of his family and entering into their world. It is Babette and "the two girls" who become his "guides to endless well-being," "puzzled but excited by [his] desire to buy." Jack reports, "My family gloried in the event. I was one of them, shopping at last" (83), and, even if Wilder and Heinrich are included in the unit "my family," Jack does not mention either one of them. The "retail therapy" Jack indulges in at the Mid-Village Mall aligns him with women and suggests his embrace ("at last") of the feminine pleasures of shopping. The language with which Jack communicates his experience certainly resonates with the language used to describe female shoppers pursuing a "shop 'til you drop" strategy of retail therapy: he "shopped with reckless abandon," being led by Babette and the girls and carried along on the wave of their desires (84). Because Lindner poses the feminine shopping Jack pursues against the masculine realm of the hardware store, his reading of the scene is dependent on a gendered logic that ties DeLillo's negative assessment of the "depthless postmodern space" (164) to the demise of the authentic, masculine self.[11]

DeLillo's interest in men's shopping is further developed through his representation of Jack and Murray in the supermarket, which contests oppositions between passive consumption and active intellectual production, between shopping and reading, and between feminine and masculine. It would be hard to argue that what goes on in the supermarket in *White Noise* is only shopping and harder still to argue that DeLillo presents shopping as passive. What Murray and Jack engage in is more like *reading* than shopping: they take pleasure in the act of interpretation in addition to the act of buying.[12] Reading is everywhere foregrounded in these scenes of shopping, from the analysis of packaging to the "paperback books scattered across the entrance" of the store (20). This is not to say that reading is, somehow, better than shopping or vice versa; it is to say that reading and shopping need not be understood as antithetical activities, the one "higher" and the other "lower." As Meaghan Morris has suggested, consumer venues can and should be understood as "spaces of cultural production" (193). For Morris, this means displacing the assumptions about cultural value (and gender) enshrined by modernism; she suggests "studying the everyday, the so-called banal, the supposedly un- or non-experimental, asking not, 'why does it fall short of modernism?' but 'how do classical theories of modernism fall short of women's modernity?'" (202). Morris gestures toward a complex set of oppositions here that poses women, stagnation, passivity, and everyday consumption against men, innovation, activity, and intellectual production. This version of modernism has spawned the particular version of postmodernism that dominates criticism of *White Noise*. The problem with this postmodernism for DeLillo's critics is not that it "falls short of women's postmodernity" but that it threatens to make men themselves appear as modernism's "other": passive, consuming, stagnant, and stuck in the materialities of everyday life.

What Morris's work suggests is that an emphasis on the material relations of consumer culture produces a very different reading of the relationships between individuals, shopping, and cultural value than does a more abstract theoretical emphasis. Much recent work in the anthropology of material culture contests the opposition between active production and passive consumption in part by focusing on the material practice of shopping and the ways in which "the commodities we acquire and experience, however mass-produced and surrounded they are by marketing hype, do deliver qualities that are of functional, symbolic and embodied importance" (Humphery 135). Sharon Zukin's *Point of Purchase: How Shopping Changed American Culture,* for example, can help us understand DeLillo's shoppers as something other than merely deluded, passive, or lacking will. Zukin talks with shoppers, analyzes their practices of consumption, and argues that shopping is best understood as one methodology for interpreting the world and our place in it, for exercising aesthetic judgments and finding aesthetic pleasures, and for actively practicing strategies of economic independence and judgment in a world that often makes us feel we have no power to do so. She goes about this project by *talking* with shoppers and draws some interesting conclusions about how shopping practices are marked by and reproduce class, gender, and racial differences.

What makes this work useful for my purposes here is that Zukin's shoppers are cannily aware of how their desires, preferences, and practices are embedded in social and political systems; they see themselves neither as the hapless dupes of consumer capitalism nor completely free of the manipulations of that system. As Zukin suggests, one's relationship to and attitude about consumerism has as much to do with gender, race, and class as it has to do with the machinations of an impersonal system. The Latino shopper who goes to Tiffany's to buy his girlfriend a bracelet has a very different experience of shopping than the privileged white woman who seeks a bargain at Walmart. While arguing that shopping does, in fact, "dominate our lives," Zukin questions the stance of "cultural theorists" who claim that "by choosing products, we create our identity. Our identity is formed by the whole activity of shopping—an activity that we experience as both freedom and necessity" (253). That freedom and necessity are conditioned by the material realities of everyday life. Zukin asks us to understand shopping not as a substitute for some other, more authentic, way of making meaning and negotiating social differences but as one activity among many that enact our social positioning, our identities, and our communities. In Zukin's analysis, shopping is active and productive, and this stance can help us understand DeLillo's shoppers as something other than merely deluded—"deceived by representation," like the mid-century housewife, "los[ing] her grip on the real" (Whiting 38).

Unlike the cultural critic who seeks a position above the practices of consumer culture, DeLillo's shoppers simultaneously analyze and enjoy, the novel suggesting that there is no disinterested position from which to launch a critique. As Linda Hutcheon argued many years ago in her elaboration of a feminist version of postmodernism, the fact of "complicitous critique" need not be cause for (modernist) despair. Rachel Bowlby offers a less moralistic analysis of shopping in the novel, suggesting that, for Jack, "there is no difference . . . between identification and resistance, or between enjoyment and critique. Like the supermarket's own multiplication of lines, he seems to be energized by, to survive on, the proliferation of theories about what the supermarket is" (210). Rather than snidely mock Jack for his supposed inability to distinguish between real and faux experiences, between activities that should and activities that shouldn't provide meaning and value in life, it is possible to read in the novel's representation of consumer *culture* a complexity we grant to the supposedly more "authentic" cultural realms of intellectual and artistic production—which, of course, come with their own practices of consumption qua "readership."

DeLillo's interest in shopping and domesticity is part of his larger interest in the "radiance of dailiness" that he describes in a much-cited 1988 interview. Asked about his "fondness" "for the trappings of suburban life" and the meaning of the "supermarket as a sacred place," DeLillo clearly differentiates his point of view from those critics who find that shopping distances us from meaning and, even, transcendence:

In *White Noise*, in particular, I tried to find a kind of radiance in dailiness. Sometimes this radiance can be almost frightening. Other times it can be almost holy or sacred. Is it really there? Well, yes. You know I don't believe as Murray Jay Siskind does in *White Noise* that the supermarket is a form of Tibetan lamasery. But there is something there that we tend to miss. . . . I think that's something that has

been in the background of my work: a sense of something extraor-
dinary hovering just beyond our touch and just beyond our vision.
(DeCurtis 70–71)

The language here—"radiance," "holiness," the "sacred," "something ex-
traordinary," something "really there"—points *not* to the falsenesses of
consumer culture but to something not reducible to a nightmare image
of the consuming self. To see the novel as "an extended gloss on Jean
Baudrillard's notion of consumer society" (Duvall 136) requires that we
declare allegiance to a brand of anti-consumerism that appears, at best,
at odds with DeLillo's statements here and, at worst, willfully uninterested in the possibility that the novel might challenge a simple opposition
between the active critic and the passive consumer helplessly seduced by
the supermarket. Without actually making an argument for what's *wrong*
with the supermarket, DeLillo's critics tend to assume that the pleasures
and reassurances sought and found there are *necessarily* inauthentic and,
so, destructive of any "real" meaning. Authenticity, wedded to masculinity, is endangered in the supermarket and mall, where the real (and the
self) is always already commodified.

As I noted above, DeLillo's interest in the simulations of contemporary
culture has prompted critics to read in his work a lament for the demise of
the real. The "real" here is not the "real" of material objects but the "real"
of some more abstract value having to do with independence from mediation, freedom from commodification, and "being" not determined by
commercial interests. This approach is exemplified by Joseph S. Walker's
attempt to pinpoint the unmediated real in DeLillo's fiction. Walker iso-
lates moments of "criminality," or more accurately moments produced
as the effect or in the wake of criminality, as the places where DeLillo
attempts to represent the real. But to even put it in these terms suggests
the problem here because, according to Walker, *any representation* of a
phenomenon—sight, experience, sound, what have you—is always already mediated. Walker suggests that the much-discussed "postmodern
sunsets" that appear with the receding Airborne Toxic Event might just
be the "book's most convincing instance of the real—indeed, it may be
the clearest instance of the real in all of DeLillo's work" (440). Although it
is not clear why it matters that this phenomenon appears in the wake of

criminality, what Walker emphasizes is how DeLillo narrates the crowd's participation in the event of the sunsets. Contrasting this viewing experience to the earlier visit to the "most photographed barn in America," Walker suggests that the instability, changeability, unpredictability of the sunsets—in short, their mystery—elevates them above all other narrated events in the novel. Because they change from day to day, and because Jack and the others do not know how to react to them, the sunsets cannot "be contained by a single image endlessly repeated, assimilated, and commercialized. The crowds that gather to watch the sunsets are unmarked by the brand names that run through much of the novel; instead of the gaudily packaged products of the supermarket," the watchers bring, as DeLillo tells us, "fruit and nuts," a "thermos of iced tea," and "cool drinks" (Walker 441; *White Noise* 324).

The idea that "fruit and nuts" are, somehow, outside commercialism or are necessarily posed against the "gaudily packaged products in the supermarket" seems unconvincing to me, evidence only of this critic's desire to imagine something "natural" that escapes from the logic of consumer culture (is iced tea "natural"?). Further, the claim that *people* in the novel are "marked by brand names" is not really convincing, either. In truth, most evocations of brand names in the novel occur in the narration's use of what one critic calls the "triptychs" such as "Visa, Mastercard, American Express" (100). Unlike, say, a novel by Bret Easton Ellis, *White Noise* has little truck with brand names and certainly does not identify its characters as embodying or seeking their identities in brand names. The critical desire to find a "pure" experience uncorrupted by "intervening mediations" (Walker 434) is fueled by an implicit assumption that "authenticity" must be sought in some pre-commercial paradise.

The search for an unmediated real in DeLillo's work is marked by a nostalgia for a (fantasized) pure past that DeLillo actually mocks in this scene by presenting the sunsets as completely mediated: "The sky takes on content, feeling, an exalted narrative life" (324). To say that the "sky takes on an exalted narrative life" is to say that this event is *framed* by the devices of narrative—that is, by representation. Like the evacuees' response to the Airborne Toxic Event, described by Jack as having an "epic quality" (122), "part of the grandness of a sweeping event" (127), the response to the sunsets can be understood only through the mediation of other narratives, other representations. To identify the sunsets as "postmodern," "rich in romantic imagery" (227), is to abandon the distinction between the genuine, the authentic, the natural and the false, the simulated, the mediated. It is also to tie the postmodern to the romantic desire to find an "authentic" self and a pre-cultural "'authentic' social relation" (D. Miller, *Material Culture* 41).

CONSUMERISM, GENDER, AND THE PRACTICES OF EVERYDAY LIFE

The critical commonplace that understands "postmodernism" in DeLillo's *White Noise* as the demise of authenticity, truth, and meaning is cousin to the critical commonplace that understands consumer culture, shopping, and commodification as distancing us from the "real" and from individual autonomy and authenticity. Both attempts to explain *White Noise*'s engagement with contemporary culture end up reinforcing a never explicitly acknowledged construction of gender. I am less interested in deciding, once and for all, what DeLillo's novel really says about the positivities and negativities of postmodern consumer culture in general, and shopping in particular, than I am in analyzing the assumptions behind the kind of critique premised on a certainty that consumerism and shopping are both trivial, unworthy of serious critical attention, and significant, heralding the demise of authenticity and the real. The anti-consumerism evident in much of DeLillo criticism is of the knee-jerk variety; while critics may spar over whether DeLillo means for us to accept or criticize Jack, and whether DeLillo is, himself, ambivalent about the possibility of cultural critique in the age of simulations, critics seem uninterested in challenging the idea that an opposition does (and should) exist between the pursuit of "higher" (art, truth, authenticity) and "lower" (commodities, simulation, inauthenticity) aims.

Further, the hostility toward consumer culture conceals a barely masked hostility toward femininity and women's arenas. Critical response to *White Noise* refuses to acknowledge domestic pleasures, the sights, sounds, and tastes of the supermarket and the kitchen; it refuses, as well, the textual pleasures produced (for this reader, at least) in the somehow realistic representation of machines and things as inhabitants of the house, entering into the narrative as participants: "Jeans tumbled in the dryer" (18). Like the student in *The Corrections* who chides her professor for holding on to a notion of false consciousness afflicting the clueless masses, one might ask these critics why they insist so vociferously that the world represented in *White Noise* is a world in crisis, a world fallen from the heights of authenticity into the depths of falsity. Too comfortable with a master narrative of declension and crisis, these critics cannot see that what's going on in the supermarkets, malls, and kitchens is also "real."

As Kim Humphery argues, much anti-consumerist discourse depends on a set of oppositions that are never fully examined. "A life that is 'really real,'" he writes, "is seen as residing principally in the world of the intellectual, the emotional and the spiritual" and is posed against the "falsity of most commodity satisfaction, particularly the ersatz and temporary fulfillment of mass-produced things and media experiences, and of mainstream commercial space such as the shopping mall" (134). The exposure of the "ersatz and temporary fulfillment of mass-produced things and media experiences" is precisely what DeLillo's critics argue is behind the novel's engagement in consumer culture, as evidenced by the nearly unanimous critical consensus that Jack experiences a "false sense of transcendence" when he hears a sleeping Steffie utter the words "Toyota Celica" (Duvall 135). But Jack concludes that Steffie's words constitute a "moment of splendid transcendence" only after submitting those words to a series of questions—that is, after he critically considers the question of consumerism and transcendence from a variety of angles:

> A long moment passed before I realized that this was the name of an automobile. The truth only amazed me more. The utterance was beautiful and mysterious, gold-shot with looming wonder. It was like the name of an ancient power in the sky, tablet-carved in cuneiform. It made me feel that something hovered. But how could this be? A simple brand name, an ordinary car. How could these near-nonsense words, murmured in a child's restless sleep, make me sense a meaning, a presence? She was only repeating some TV voice. Toyota Corolla, Toyota Celica, Toyota Cressida. Supranational names, computer-generated, more or less universally pronounceable. Part of every child's brain noise, the substatic regions too deep to probe. (155)

The critical consensus on this scene is that Jack is deluded, that he mistakes a "false transcendence" for genuine transcendence by failing to see that Steffie's words represent "a key moment in the production of consumers" (Duvall 135). But Jack has already considered this position and nevertheless concludes that the transcendence is real and is "splendid"—what DeLillo describes, elsewhere, as "something nearly mystical about certain words and phrases that float through our lives" (Begley 97). That Steffie is simply "repeating some TV voice" does not disqualify her utterance from significance; what Jack reaches for here is a way to interpret a transcendence that goes against the philosophical certainty that it shouldn't *count as* transcendence and so must be inauthentic. While DeLillo might be mocking Jack's exaggerated response—"it was like the name of an ancient power in the sky, tablet-carved in cuneiform"—this passage also suggests a desire to connect the "ordinary" to the "beautiful and mysterious." We need not dismiss this desire as inauthentic just because it is fully implicated in consumer culture.

Indeed, if we look more closely at how DeLillo describes the everyday life of this family, surrounded by their familiar and not-so-familiar objects, engaged in conversations that often veer toward "nonsense" but nevertheless hit on key truths, it is hard to sustain an interpretation of the novel as a hard-nosed critique of consumerism and its abnegation of the "real." As the critical interest in "things" has taught us, literary and cultural critics have often been content to look *through* things to find the higher truths of literary value or cultural commentary. *White Noise* dwells on things, and its characters evince a fascination with the possibility that these things—objects, and their sounds, smells, tastes—might yield useful knowledge or provide genuine satisfactions. Jack often catalogs things, as in the "day of the station wagons" when the affluent students return each fall to the College on the Hill. Commenting on this scene with a sense of moral outrage, Christoph Lindner looks through the actual nomination of the things to see in the catalog evidence of DeLillo's disdain for this "parade of commodities": the focus of this description "is not on the students themselves," as clearly Lindner thinks it should be, "but on the mass of belongings they bring with them—or more exactly, on the strangely mesmerizing spectacle created by that mass of belongings. . . . The list of objects is exhaustive, but that of course is the entire point of the passage. The sheer volume of goods signals that *White Noise* belongs to a world dominated by commodities, congested by their presence, glutted by their consumption" (138).

But does this catalog, in fact, function to show "consumer objects hijacking the thoughts and driving the imagination of a mesmerized spectator" (138)? Or is Lindner projecting onto the text what Humphery names an anti-consumerist "disenchantment story," a "tale of modernity as loss, of existence as alienated and of society as decayed" (150)? Does the mere fact that a novel dwells on things support the nightmare vision of a world "glutted by consumption"? On the contrary: to recall Bowlby's comments on Jack's active critical engagement with the supermarket, here, too, he "seems to be energized by, to survive on, the proliferation of theories about what" consumerism is (209–10). Like the catalog of items that compel Jack in the hardware store—"rope hung like tropical fruit, beautifully braided strands, thick, brown, strong" (82)—Jack's response to the parade of goods on the day of the station wagons need be read as alienating only if we start from the premise that any and all desire to consume goods or the spectacle of goods can only and always be evidence of false consciousness, that the only relation one can have to commodities is "fetishistic displacement" (Lindner 140), and that the failure to resist the lure of consumer culture means the loss of some (unidentified) authentic reality or meaning. Lindner's reading works, like other anti-consumerist discourses, "to place the [very] act of consumption at the dead centre of western socio-moral decay" (Humphery 46).

The critical insistence on a moral difference between the "real" and the "false" or "illusory" evidences a fantasy of unmediated reality that Don DeLillo does not share. Rather than lament a state of crisis in which we can no longer distinguish between "real" and "false" emotions, commitments, and experiences, DeLillo instead is interested in representing the shifting epistemological ground of postmodern culture and, particularly, the blurring of the boundaries between the real and the simulated, the authentic and the copied. We can see this interest in his representation of the Gladney children responding to each newly announced symptom of Nyodene D exposure: "What did it all mean? Did Steffie truly imagine she'd seen the wreck before or did she only imagine she'd imagined it? Is it possible to have a false perception of an illusion? Is there a true *déjà vu* and a false *déjà vu*?" (125–26). Even though playing this scene for laughs, DeLillo nevertheless suggests here that, even if we could confidently tell the difference between the "real" and the "false," it would not matter because Steffie feels herself experiencing déjà vu, even if it is an illusion of an illusion. In insisting that consumer-mediated experiences are false or inauthentic *because* they are consumer-mediated experiences, we can only conclude that those experiencing them are suffering from a form of false consciousness. Indeed, even Baudrillard, railing against John Kenneth Galbraith's insistence on the difference between "authentic" and "artificial" "satisfactions," argues that the enjoyment of consumer products and services is experienced as "true" and "real," not as "alienation." "Only an intellectual," Baudrillard claims, "would say such a thing, from the depths of his moralizing idealism, but this at most marks him out as being, for his part, an alienated moralist" (73).[13]

The absolute self-evidence of the claim that consumer culture substitutes the false for the real and, thus, distances us from both an authentic selfhood and an authentic engagement in the social betrays an investment in what Daniel Miller calls the "discourse of shopping," the dominant story that intellectuals tell about consumer culture: consumer culture is necessarily trivial, and the "giant malls" are "symbols of sheer emptiness, crammed full of pure ephemera that have the power to dissipate the seriousness of labour into an objectifying of nothing" (*Theory of Shopping* 96). This narrative serves the purpose of perpetuating the "exclusively masculine jeremiad of postwar American culture" (Gould iv), here couched in the vocabulary of postmodern critique. Miller argues that "the academic theory of postmodernism provides admirable service to our need for a vision of destructive consumption as pointless waste" (*Theory of Shopping* 96), suggesting that this theory is less interested in describing a contemporary reality than it is in constructing that reality as a fall from an earlier, better, pre-consumerist reality. This "need for a vision of destructive consumption as pointless waste" both stems from and further entrenches a set of hierarchical distinctions that "we" need only if we are intent on safeguarding high culture from low, real value from sham value, consumption from production, masculinity from femininity.

When asked by an interviewer to comment on the "relationship between consumerism, the indifference of the masses and the loss of personal identity," DeLillo zeroes in not on the figure of the zombie shopper compulsively consuming, or on the alienated individual subject to commodification, but on the homeless he represents in *Mao II,* who "live in refrigerator boxes and television boxes. If you could write slogans for

nations similar to those invented by advertisers for their products the slogan for the US would be 'Consume or die'" (Naidotti 115). What DeLillo
is getting at here is more than an abstract dissatisfaction with the postmodern condition of simulation, consumerism, and inauthenticity; he is
foregrounding the ways in which such an abstract stance—as indicated in
the interviewer's question—fails to get at the lived realities of consumer
culture. Clearly, DeLillo sees the problems engendered by capitalism, but
he does not necessarily see these problems as producing the existential crisis his critics most often invoke in their readings of *White Noise*. Further,
the implicit anti-consumerism that characterizes this criticism continues
to insist on an increasingly unstable distinction between the social and the
commercial, the authentic and the inauthentic, and intellectual production and passive consumption.

Offering a more negative assessment of *White Noise*'s critical interven-
tion than do most of the novel's critics, Andrew Hoberek suggests that
White Noise's focus on processes of commodification obscures the larger
economic forces affecting the middle class and, thus, repeats Jameson's
"symptomatically postmodernist turn away from production and toward
consumption" (118). For Hoberek, DeLillo's failure to "allude to the possibility of some social horizon beyond [his] protagonists' alienation" means
that *White Noise* "eschews even the possibility of a *social* solution to [Jack's]
alienated, commodified existence" (125; emphasis added).[14] While it is certainly true that DeLillo does not, in this novel, offer the kind of analysis
that Hoberek traces in his argument about the "proletarianization of the
middle class," I wonder why it's necessary to uphold a clear distinction
between the social and the (merely) personal, between a focus on labor
and modes of production and a focus on consumption; the practices of
consumption that DeLillo (and others) represent are political, but they are
not always political in a clear or one-dimensional way.[15]

Further, I am not sure it's completely useful, or even accurate, to speak
of Jack or any DeLillo protagonist as "alienated" because notions of alienation rely on often unspecified assumptions about what would constitute
the "unalienated"—a concept that is as problematic in DeLillo's work as
the concept of an "unmediated" representation. DeLillo has, in all of his
work, displayed an abiding interest in thinking through the mutual en-
tanglement of subject and system, the complex ways in which individual

agency is both constrained by and made productive through the networks of power and social organization that can work only through the individual's participation in them. The narrative of decline that marks criticism of *White Noise* fails, in my view, to fully acknowledge this aspect of DeLillo's work and, instead, gets hijacked by a modernist impulse to recapture a lost authenticity and an unalienated subject always threatened by large, impersonal systems. It also unwittingly reproduces the account of postmodernism as decline and relies on the assumption that there is a social, political, or even literary realm that is, somehow, more real or authentic than the realm of consumption. In postwar social critique, white middle-class alienation is figured as a fall, not only in class terms but in gender terms as well. The tendency to code the crisis of late capitalist, postmodern consumer culture as a crisis of masculinity—in readings of DeLillo's novels and elsewhere—severely limits our understanding of both that culture and the possible modes for critiquing it.

ANXIETIES OF (MASCULINE) OBSOLESCENCE: TECHNOCONSUMERISM AND AMBIVALENT CRITIQUE IN THE CORRECTIONS

Jonathan Franzen invokes DeLillo in his much-discussed essay, originally published in *Harper's* as "Perchance to Dream" and later edited and republished as "Why Bother?," in his essay collection *How to Be Alone*. Here, as elsewhere, Franzen pays lip service to the idea that what he calls "techno-consumerism" has damaged American culture and impoverished American lives, but his real interest is in how this imagined consumer culture has made the serious fiction writer obsolete. Hailed by *Time* and the *New York Times* as the next "great American novelist," Franzen nevertheless spills a great deal of ink bemoaning his own irrelevance and, perhaps more strikingly, expressing his own ambivalence about the relation of "serious" fiction to mass culture. Although his relationship to "postmodernism" is by no means clear—he aligns himself with DeLillo but distances himself from the "difficulty" of a William Gaddis—he has been heralded as a writer interested in critiquing consumer culture and in detailing the damage to human community and authentic relationships wrought by that culture. For example, a brief essay in *Notes on Contemporary Literature* states that *"The Corrections* underscores the pernicious effects of consumerism that perverts work ethics, familial values, individual psychology and even sexuality" and concludes that the novel "sustains a critique of the massive American consumer society in registering how it irreversibly depletes human values often testified to in the alienation of individuals" (Chatterjee and Neelakantan 6). *The Corrections* is widely read as a commentary on how the consumer and financial excesses of the 1980s had detrimental effects on a family of "ordinary" middle Americans and, in particular, how consumer culture offers easy fixes for complex problems. These easy fixes fail, of course, to deliver what the characters desire (except, perhaps, for the two mother figures in the novel, to whom I will return), even if the characters can be said to know what they desire in a world where everything has become inauthentic: from real railroads to museums of transport, from industrial production and inventor entrepreneurship to rampant consumption and fraudulent technology-mediated schemes, from good American values of honesty and thrift to superficial pursuits of consumer goods and lifestyle pleasures.

The assimilation of *The Corrections* to an anti-consumerist narrative—relatively common, given Franzen's own statements against "techno-consumerism" in his published essays—ratifies the anti-consumerist worldview that makes individuals the victims of a system that destroys the more traditional values imagined to have dominated in a pre-consumerist world. But as my opening salvo from the novel suggests, Franzen is by no means an unambivalent spokesperson for the kind of anti-consumerism that marks criticism of *White Noise*. In fact, the question I would like to raise here is whether *The Corrections* mounts anything like a sustained critique of any social system or whether the novel uses a fantasy of a lost authenticity to mount a masculine protest against a vaguely drawn society that thwarts the straight white male. That reviewers and critics read in this personal, individualist, and essentially masculine narrative of decline an indictment of our contemporary national reality suggests that, once again, the fate of the white man in a post-liberationist, late capitalist world is the tragedy of our era. When Franzen confesses to "succumbing, as a novelist, to despair about the possibility of connecting the personal and the social" in order to determine whether his distress "derive[d] from some internal sickness of the soul, or was it imposed on me by the sickness of society" (*How to Be Alone* 57–58), he is positioning himself solipsistically as the barometer of the goods and ills of his society. James Wolcott speaks for many reviewers when he writes, "As a cultural analyst, Franzen is simply the latest to join the chorus line of declinism. . . . The difference is that Franzen makes his state of mind the social indicator, his mood at any given moment the measure of literature's misery index" (38).[16]

As perhaps might have been expected, *The Corrections* includes several memorable scenes of shopping, and one in particular seems an homage to *White Noise*. The scene takes place in the first part of the novel, the part devoted primarily to telling Chip's story and titled "The Failure." Having been fired from his teaching job for sleeping with, and stalking, his erstwhile star student Melissa, Chip's fortunes have plummeted. He decides to "purge the Marxists from his shelf," selling them in order to have the money he needs to prepare dinner for his visiting parents. Franzen tells us that Chip "turned away from [the books'] reproachful spines, remembering how each of them had called out in a bookstore with a promise of a radical critique of late-capitalist society" (92), choosing to sell them because of his lust for, and desire to keep, his girlfriend, Julia, who is about to dump him. With his measly $115 in hand, this fallen Marxist goes to what he terms "the new Nightmare of Consumption ('Everything for a Price!')" (93). This scene perfectly captures the odd blend of self-denigration and pompous whininess that characterizes Chip (who, in fact, has much in common with his creator), whose individual and often salacious desires come into conflict with his quasi-intellectual disdain for the consumer culture that offers to satisfy those desires. Chip is mortified by the "Nightmare of Consumption," not only because it is the epitome of hip consumerism pursued by "the supergentry of SoHo and Tribeca" (93) but also because he really does not have the financial resources to participate in the rituals of this class and culture. (Franzen tells us, in an aside, that "Chip hated cell phones mainly because he didn't have one" [102].) When he finds that the Norwegian salmon he has asked for will cost him $78.40, he stuffs it into his pants, and what follows is a farcical scene in which Chip tries to keep the salmon from slipping out, forcing him to keep putting his hands on his crotch to adjust the fish.

In this setting, he encounters Doug O'Brien, the husband of the agent to whom he has given his ridiculously bad screenplay in the hopes that she will be able to get him in touch with interested producers. What follows is a scene that pays homage to Murray and Jack, with Chip and Doug having a conversation that is DeLillo-esque in its rhythms. Like the scenes in *White Noise* where Murray and Jack have serious intellectual conversations in the supermarket, this scene has Doug and Chip discussing new technologies for "cerebral rehab"—that is, a personality makeover courtesy of a brain rewiring.

> "You get to keep your handsome façade," Doug said. "You still look serious and intellectual, a little Nordic, on the outside. Sober, bookish. But inside you're more livable. A big family room with an entertainment console. A kitchen that's roomier and handier. You've got your In-Sink-Erator, your convection oven. An ice-cube dispenser on the refrigerator door."
>
> "Do I still recognize myself?"
>
> "Do you want to? Everybody else will—at least, the outside of you." (97)

Unlike Jack, Chip does not fully enter into the spirit of this conversation, does not completely follow Doug into his hypothetical scenario, balking at the idea that his uniqueness as an individual could be captured in metaphors about appliances and furnishings. But Chip's anxieties about the implications of this technology do not come off as sincere, nor does his disdain for the Nightmare of Consumption convince, because all other thoughts are overshadowed by the fact that a stolen "salmon filet was now spreading down into Chip's underpants like a wide, warm slug" (97). Chip's anti-consumerism, thus, is exposed as inauthentic. What of Franzen's?

The Corrections, weirdly, wants to mount a critique of consumerism but also wants to mount a critique of critiques of consumerism. Franzen's famous ambivalence—captured perfectly in his essays and in his response to being chosen as an Oprah author—makes it difficult to decide whether *The Corrections* is, in fact, an anatomy of late capitalism affecting the generation coming of age at the end of the industrial era and the consequent decline of the Protestant Ethic, as some readers and critics have averred;[17] or whether it is articulating a more personal complaint about how the "acids of modernity," to recall Conroy's comments on *White Noise,* have eroded the guarantees of autonomy and authenticity enjoyed by middle-class white men. Like many other anti-consumerist texts, *The Corrections* seems inevitably, and nostalgically, drawn to the 1950s as an era in which men were men and consumer culture had not destroyed masculine authenticity. Susan Faludi's best-selling *Stiffed: The Betrayal of the American Man,* published just two before *The Corrections,* memorializes the mid-century man who, trying heroically to pursue the Protestant Ethic even as consumerism aims to squash it, was the gold standard for American masculinity. Reaching for melodrama in her description of an epochal shift in masculinity, and unwittingly repeating the mid-century critique of writers like David Riesman, Faludi writes, "The fathers did give the sons a New Frontier, but it was a land made sterile by the onrush of mass consumerism. The more productive aspects of manhood, such as building or cultivating or contributing to a society, couldn't establish a foothold on the shiny flat surface of a commercial culture, a looking glass before which men could only act out a crude semblance of masculinity" (37). *The Corrections* follows this narrative pretty closely in its representation of Alfred, who feels "stiffed" by what Jeremy Green calls "the feminized decay of the Erie Belt" (109) and who suffers his own series of "feminizations" because of his decline from Parkinson's disease and Alzheimer's. Alfred is angry at being forced to inhabit a world in which the feminizations of consumer culture amount to the broken promises of an "authenticity guaranteed."

Alfred articulates Franzen's crankiest critique of techno-consumerism, allowing his creator to give voice to some "old-fashioned" truths without endangering the "cool" that Chip embodies.[18] Alfred is irritated by the "take it easy, pal" attitude he sees all around him: "On the high prairie where he'd grown up, a person who took it easy wasn't much of a man. Now came a new effeminate generation for whom 'easygoing' was a compliment" (243). Alfred links the real and the authentic to a time before the empty promises of consumer culture made everything easy; he "believed that the real and the true were a minority that the world was bent on exterminating. It galled him that romantics like Enid could not distinguish the false from the authentic: a poor-quality, flimsily stocked, profit-making 'museum' from a real, honest railroad" (256). Later, as Alfred wrestles with a set of Christmas lights that refuses to respond to his old-fashioned know-how, the narrator tells us that throwing away a string of lights that should work fine "offended [Alfred's] sense of himself, because he was an individual from an age of individuals, and a string of lights was, like him, an individual thing. No matter how little the thing had cost, to throw it away was to deny its value and, by extension, the value of individuals generally: to willfully designate as trash an object that you knew wasn't trash. Modernity expected this designation and Alfred resisted it" (460).

If this scene is meant as a moment of social critique, it fails pretty badly—partly because Alfred's logic depends on an arrogant understanding of things in the world as always and only a reflection of his self; but also because, like Franzen's rant against "touch-tone hegemony" in his essay "Scavenging," there's a romantic effort here not so much to critique "modernity" as to imagine one's superiority to it. When Alfred gives in, the narrator concludes that "and so the goddamned lights made a victim of him, and there wasn't a goddamned thing he could do except go out and *spend*" (461; emphasis in the original). Now, while Alfred might be a victim of something—his own repressive psychology, the diseases that are robbing him of his autonomy and independence—to say that he is a victim of consumer culture or of modernity suggests a retreat from a viable critique of economic or cultural forces into just one more example of masculine complaint. It is Alfred's *manhood* that is offended by the lights, not just his individuality. Like the men Faludi follows in *Stiffed*, Alfred represents a version of masculinity endangered by the dominance of consumer logics, and his depression emphasizes his sense that he is out of sync with the current zeitgeist. But while Franzen clearly sympathizes with Alfred and his conservative worldview, Alfred's form of masculine complaint does not rise to the level of a social critique: he is cranky and depressed, unsympathetic to his wife, judgmental about his sons, and, perhaps, most important, subject to a series of humiliations that stem *not* from his out-of-sync-ness with his culture but from his own emotional and psychological pathologies. If Alfred represents a response to a "sick" culture, his sickness is entirely personal and individualized rather than culturally or socially symptomatic.

Indeed, *all* of the characters in this novel suffer from something like depression, with the exception of the two mother figures, Caroline and Enid, but the male Lamberts of both generations suffer the most. The two mothers fully embody the feminization of consumer culture in the sense that they are enthusiastic participants in consumer activities, and, although they do not represent the *same* relationship to consumerism, they each represent a complete embrace of the values and promises of that culture. Enid is the stereotype of the mid-century midwestern suburban housewife, while Caroline is the stereotype of the 1980s eastern suburban soccer mom, and the novel stages a conflict between these two models of feminine conformity. This becomes clearest as the two women square off over the question of how and where to celebrate Christmas, that most commercial of holidays. Caroline bribes her sons with promises of spending and getting in order to mount an offensive against Enid's request that all the Lamberts spend "one last Christmas" in St. Jude. While Enid might be said to represent an older, non-materialist approach to the holiday and to desire an alternative to its consumer-centered celebration, this would be a misreading of her desires. If she lacks Caroline's economic resources and her elitist disdain for the tackier aspects of midwestern culture, she has her own love for the trappings of consumer culture: she clips coupons, she has a stock of items she has collected over the years to be used for emergency gifts, she collects souvenirs from her travels. Further, she associates social mobility with the ability to purchase goods and to display those goods as a sign of value and worth; she envies her richer neighbors, whose husbands, unlike hers, have not resisted, on moral grounds, the lures of late capitalism.

Caroline disdains her mother-in-law, encouraging her sons to mock the kitschy gifts she chooses and waging war against the midwestern tackiness she sees embodied in St. Jude. Franzen uses the older Lambert son Gary to express a more masculine and class-based form of Caroline's cultural elitism. Gary worries that the distinction between the East Coast and the Midwest is collapsing and taking with it his sense of his own superiority.[19] Articulating the kind of elitist attitude toward "cool" versus "uncool" forms of consumption that I will discuss in chapter 5, Gary worries that the "shoppers at the mall near his parents' house had an air of entitlement off-puttingly similar to his own. . . . Gary wished that all further migration to the coasts could be banned and all midwesterners encouraged to revert to eating pasty foods and wearing dowdy clothes and playing board games, in order that a strategic national reserve of cluelessness might be maintained, a wilderness of taste which would enable people of privilege, like himself, to feel extremely privileged in perpetuity" (195). *The Corrections* is full of these very funny moments when Franzen's exposure of his characters' self-delusions hits the mark exactly; like Chip, Gary is exposed as superficial, his "liberal" and "cool" views unable to withstand his own selfish need to be smarter, better, richer than others. But as would become clear with Franzen's ill-conceived feud with Oprah over *The Corrections,* Franzen could be said to harbor the same elitism expressed by Gary here, the same desire to differentiate the middlebrow from the highbrow, the same desire to keep in place a cultural hierarchy that, as also became clear in the Oprah Book Club fiasco, is a gendered hierarchy. While Gary might not explicitly identify the "cool" with the masculine, his creator most definitely identifies the middlebrow with the feminine, as in his (in)famous lament that "branding" his book with Oprah's seal would mean the loss of *male* readers and the appropriation of his "high literary" novel by women. Indeed, Franzen has expressed a good deal of ambivalence over the fact that *women* constitute the main audience for fiction, a fact that male writers have been worrying about since the nineteenth century.

Franzen's desire to be read as a novelist in the "high literary" tradition is at odds with his desire to distance himself from the form that tradition takes at the end of the twentieth century. In an essay originally published in the *New Yorker,* slightly revised and reprinted in *How to Be Alone,* Franzen uses William Gaddis, whom he dubs "Mr. Difficult," to launch into a critique of "Hard-to-Read-Books." Franzen argues that there are two "wildly different models of how fiction relates to its audience," and, perhaps not surprisingly, Franzen (who might be called "Mr. Ambivalence") confesses to being torn between them. The "Status" model carries an elitist stance, "invites the discourse of genius and art-historical importance," and disrespects the "average reader" as a "philistine." Franzen identifies with this model because of his father, who "admired scholars for their intellect and large vocabularies." The "Contract" model, on the other hand, is based on an idea of writing and reading as communication rather than virtuoso performance. His attraction toward this model of writing and reading comes from his mother, a "life-long anti-elitist who used to get a lot of mileage out of the mythical 'average person'" (*How to Be Alone* 239–40). Yet while Franzen says that he ultimately prefers the Contract model and bases his rather savage attack on Gaddis on the latter's complete failure at

it, what really comes through in the essay is a wishful claim that high literary postmodernism is passé and irrelevant, coupled with a whiny lament
that his own work—his own very midwestern, "average person," ordinary language and craft—has not found a place among the "canon of intellectual, socially edgy, white-male American fiction writers"—"Pynchon,
DeLillo, Heller, Coover, Gaddis, Gass, Burroughs, Barth, Barthelme,
Hannah, Hawkes, McElroy and Elkin" (246).

In some ways, "Mr. Difficult" appears to be completely sympathetic
with the argument I am making in this book, for Franzen mocks a postmodern "literature of emergency" that relies on a master narrative of
cultural decline and a desire to "resist absorption or co-optation by an
all-absorbing, all co-opting System" (258). He even turns to homely, dare
we say "feminine," metaphors to describe an alternative to this literature
with its "notion of formal experimentation as a heroic act of resistance"
(259). Against this "five-alarm avant-gardism," he imagines a fictional
ethic of domestic care. "My small hope for literary criticism," he confesses,
"would be to hear less about orchestras and subversion and more about
the erotic and culinary arts. Think of the novel as lover . . . Or the novelist as cook who prepares, as a gift to the reader, this many-course meal"
(261). Yet this just does not ring true from a novelist who whipsaws back
and forth between a desire to join the big boys of postmodernism (and
they are all boys) and a desire to be "relevant," to please readers. Pleasing
readers means acceding to their demands; after all, this essay begins with
an account of the "angry mail from strangers" Franzen received after the
publication of *The Corrections*—and, one presumes, after his very public
expression of anxiety about being chosen as an Oprah writer and his ill-
advised complaint about the *type* of reader who would be attracted to his
book once emblazoned with the Oprah brand.

There is something a little disingenuous about Franzen's characteriza-
tion of Gaddis as wanting to separate himself from his readers, and his
culture, by denying the public access: "Strict prohibitions like this," writes
Franzen, "are a way in which threatened religious minorities resist the
seductions of the majority culture" (251). This is, in essence, a key com-
ponent to Franzen's discomfort with being an Oprah author and being
"forced" (for a great deal of money) to market not only his book but his
self as well. Indeed, in an earlier essay, he says that Gaddis taught him that
"the artist who's really serious about resisting a culture of mass-marketed

image must resist becoming an image himself, even at the price of certain obscurity" (*How to Be Alone* 86). Has Franzen learned a lesson from his experience with Oprah, or is he trying to have it both ways? Is his desire to distinguish himself from high literary postmodernists a desire to be a populist author, or is it a desire to remake the "high literary" into a category that better suits his own ambitions and talents? In either case, one suspects that Franzen, despite his insistence on "authenticity" here and elsewhere, is merely *performing* sincerity and conviction. Interestingly, what emerges from "Mr. Difficult" is an anti-populist populism, an anti-elitist elitism, and anti-postmodernist postmodernism.

I want to end this chapter by looking briefly at a passage from Fredric Jameson's *Postmodernism; or, The Cultural Logic of Late Capitalism* and to suggest how the set of arguments I have analyzed in this chapter are less about elaborating on what postmodernism is than they are about resisting the deconstruction of a romantic version of the self that is still fully operative in modernism. In order to make his case about the "flattening of affect" and the waning of historicity in late capitalism, Jameson performs an interpretation of several images of shoes, most notably Van Gogh's *A Pair of Boots* and Warhol's *Diamond Dust Shoes*. Jameson reads in Van Gogh's boots a modernist invitation to a hermeneutic gesture, pointing toward the "whole life world" that gives the boots meaning. Quoting Heidegger's response to the same painting, Jameson writes, "'In them,' says Heidegger, 'there vibrates the silent call of the earth, its quiet gift of ripening corn and its enigmatic self-refusal in the fallow desolation of the wintry field'" (8). That Heidegger sees the boots as peasant *women's* boots is interesting, if a bit surprising, but Jameson uses this lever to wedge open his own reading of another pair of shoes, the Warhol shoes. Unlike the Van Gogh women's boots, the Warhol women's rather more stylish pumps/flats (we can't tell which), insists Jameson, signify "flatness or depthlessness." For Jameson, Warhol's piece "evidently no longer speaks to us with any of the immediacy of Van Gogh's footgear; indeed, I am tempted to say that it does not really speak to us at all." He writes:

> There is therefore in Warhol no way to complete the hermeneutic gesture and restore to these oddments that whole larger lived context of

the dance hall or the ball, the world of jetset fashion or glamour magazines. Yet this is even more paradoxical in the light of biographical in-
formation: Warhol began his artistic career as a commercial illustrator
for shoe fashions and a designer of display windows in which various
pumps and slippers figured prominently. Indeed, one is tempted to
raise here—far too prematurely—one of the central issues about postmodernism itself and its possible political dimensions. Andy Warhol's
work in fact turns centrally around commodification, and the great
billboard images of the Coca-Cola bottle or the Campbell's soup can,
which explicitly foreground the commodity fetishism of a transition
to late capital, *ought* to be powerful and critical political statements.
If they are not that, then one would surely want to know why, and
one would want to begin to wonder a little more seriously about the
possibilities of political or critical art in the postmodern period of late
capital. (8–9; emphasis in the original)

There's a lot going on in this passage, and in the extended discussion of the
two renderings of shoes. Jameson is rather coy here, with his "evidently"
and his "one is tempted," his invitation, slightly hesitant, to consider
Warhol's shoes the very embodiment of his, Jameson's, argument about
the "cultural logic of late capitalism." But why is Jameson so sure that
these two renderings of women's shoes should figure the epochal change
that is his subject, and on what does he base his certainty that Warhol's
shoes do *not* point toward the "lived context"? Because they are photographed and photographically enhanced? Because they are multiple, not
singular? Because they are "fashionable," even "glamorous," as opposed
to the "worn and broken instruments of labor" he reads, via Heidegger,
in Van Gogh's shoes?

We can read here the set of themes that I have analyzed in criticism of
White Noise and characterizations of its postmodernism. The Van Gogh
shoes are authentic because they are connected to labor; the Warhol shoes
are inauthentic because they are connected to consumer culture, the "jetset world of fashion or glamour magazines." And despite Jameson's repetition of Heidegger's gendering of the boots as female, Van Gogh's boots
do *not* signify femininity, while Warhol's shoes clearly do. Jameson sees
Warhol's shoes as the epitome of commodity fetishism and Van Gogh's

as outside the circuit of consumer exchange. For Jameson, it goes without saying that Warhol's shoes are not "political" in the Marxist sense; they don't even rise to the level of representing the alienation of the (post) modern subject. Jameson's desire to understand postmodernism through a narrative of loss and decline leads him to assimilate Warhol's shoes to an interpretative frame that makes them *lesser* than Van Gogh's and, further, makes them embody the death of the subject, the demise of affect, the end of artistic uniqueness. That this decline is represented by an explicitly feminine image suggests pretty forcefully how the narrative of postmodern decline is also a narrative of feminization.

As the art historian Cecile Whiting has demonstrated, the very shop windows that Jameson references as indicating Warhol's retreat from a modernist critical engagement with commodity culture—that is, a surrender to it—are more complicated than the theorist of postmodernism gives them credit for. For Jameson, the window display in the department store can be nothing more than evidence of the wastes of late capitalism and the consequent loss of the values of authenticity, historicity, and genuine affect. But Whiting points out that the display window had been developing as a space for the exhibition of modern art since the 1930s, a development that culminates in the windows designed for Bonwit Teller by Gene Moore—one of which featured female mannequins in fashionable dresses among a set of canvases by none other than Andy Warhol. Rather than seeing these displays as further evidence of the decline of "art" in a postmodern age, Whiting argues that these displays "regularly permitted a sophisticated group of women to wield the cultural resources of modern art when window-shopping. . . . Combining paintings by Warhol with *haute couture* in a window organized with an eye toward line, form, and color bid the female shopper to evaluate the aesthetic quality of the art, of the dresses, and of the display itself. The window display thus transformed the activity of shopping into a form of art appreciation; the shopper did not covet so much as contemplate and appreciate" (18–19). While Whiting acknowledges that the displays might also be said to frame the paintings as so much "merchandise" for sale alongside the dresses, she concludes that the "potential collapse of the difference between art and commerce, however, need not be taken as a failing of the Warhol window" (20); on the contrary, the window, and others like it, can be read as promoting an active engagement in the aesthetics of consumer culture, something that DeLillo's shoppers also demonstrate. Shopping and reading, shopping and art appreciation, shopping and cultural analysis—these combinations work to challenge the commonsense construction of consumerism as the opposite of politics and consumerism as the force that turns active, autonomous, and male individuals into passive and feminized dupes. In the next chapter, we will see another version of how shopping and other consumer activities mark the decline of American culture, in this case more overtly and explicitly about the effects of late capitalism on men and on masculinity.

CHAPTER 4

THE REAL DEAL

Fighting the Feminizations of Consumer Culture

As we saw in the previous chapter, the anti-consumerism expressed by theorists of the postmodern relies on a set of unexamined premises that pose the inauthenticities of consumer culture against the fantasized authenticities of modernist culture. That modernist culture is imagined to predate and offer a superior alternative to the postmodernist culture that represents the triumph of the commercial over the artistic, the fake over the real, the feminine over the masculine. In this chapter, I turn to a set of texts, all from 1999, that begin from a similar set of premises and also look backward, nostalgically, to an unidentified moment before the rise of consumerism subjected men and America to the inauthenticities of a feminized culture: David Fincher's *Fight Club*, Sam Mendes's *American Beauty*, and Susan Faludi's *Stiffed: The Betrayal of the American Man*. These premises are amply demonstrated in each of these texts but can be seen with particular clarity in a scene in *Fight Club* when the narrator (Ed Norton) and his alter ego, Tyler Durden (Brad Pitt), face a Gucci underwear ad on a bus and ask, "Is that what a man looks like?" This is a rhetorical question because, by this point in the film, we've seen what "real" men are up to: beating each other to a bloody pulp rather than pursuing fashion, brands, and a "life-style obsession." "I felt sorry for guys packed into gyms, trying to look like Tommy Hilfiger and Calvin Klein said they should," the narrator concludes, suggesting that real men should be working in gyms, not preening in them. The commodification of men is just one symptom of what the film represents as a new cultural dominant that substitutes consumption for production, simulation for reality, superficiality for depth. The trendy retailer Ikea epitomizes what the film paints as a numbing consumer culture, a culture that has replaced pornography—that old instrument of male affect—with home-furnishing catalogs. As numerous film reviewers noted, there's an almost uncanny resemblance between *Fight Club*'s representation of the demasculinizing forces of consumer culture and Faludi's critique of the demasculinizing forces of ornamental culture in *Stiffed*. This resemblance is consolidated by Faludi's own review of *Fight Club* for *Newsweek*, where she hailed it as "an incisive gender drama" that supports her own narrative of a masculinity pushed into crisis by a culture of display that vests identity in products and image.

Both *Fight Club* and *American Beauty* imagine violence as the "logical" response to the feminizations wrought by consumer culture, and they both seek "authenticity" by turning back the clock to a fantasized moment when men were, purportedly, not subject to such feminizations. As we have seen in a number of contexts in this book, the historical point of reference for these films' articulation of a crisis in American consumer culture (and masculinity) is the 1950s. *Stiffed* also harks back to an early postwar context, repackaging a venerable narrative about the feminization of American culture in arguing that the current crisis of American manhood stems from the fact that men have become consumers instead of producers, passive reflectors of consumer culture rather than active participants in it. The fact that this narrative persists until the end of the twentieth century, despite massive challenges to our understandings of the relationships between individual and society (or subject and structure), testifies to the seemingly irresistible pull of transhistorical master narratives—even in a postmodern age, as we saw in the last chapter, when such narratives are supposed to have lost their legitimacy.

The tensions between the transhistorical and the historical are everywhere in *Stiffed*, which manages to imply that the commodification of men and masculinity at the cusp of the twenty-first century is *both* a particular symptom of postmodern, postindustrial, celebrity culture—a recent development that underlines what men have lost through recent social, economic, and political changes—*and* a contemporary version of a timeless, ahistorical "truth" of gender. Such contradictions cannot be resolved as long as we insist on coding anti-consumerist critique in the language of gender. As we will see, *Fight Club* is also riven by the tension between the historical and the ahistorical, but whereas we might say that Faludi wants to ameliorate the current historical condition of men by looking to the past, *Fight Club* wants to lift men out of history altogether. In the place of the contemporary context in which men are forced to define themselves by "the stuff they own," the film installs a fantasized space outside of history where men can evade the "society" that always aims to curtail their activities, their potential, and their self-determination. This fantasy of authenticity depends not only on the evacuation of women but also on the reassertion of a clear, stable gender difference secured by the logic of feminization. As we have seen in other contexts, the narrative of men rebelling against consumer culture makes possible a transhistorical construction of masculinity as always under threat and, thus, in need of restitution. *American Beauty* is both more subtle and less sweeping in its representation of the crisis in contemporary masculinity wrought by consumer culture. It focuses its attention more on the individual than the system, identifying the protagonist, Lester Burnham, and his antagonist-wife, Carolyn Burnham, as the object and agent of feminization. As in *Fight Club,* women are tied to the falsities of consumer culture, and Lester seeks authenticity by going back to an earlier moment. Lester's nostalgia for his high school years is presented less as a pathetic return to an adolescent worldview than a "logical" solution to his stagnation and dissatisfaction with his present. The film is more ambivalent about both the problem and its solution than is *Fight Club,* but it shares with the other film a certainty that men in the 1990s are experiencing a series of losses that distance them from an authentic way of being in the world.

FEMINIZED MEN AND INAUTHENTIC WOMEN

From the moment of its release, David Fincher's *Fight Club* has provoked a great deal of theorizing about gender both inside and outside of academia. Such a cultural event, interesting wide swaths of the moviegoing public, media pundits, and academics, is rare enough, but when the topic at hand is gender and, more specifically, the pull of gender on men, the response to the film becomes almost as interesting as the film itself. Early response to *Fight Club* focused attention on the question of violence, as audiences, critics, and academics debated whether the film recommends violence as a solution to a perceived crisis in the lives of a generation of American men who lack the power to find meaning in the wastes of consumer culture.[1] Critics and fans alike, however, accepted the underlying premise of the film; whether arguing for or against the oppositional potential or effect of the film, everyone seemed willing to accept the "fact" that we are experiencing a widespread cultural crisis, that that crisis most poignantly affects men, and that the cause of that crisis is a consumer ethos that reduces identities to brand names and replaces meaningful work with status-oriented consumption.[2] Men, the film insists, are feminized by consumer culture, an insistence that seems to have raised very little objection in the ample commentary that greeted the film's release and the dozens of scholarly articles that have been published in the intervening years. While many scholars have challenged the film's retrograde version of a violent masculinity rooted in the male body,[3] and others have analyzed, both positively and negatively, the film's critique of late capitalist consumer culture,[4] no one has directly challenged the film's articulation of its anti-consumerist critique *through gender*. In fact, some critics have explicitly argued that the film is not "about" gender and that attention to its constructions of masculinity only obscures the "larger" issues it explores.

Omar Lizardo, for example, argues against a focus on masculinity in analyses of the film, insisting that "beneath the gendered readings of *Fight Club* lies a more compelling and important story" (241) about the contradictions of capitalism. It is not clear why the contradictions of capitalism make for a more compelling story than the contradictions of gender, although this logic is a familiar one. But what Lizardo does not see is that *Fight Club* can launch the critique it wants to make only by using gender. Even if we were to accept the premise that the film offers a coherent critique of capitalism (a premise that is arguable, at best), we might still question the logic by which the "feminization" of men is evidence of the contradictions produced by capitalism. Indeed, even while arguing that the film is not "about" gender, Lizardo accepts as unproblematic the fact that it is only *men* whom the film represents as suffering from the contradictions of consumer capitalism and that suffering is best understood as a condition of "feminization." He writes:

> What is missed by this [gendered] reading of the film, is precisely the sociocultural and class-based origins of this feminization of men.

As is plain throughout the film, the feminization of men begins not at the point at which they are forced to become consumers, but in their everyday existence as *laborers* in the service society. Thus, it is the new service jobs that "this new generation" of men—who do not have a great war to commemorate, but whose war is instead a "spiritual war"—is forced to work that begin the process of feminization. Becoming entangled in consumer culture is simply the complement of the more fundamental "feminization" that has occurred at the *point of production* with the move toward the post-industrial organization of the economy. (232; emphasis in the original)

What Lizardo misses here is what should be an obvious question: Why represent the "post-industrial organization of the economy" as a *feminization*? It makes no sense to accept this premise and, at the same time, argue that the film is not "about" gender—even if we accept the shaky proposition that gender is *not* a "sociocultural" condition. Lizardo does recognize that the film obscures the fact that "the service class, in 'real' contemporary society, is not dominated by men but by women" (234), but he calls this a "big gender irony" rather than what it actually is: an attempt to recode the contemporary reality as a crisis in masculinity and, thus, to erase literal women from the scene while making metaphorical women (that is, "feminization") the source of the crisis. "We are a generation of men raised by women," says Tyler in what is easily the most quoted line of the film, putting into play the logic of a critique that poses a masculine rebellion against a feminizing condition. It matters not a bit whether the feminization at the "point of production" comes before the feminization at the point of consumption, nor does it matter whether the gender trouble is caused by class inequities or vice versa. In either case, the film (and Lizardo's critique of it) accepts the self-evidence of the proposition that men are the victims of an economy that makes them more like women. Such a logic authorizes the film's excesses of violent masculinity and, also, as we will see, its hostility toward women. As Suzanne Clark notes in her comments on *Fight Club,* "It is particularly important to realize that gender plays a part in rhetoric when struggles over issues seem not to be about gender. This is not because gender necessarily organizes cultural history in predetermined ways, but because gender has defined so much of American cultural history. Thus, it determines the rhetorical force and implications of arguments at a level that could be called a 'gendered unconscious'" (416). If the issues at the heart of *Fight Club* "seem not to be about gender," it is perhaps because the logic and rhetoric of American social critique have for so long relied on a metaphorics of gender that we can no longer even see its functioning.

The film's articulation of its anti-capitalist rebellion as a fight against feminization not only relies on and perpetuates a stable, transhistorical idea of gender difference but also imagines contemporary social realities as serving the needs of women at the expense of men. What narratives about feminization all have in common is that they imagine the individual as an autonomous, self-determining agent who battles against a "society" or vaguely drawn array of social forces that always aim to curtail his autonomy and agency. The social force against which *Fight Club*'s male characters rebel is figured as a consumer or corporate culture that promotes phoniness over authenticity, the pleasures of indulgence over the rewards of self-denial, mass psychology over individual will and agency, and dependency over self-reliance. As we will see, one persistent and unavoidable effect of the logic of masculine protest is a willingness to entertain the possibility that women—embodying consumerism—threaten a masculine authenticity and are, thus, eradicable.

Echoing countless social critics who bemoan the emasculating effects of consumer culture on once self-defined and autonomous individuals, *Fight Club* clearly delineates the lure of commodities and the false promises of a therapeutic individualism. The effects of this feminization are everywhere evident: in male characters' obsession with shopping, in the dominance of a therapeutic model of affect, in the passivity produced within a bureaucratized white-collar workplace. The temptations of consumer culture are amply represented in a striking early scene of the film, which offers a visual pleasure and sheer cleverness that would seem to belie the logic through which we are invited to reject consumer culture as vapid and enervating. The scene has the narrator sitting on the toilet and then wandering around his apartment, phone attached to his ear, ordering "the Erika Pekkari dust ruffles." While the voice-over tonelessly itemizes the commodities he's purchased for his home, his apartment becomes a virtual catalog, with individual items, their names, prices, and capsule descriptions appearing on the screen: "Like so many others, I had become a slave to the Ikea nesting instinct. If I saw something clever, like a little coffee table in the shape of a yin yang, I had to have it. . . . I'd flip through catalogues and wonder, 'What kind of dining set defines me as a person?'" From the beginning of the film, the feminization produced through an acceptance that commodities can define the self is posed against an ideal of authenticity that promises to ward off that feminization and to lead the narrator back to the "real." Mimicking the promises of virtual reality to improve on "real life," this sequence functions to emphasize the narrator's lack of contact with anything not mediated through consumer culture. In the logic of the film, these commodities are fetishes that hide the narrator's lack of identity, his addiction to shopping, his lack of purpose; as Tyler Durden teaches the narrator, being a consumer—"the byproduct of a lifestyle obsession"—deprives him of any relation to authenticity and, thus, separates him from masculinity. Tyler makes this point perfectly clear in his response to the narrator's plaintive cry about losing his apartment and its accouterments: "You know it could be worse—a woman could cut off your penis while you are sleeping and throw it out of the window of a moving car." Castration is simply a more literal form of the emasculations produced by a fantasized consumer culture aligned with vicious women intent on maiming men.

Fight Club bases its social critique on the premise that a feminizing consumer culture destroys authenticity. Perhaps more than any other text under consideration in this book, *Fight Club* indulges in a fantasy of authenticity. The narrator comments again and again about the absence of the real in consumer/corporate culture, and the film continuously defers both the narrator's and our access to that real. The real is a horizon that is always out of reach because consumerism and its processes of feminization have replaced the real with simulacra—a familiar narrative about the postmodern condition, as I argued in chapter 3. The real that the narrator yearns for is an emotional release that might enable him to escape his chronic insomnia and get a good night's sleep. "With insomnia," he tells us, "nothing's real; everything's far away. Everything is a copy of a copy of a copy." His physician corroborates the narrator's sense that he suffers from inauthenticity when he refuses to prescribe drugs, instead counseling the narrator to take herbal remedies; "good, healthy, natural sleep is what you need," he says. When the narrator complains that he's in pain, the doctor prods him to discover the difference between his pain and *real* pain by suggesting he visit the support group for testicular cancer sufferers. These guys, the doctor says, are in pain. The doctor's cure works, but not for the reasons he suspected; the narrator is able to find a real emotional release—evidenced by tears—in the support group, and this emotional release enables him to "sleep like a baby." The malady caused by the dominance of the inauthentic in his life is cured by an authentic release of emotional pressures.

Therapeutic culture does not, however, offer the narrator the rebirth and refreshment he needs because it, too, turns out to be inauthentic. The film's nameless narrator is represented as completely removed from any clear sense of identity, authenticity, or individual autonomy. Although nearly everyone who discusses this film refers to Edward Norton's character as "Jack" (because he reads from a children's book that anthropomorphizes parts of the body, as in "I am Jack's colon"), such a naming works against the film's representation of him. The credits list him as "The narrator," and I would argue that the "I am Jack's" conceit, far from identifying him as an individual, testifies to his psychologically flat, affectless state; indeed, he signifies not an individual with an individual history but an Everyman whose generalized or representative emotional and physical state fails to compensate for his lack of individual uniqueness and autonomy. As his twelve-step tourism indicates, one self with one history is easily interchangeable with another self with another history, and such inauthentic selves cannot harbor authentic emotion. It is this cultural condition that will, eventually, be eradicated through Fight Club.

The later fighting scenes contrast the earlier scenes in which the narrator and Marla Singer (Helena Bonham Carter) spar over ownership of the various support groups they visit. When the narrator cries at the testicular cancer survivors' meeting, he is merely faking emotion, thus exacerbating, rather than curing, his condition. When Marla appears on the scene and her support-group "tourism" exposes his for the sham it is, he tells us, "Her lie reflected my lie. I couldn't cry, so I couldn't sleep." This is a culture of inauthenticity taken to its extreme limits, a fact driven home by Marla's participation in the testicular cancer support group. No one in the group seems disturbed by a woman's presence, and, as Marla herself insists to the narrator, she has just as much right to be there as he does—more, in fact, because, unlike the narrator but like the "real" members of the group, Marla has "no balls." Gender is meaningless in this therapeutic culture, reduced to a tautology that fails to illuminate experience or reverse the effects of feminization. The men hug each other and intone, "Yes, we are men; men is what we are."

It is no accident that the film dwells on the testicular cancer support group or that it uses Marla's participation in it as the narrator's break-ing point. Both the narrator and Marla are faking all the illnesses whose support groups they attend; neither has blood or brain parasites, neither has tuberculosis, neither has any form of cancer. But what makes Marla's faking of testicular cancer particularly galling to the narrator and signifi-cant to the film's logic is that it proves that gender itself can no longer be authenticated. Later, after the narrator has given up support groups for the "release" found in bare-knuckled fighting, he tells Marla that he has "found something else" to replace his support-group fix and triumphantly announces, "It's for men only." Unlike "that testicular thing," Fight Club is something that Marla can't fake because Fight Club reinstates a real masculinity. Further, this real masculinity is rooted in the body, and even "feminized" male bodies embody it; whereas the suffering Bob (Meat Loaf) can be said to "perform" femininity through his bodily attitude and emotional display, Marla cannot perform masculinity because, accord-ing to the film's logic, masculinity is that which cannot be performed or faked. It is the culture of inauthenticity, represented by a feminizing con-sumerism and its "self-help" ideologies, that snuffs out masculinity.

Fight Club does not simply argue that an authentic masculinity needs to be rescued from the wastes of an inauthentic and feminizing consumer culture; it argues that we need to think about masculinity as *outside* of culture itself. The logic goes something like this: while femininity is a social construction—and, thus, "fake"—masculinity, rooted in the male body and its elemental sensations and desires, is a brute fact of nature. This particular construction of gender difference can be seen as a legacy of the decades-long critique of masculinity that has aimed to attack male dominance by demonstrating that masculinity, like femininity, is a so-cial construction. *Fight Club* wants to forget this critique and to reset the clock to a time when masculinity was understood as a value to be earned rather than an identity to be deconstructed. In order to do this, the film must position masculinity as the location of authenticity—the thing that cannot be bought or faked or constructed. The film pursues a masculine authenticity rather than an authentic masculinity, and masculinity, thus, becomes the location of the real, the authentic. What this logic produces is a closed circle in which the ideal of masculine authenticity becomes the only goal of anti-consumerist, anti-capitalist, countercultural critique; and only men can articulate that critique because women are the very embodiment of the problem. That this inauthenticity is understood as contagious, spread by the feminizing effects of consumer culture, means that women are positioned with or in the forces that always threaten to undermine masculinity and cultural authenticity itself. Such a logic feeds into a fantasy of constructing a world without women, a world where the feminine disappears, along with consumer culture, in a spectacular display of destruction.[5]

This fantasy seeps into *Fight Club* through the narrator's hostility toward Marla but also in Tyler Durden's discourse on women, inauthenticity, and consumerism. One particularly troublesome example of this comes in the scene when the narrator and Tyler break into the yard of a liposuction clinic to steal human fat to make their high-end soap. Tyler's delight at the idea of "selling rich women's fat asses back to them" in the form of designer soap seems a clever exposure of the ironies of consumer culture. But the joke depends on the audience's acceptance of the premise that body-conscious, self-indulgent, fake women embody the ills of a consumer culture drunk on "self-improvement" and deserve to be duped by these masculine, svelte working men. The target of this clever, highly ironic critique might be the inauthenticities of consumer culture, but the fact that this critique is articulated through a giddy image of female bodies mutilated in the service of "self-improvement" exposes the film's pleasure in the possibility of eradicating women along with the consumer culture they embody. The silly self-mutilation of rich women, the epitome of inauthenticity and quite literally the butt of the joke, contrasts with the serious self-destruction of hungry young men in the quest for authentic experience in a false world. The ills of consumer culture are embodied not only in the "rich women's fat asses" but in the "feminine" value of self-improvement. The men who trick the women are positioned as *producers*, not consumers, and, thus, their own implication in the consumer system goes unremarked.[6] It is also worth noting that Tyler slyly refers to this substance as "the fat of the land," suggesting that women are also aligned with a (passive) nature that exists only for the exploitation of enterprising men.

ESCAPING HISTORY, SEEKING AUTHENTICITY

The film's logic depends on the assumption that, like masculinity, "authenticity" is not socially constructed—that is, authenticity is a pure ideal, *outside* of culture. Culture, or more specifically, consumer culture, is what endangers masculinity rather than what might be said to produce it. The effort to locate masculinity outside of culture, outside of history, is a characteristic of narratives that depend on the feminization thesis to explain the causes of cultural crisis. As I noted above, one particularly relevant example of this can be found in Susan Faludi's *Stiffed: The Betrayal of the American Man,* which was released the same month as *Fight Club.* In addition to complaining about the indignities of consumer culture, Faludi's informants also blame feminist work on the construction of gender for raising the idea that masculinity might be "fake." Of course, understanding gender as socially constructed does not necessarily mean that it is any less "real." *Fight Club* avoids such theoretical nuances by pursuing a fantasy of destroying everything "fake," a fantasy that involves evacuating women almost entirely and purging the world of the "feminine" trappings of consumer culture. Like Faludi's "stiffed" men, who can accept the idea that *women's* identities are constituted through the practices of consumer culture, the Fight Clubbers battle the possibility that *men's* identities might be so constituted because such a possibility endangers both "authentic" masculinity and masculine authenticity.

Fight Club's efforts to reinstate an ahistorical truth through its pursuit of a masculine authenticity depend on what T. J. Jackson Lears identifies as a persistent strain of "antimodernism" in U.S. culture, one of whose chief manifestations is a martial "fascination with pain" as an "attempt to move beyond the pleasure principle of a democratic, industrial culture" and a "groping for transcendence" (*No Place of Grace* 118). Such an antimodernism expresses a desire to escape from history and contemporary cultural systems, as we can see in *Fight Club*'s celebration of pre- or anti-consumerist spaces. The film's social critique and its masculine protest are most clearly articulated in Tyler Durden's didactic pronouncements on the state of modern masculine selfhood: "We are the middle children of history, slaves with white collars, an entire generation pumping gas, waiting tables. Advertising has us chasing cars and clothes, working jobs we hate so we can buy shit we don't need." The "middle children of history" are *outside* of history, stuck in a moment of stasis, looking back nostalgically to a (fantasized) moment when masculinity and authenticity were guaranteed and forward longingly to a moment of rebellion through which that masculinity and authenticity might be restored. The film implicitly identifies that earlier masculinity and authenticity with the working class and suggests that the middle-class narrator's malaise can be cured by downward mobility.

Chuck Palahniuk's novel, on which Fincher's film is based, is even more explicit in its narrator's desire to find a space outside of history. The novel uses *history* as a code word to nominate a fake culture and society and to pose an appealing masculine fantasy against a history that aims to constrain that fantasy. The narrator sees the goal of Project Mayhem as "destroying every scrap of history" and imagines that the actions taken by the project to explode corporate buildings could not be found "in any history book" (12–13). It eventually becomes clear that the problem with "history" is the same problem with "society" in the standard "individual-versus-society" narrative: history requires the individual to submit himself to a larger force or forces and, thus, works against the radical individual autonomy the narrator and other members of Fight Club seek. "For thousands of years," the narrator says, "human beings had screwed up and trashed and crapped on this planet, and now history expected me to clean up after everyone. I have to wash out and flatten my soup cans. And account for every drop of used motor oil. And I have to foot the bill for nuclear waste and buried gasoline tanks and landfilled toxic sludge dumped a generation before I was born" (124). The whininess of this response points to the same sense of wounded entitlement we see in the film, where "the middle children of history" feel that they have been ripped off by a consumer culture that promises more than it can deliver. Importantly, the burden of this sense of history and responsibility can be alleviated by the destruction of a figure who represents the feminine to the narrator—the man he calls "beautiful mister angel face" whom he fantasies about, and eventually succeeds in, defacing. "Put him in a dress and make him smile, and he'd be a woman," the narrator growls (128). The goal of Project Mayhem is "to teach each man in the project that he had the power to control history. We, each of us, can take control of the world" (122). The film, too, uses the concept of "history" not to imagine the men's grounding in the material conditions of their reality but, on the contrary, as the false and falsifying narrative against which the *fantasy* of authenticity can be launched.

The film's protest against feminization and its search for a masculine authenticity outside of culture and, even, of history are both literally and metaphorically rendered. The film proceeds by a relentless narrative and visual movement *downward* and *backward,* encapsulated each time we see the narrator, Tyler, and other characters descending toward the dark, dank basements in which they fight and make bombs, and encapsulated as well in Tyler Durden's credo that "hitting bottom" is the prerequisite for rebirth. The backward movement of the narrative works on two levels: in the structure of the film, which begins at the end and several times backs up explicitly and dramatically, and in the thematic concern with an "evolution" that is actually a regression that leads to nihilism. The film, like other late-twentieth-century attempts to find the "inner warrior" in men, draws on an anti-modernism that aims to find "character" behind the veneer of "personality." The narrative of feminization depends on an anterior order against which the contemporary disorder can be posited. *Fight Club* finds that anterior order in the raw, physical culture of fighting and the homosocial bonding it promotes; the real is reinstated in these exclusively male spaces where gender difference—that is, woman's difference from man—can be reasserted. The authenticity of what the men experience in Fight Club is explicitly contrasted with the falseness of their everyday lives; if "everything is a copy of a copy of a copy" outside of Fight Club, within it life is *"real,* not like TV." "After fighting," the narrator reports, "everything else in your life got the volume turned down. You could deal with anything," including a "smarmy" boss with his "primary action items."

The film, of course, resides fully within the realm of consumer culture, itself forwarding corporate interests, despite its cool aura of hip critique.

In the late-twentieth-century consumer culture that is the ground of *Fight Club*'s representation, locating authenticity outside of, or prior to, consumerism requires a concerted effort to ignore the ways in which authenticity itself is the primary commodity marketed by consumer culture. As I noted in chapter 1, authenticity concerns advertisers, marketers, managerial theorists, and business school professors as much as it does cultural studies scholars, countercultural rebels, and public intellectuals. *Fight Club*'s anti-modernist stance is dependent on the idea that consumer culture (including business culture) *endangers* authenticity, but such a stance seems nostalgic at best, disingenuous at worst. As one reviewer suggested, "When the movie, after satirizing the gym-enhanced bodies of men in Gucci subway ads ('Self-improvement is masturbation,' Tyler pronounces), cuts to the impeccably lean and cut body of its leading man, it is in the grips of a style-content contradiction that this slick denunciation of surface values battles throughout" (Ansen).

While this comment is meant to chide the film for bad faith, it falls into the same trap as the film by reproducing a nearly mythic narrative based on the opposition between countercultural rebellion and capitalist social forms. This is the same trap that critics of *On the Road* fall into when they accuse Kerouac of being inconsistently anti-consumerist—as if there is a kind of authenticity meter that registers degrees of rebellion. As a number of recent studies of the relationship between consumerism and countercultural critique have suggested, American discourses critical of capitalism and consumer culture have been repackaging this myth for quite some time, despite constant and rapid changes in the global economy. In addition to Heath and Potter's *A Nation of Rebels,* which I addressed in chapter 1, Thomas Frank's *The Conquest of Cool* challenges the deeply held idea that there is a "real" counterculture mimicked and diluted by its "fake," commodified version. Rather than offering another lament over the co-optation of rebellion by consumer culture, Frank analyzes how business culture, particularly advertising, has played an essential and complicated role in the history of counterculture in the latter half of the twentieth century. Underlining the irony of a mass-society critique "adopted by millions of Organization Men," Frank argues for a more nuanced understanding of how co-optation has actually worked. The standard "co-optation thesis"—like the standard "feminization thesis"—is recognizable in a wide range of discourses and representations. "According to the standard binary narrative," Frank writes, "the cascade of pseudo-hip culture-products that inundated the marketplace in the sixties were indicators not of the counterculture's consumer-friendly nature but evidence of the 'corporate state's' hostility. They were the tools with which the Establishment hoped to buy off and absorb its opposition, emblems of dissent that were quickly translated into harmless consumer commodities, emptied of content, and sold to their very originators as substitutes for the real thing" (16). Analyzing the rise of "hip consumerism" and its architects, Frank notes that "in the counterculture, admen believed they had found both a perfect model for consumer subjectivity, intelligent and at war with the conformist past, and a cultural machine for turning disgust with consumerism into the very fuel by which consumerism might be accelerated" (119).

This is not the story of a powerful corporate entity destroying the counterculture and imposing mindless consumerism on brainwashed "mass man," as the critique of mass society would have it; it is the story of the cultural cachet of the "outsider" in all realms of life, in corporate culture as well as counterculture. The official website for *Fight Club* provides a perfect example of how "hip" anti-consumerist consumerism functions as countercultural critique. This tongue-in-cheek spread, an edgy cousin to culture jamming, has much in common with the advertising Frank associates with the "Creative Revolution" in the sixties and seventies, which functioned, ironically, to reassure consumers that, unlike the great unwashed masses, *they* could see through the tactics of "malicious robber barons and their unscrupulous Madison Avenue minions" (145). The website for *Fight Club* features "Additional Fashions" for Jack, Tyler, and Marla as well as "Home Furnishings." Tyler's "Huggybear Silk Shirt" ($125, "handcrafted in an Indonesian sweatshop by Frida, a single mother of seven whose monthly salary is equivalent to six american dollars") and "Retro Leather Jacket" ($725, "made from the hide of an 8 month old Jersey calf. These calves are bred for the sole purpose of supplying leather for the production of bags, belts, shoes, and this exquisite jacket"). Slickly packaging its tongue-in-cheek anti-consumerism, the website is an incoherent stew of hip consumerism and hip anti-consumerism. The subject of its address can appreciate the cool things on offer while simultaneously occupying a rebellious posture in relation to those things and their marketing. By drawing attention to genetically engineered calves and exploited workers, the website offers a critique of the political and social effects of a malicious global capitalism but also allows its viewers to take a superior position by participating in an edgy anti-consumerist consumerism.

These are not real commodities, and the website isn't actually selling them; what it is selling is a relationship to consumer culture that evades feminization. As I have noted in other contexts, anti-consumerist discourses often distinguish between active and passive consumerism, between forms of consumption that secure authenticity and those that endanger it. Viewers are invited to imagine themselves, like Tyler, as consuming rebels against consumer culture and its politically suspect practices. The website, thus, performs the same kind of critique that the film does. As Henry Giroux argues, the film is "less interested in attacking the broader material relations of power and strategies of domination and exploitation associated with neoliberal capitalism than it is in rebelling against a consumerist culture that dissolves the bonds of male sociality and puts into place an enervating notion of male identity and agency" (5). That male sociality is reinstated within the film by Fight Club and, later Project Mayhem. But it is also, I would argue, reinstated by the relationship the film has with an audience schooled in the modes of (masculine) rebellion against the feminizing forces of consumerism and other social structures. The masculine protest that leads to Fight Club, like all forms of social critique, produces insiders and outsiders—those in the know and those in the dark. The film plays on this effect of rebellion by showing that only true members can recognize each other, as happens in the many scenes when men salute in each other the "badges"—the Band-Aids, the black eyes, the swollen noses—of authenticity that come from participating in this secret society. The fact that actual fight clubs started showing up around the United States after the release of the film suggests that its mode of masculine protest was not limited to what happens on the screen.

In line with much anti-consumerist discourse, *Fight Club* might appear to be offering an economic analysis of the social effects of consumer and corporate culture, but it ultimately is more interested in representing how this culture affects the individual man and possible strategies for fighting against feminization. Consumerism is represented in the film as "an ideological force and an existential experience" rather than an economic or political system (Giroux 14). Tyler Durden expresses the limits of the film's social critique when he lectures the narrator on what really matters and what is worth rebelling against: "Murder, crime, poverty. These things don't concern me. What concerns me are celebrity magazines, some guy's name on my underwear, Rogaine, Viagra, Oloestra." The limits of this individualistic focus are evidenced by the denouement of the film. As the masochistic pleasures of self-destruction in Fight Club give way to the mechanized destruction of Project Mayhem, the film suggests that the regenerative powers of violence can be taken too far. But the problem is not that violence is bad or that the adolescent antics of the gang appear randomly destructive. In fact, the film appears to be suggesting that the remasculinization enacted by Fight Club leads into another feminization, as the newly de-individualized foot soldiers of Project Mayhem find themselves right back where they started: in thrall to a system or organization that cares nothing for individual will and initiative and everything for conformity to a collective vision. As Jennifer Barker notes, Fincher represents Project Mayhem as a fascist organization; like his version of corporate capitalism, his version of fascism renders the masculine individual a passive conduit for its values. However, Project Mayhem is *not* the same thing as the consumerism the narrator leaves behind at the beginning of the film. It is the creation not of some nameless bureaucratic entity but of a fully masculinized, charismatic *individual*. Despite the narrator's eleventh-hour renunciation of Tyler Durden and the organized violence he engineers, the film never wavers from its worship of Durden *or* its pleasure in the spectacle of violence it proffers as a cure for what ails modern man. Edward Norton never comes close to the power emanating from Brad Pitt, and even though the narrator ultimately exorcises Tyler, the film nevertheless ends with an aestheticized spectacle of destruction that pays tribute to that alter ego.

The film demonstrates what Lears notes in an earlier version of antimodernism in American culture: that "desperate quests" for "primal irrationality" and "pristine savagery" do not offer a way out of the dilemmas of modern consumer culture but instead end up simply reaffirming a nihilistic acceptance of that culture. The "militaristic obsession with authenticity, like other cults of risk-taking," can become "a circular and self-defeating quest for intense experience—a characteristic mode of *adjustment* to a secular culture of consumption. Reacting against therapeutic self-absorption, the cult of martial experience prove[s] unable to transcend it" (*No Place of Grace* 138; emphasis added). The aestheticized and commodified spectacle of violence at the end of the film is as much sanctioned by consumer culture as is the equally aestheticized and commodified spectacle of an upscale furniture catalog come to life. But the film insists that there is a difference between the two, and that difference is a gendered difference. Even if Tyler Durden goes too far in pursuing his vision of exploding consumerism, the film still insists, along with him, that "guys like us" should not know "what a duvet is," because such knowledge is not "essential to our survival in the hunter-gatherer sense of the word." Ikea has been exorcised, and there are no duvets in the narrator's future. Much has been made of the film's clever twist and its possible meanings, but does it really matter if Tyler Durden is just a figment of the narrator's imagination? The film is a fantasy with a certain critical self-awareness, but representing the violence of Fight Club and Project Mayhem as a hallucination does not in any way change the film's ideological investment in a mode of social critique that figures virile, anti-capitalist rebels purging the world of the inauthenticities of the feminine and a feminizing consumer culture. While the film does not direct its violence against women, the gendered logic of its anti-capitalist critique begs the question of what happens to women when a masculine authenticity triumphs over the feminizing forces of consumer culture for a "generation of men raised by women."

Project Mayhem returns the men in the film to a de-individualizing force, an even more total loss of individual will than that produced by consumer culture. It is the fact that Project Mayhem represents the "logical" conclusion of Fight Club—the next step in the evolution of its newly masculinized secret society—that might lead us to see the film as renouncing an atavistic return to a pre-cultural masculinity. The film seems close to understanding the cost of seeking an authentic masculinity that expresses itself *against* the social body, *against* women, *against* structures and systems and institutions—that is, against *everything* other than itself. Such a masculinity can be nothing but combative, defensive, antisocial, and dangerous; perhaps more importantly, the version of masculine authenticity offered by the film propels itself right out of history as a kind of transhistorical real that is not shaped by anything other than its own will.

But while the film backs down, along with the narrator, from the implications of Project Mayhem, that does not mean that the version of the real it offers in the form of Fight Club is thus delegitimated—on the contrary, as has been demonstrated by the number of actual Fight Clubs that have arisen in response to the film. The film wants to have it both ways: it wants to save the pleasures of Fight Club (physical, homoerotic, masochistic, atavistic) and to disavow the pleasures of Project Mayhem.[7] It should come as no surprise, then, that the ending of the film is torn neatly along a seam of irony, offering us the pleasurable spectacle of mass destruction at the same time that it asks us to see the events leading up to this spectacle as troubling. The film has propelled itself entirely out of the real by this point, the narrator having shot himself in the mouth with little damage, thus perhaps obviating the need to decide which of the two cultures (consumer or pre-consumer) is the disease and which the cure.

ORNAMENTAL CULTURE, FEMINIZED SUBURBIA, AND MASCULINE REGENERATION

While it seems clear that the coherence of *Fight Club*'s narrative logic depends on our accepting as true the premise that consumer culture is a de-individualizing, de-masculinizing, de-authenticating force, it is also the case that the film's ending nudges us to consider the effects of going backward. In this, the film seems more canny and more historically aware than Faludi's romanticized version of a return to authentic masculinity. As in the cultural histories of the feminizing effects of the marketplace articulated to explain and defend the binary relationship between masculine production and feminine consumption, Faludi's account reinvests in a transhistorical narrative in which stable gender categories underwrite her sense of the crisis in masculinity:

Ornamental culture has proved the ultimate expression of the American Century, sweeping away institutions in which men felt some sense of belonging and replacing them with visual spectacles that they can only watch and that benefit global commercial forcers they cannot fathom. Celebrity culture's effects on men go far beyond the obvious showcasing of action heroes and rock musicians. The ordinary man is no fool: he knows he can't be Arnold Schwarzenegger. Nonetheless, the culture reshapes his most basic sense of manhood by telling him as much as it tells the celebrity that masculinity is something to drape over the body, not draw from inner resources; that it is personal, not societal; that manhood is displayed, not demonstrated. The internal qualities once said to embody manhood—surefootedness, inner strength, confidence of purpose—are merchandised to men to enhance their manliness. What passes for the essence of masculinity is being extracted and bottled—and sold back to men. Literally, in the case of Viagra. (*Stiffed* 35)

Ornamental or celebrity culture is a culture of inauthenticity, and, according to Faludi's reading of the thermometer of male angst, such a culture is producing a wide range of symptoms, from domestic violence to sexual harassment to the spectacle of white male anger featured on TV talk shows and in venues as different as a Cleveland football stadium and the Citadel. Nowhere in Faludi's long book does she suggest the possibility that the demise of a producer masculinity is historically grounded in economic and social changes that are not likely to be reversed, nor does she entertain the possibility that new forms of masculinity—oriented toward consumer pleasures, for instance—are emerging out of the demise of the old. Further, her belief in the possibility (and the desirability) of an "essence" of masculinity—a *real* masculinity—is troubling, coming as it does from someone who has argued elsewhere that the "essence" of femininity is a sham.

Fight Club buys into the logic of Faludi's analysis, as it moves from surface to depth, from the inauthenticities of consumer culture to an experience of the real meant to signify the apotheosis of consumer culture. But in the narrator's search for *real* experience, each step in the process ups the stakes and, not incidentally, the violence quotient: from the numbness of corporate-consumer insomnia and a free-floating emotional release to a celebration of physical pain and a spectacle of apocalyptic destruction, this search for the real can end only in violence. An ever-receding real, thus, becomes a motivation for escalating violence—as when Tyler Durden teaches, "without pain, without sacrifice, you have nothing," while he forces the narrator to endure a particularly excruciating ritual. Early in the film, in the first fight scene, the narrator, surprised by the fact that getting punched actually causes physical pain, says, "It *really* hurts. This is *real*, not TV. Hit me again." The film here resonates with a tradition of cultural critique that sees televised reality as mediating and even replacing experiential reality and sees in the rise of simulacra a possible explanation for the troubling evidence of violence in our world. Such critiques often imply that it is advisable, if not particularly easy, to turn back the clock to a moment before the rise of electronic media and the other mediating forms of consumer culture, to seek some access to authentic experience behind the mediations.

American Beauty locates this moment in the 1970s. The film has been received in much the same way as *Fight Club*, although without the controversy that came along with the violence of Fincher's film. Like reviewers of *Fight Club*, reviewers of *American Beauty* eagerly assimilated the film to a vaguely apprehended crisis in American culture that afflicts straight white middle-class men. Screenwriter Alan Ball locates the script and the film within the anti-consumerist narrative I have read in *Fight Club*, and although he does not identify consumer culture as "feminizing," he does suggest that consumer culture has made it "harder to live an authentic life" (Chumo 8). Like the narrator in *Fight Club*, Lester Burnham was read as an Everyman, a representative figure for what currently ails American masculinity: working at a dead-end job, made a "whore to the advertising agencies," aware that "both [his] wife and daughter think [he's] a gigantic loser," Lester is emasculated until he learns to regenerate himself by taking a step back into his past. He becomes increasingly aggressive and begins to talk like Tyler Durden; during a fight with his wife, he articulates the same kind of lament that audiences and critics ate up in *Fight Club*: "This is just stuff, it's not life. It's become more important to you than living. I'm only trying to help you." Lester's violence remains more or less simmering below the surface, exploding only a couple of times and mostly in language rather than action.

Against Lester, the film poses Ricky Fitts, an artist figure who offers a seeming alternative to the consumer-driven lifestyle the Burnhams are trapped within. I say "seeming" because, like *Fight Club*, *American Beauty* only pretends to find an alternative to consumer culture; both Lester and Ricky find their power and their "beauty" through consumerist means. Lester finds satisfaction by fantasizing about a Barbie doll–like teenager, buying the car of his teenage dreams, smoking a lot of pot, and listening to anthems of youthful rebellion circa 1970. Ricky finances his art and his escape from his emasculating father through selling drugs—an activity that the film represents as an alternative to the dead-end jobs Lester has, a professional, entrepreneurial, and empowering form of business that offers Ricky a way out of his otherwise unpromising life. Like the soap making that goes on in *Fight Club,* Ricky's drug business offers an alternative economy, but an economy that allows men to benefit from consumer culture rather than become victims of it. The two films, thus, carry on a tradition of cordoning off certain forms of male consumption in order to evade feminization. Like the paeans to the "man cave" and the "inner-directed" consumption celebrated by David Riesman, *American Beauty*'s representation of appropriately masculine consumption works to secure gender difference; Lester's project of self-improvement, pumping iron in his own version of the man cave, escapes from the logic of feminization through the tried-and-true method that Mark Swiencicki identifies in the marketing of sports. Because sports "have been so heavily promoted by the discourse of heterosexual masculinity, the commodities that men used while engaging in these activities (i.e., balls, uniforms, running shoes, gyms, rackets and golf clubs) have generally been viewed as props in the rituals of militaristic training rather than as products which transform their participants into consumers" (791–92).

Lester's story begins with his death but then rewinds to the events leading up to it—much like *Fight Club.* As the camera zooms in on his suburban neighborhood, Lester immediately foregrounds the superficiality of his existence by offering a narrative that is as familiar to American audiences as the suburbs, and so functions as a shorthand description of typical American middle-class male angst: "This is my neighborhood, this is my street, this is my life." Immediately following this gloomy statement, we see Carolyn Burnham cutting down what the film's critics were very quick to see as a symbol of "real" (rather than false) beauty: her prized American Beauty roses. Lester's indictment of his wife—"her pruning shears match her gardening clogs exactly"—makes it clear that any happiness she might experience or express is only the false happiness of a successful *consumerist* life. But, further, the film accuses Carolyn of emasculating Lester; one reviewer ratifies this view by commenting that the roses in this early scene represent "the flower of Lester's virility [!], which his wife has clipped" (Denby 134). As in a later scene where Lester accuses Carolyn of having lost her "joy," the film asks and expects its audience to accept as true Lester's assessment of his wife and as self-evident the "fact" that her happiness cannot be real because she is, in Lester's estimation, a "bloodless, money-grubbing freak." As I will suggest later, it's possible to interpret Carolyn in a different way and to understand *her* crisis as different in kind and origin from Lester's; but Lester's story depends on framing Carolyn in this way, on positioning her as the representative of all that Lester needs to escape from. Articulating a version of Faludi's narrative in *Stiffed,* Lester says, "I have lost something. I'm not exactly sure what it is. I didn't always feel this sedated." That Lester need not be more specific here testifies to the dominance of the commonsense understanding of the position of straight white middle-class men in the 1990s: in Faludi's terms, for the men who grew up under the shadow of the Cold War, their "mission to manhood shows up in their minds not as promises met but as betrayals, losses, disillusionments. It is as if a generation of men had lined up at Cape Kennedy to witness the countdown to liftoff, only to watch their rocket—containing all their hopes and dreams—burn up on the launchpad" (27).

Faludi's diagnosis here—complete with phallic rocket petering out— became in the 1990s such a truism that *Time* could suggest that men were suffering from a backlash and masculinity getting a bad rep. "Are Men Really That Bad?" was the plaintiff cry on its cover. It's worth noting that the 1990s narratives not only echo but virtually *repeat* the laments over lost manhood in the 1950s. As we saw in chapter 2, Arthur Schlesinger 1958's "The Crisis of American Masculinity" is an earlier chapter in the narrative excoriating consumer culture and its female engineers for orchestrating the demise of masculinity. In the *Time* article, Lance Morrow trots out Allan Carlson, president of a "conservative think tank," to offer this diagnosis: "We are at the tail end of the deconstruction of patriarchy, which has been going on since the turn of the century. The last acceptable villain is the prototypical white male." Offering a textbook example of the narrative of declension I have been tracking throughout this book, Carlson raises an alarm about the rising tide of feminization and predicts, à la *Fight Club,* a reckoning that could be apocalyptic: "I think matriarchies are always a sign of social disintegration. . . . In history there are not examples of sustained, vigorous matriarchal societies. . . . I think we're a society in decay and destruction" (54).

Given the 1990s rebirth of the 1950s crisis in masculinity, it perhaps comes as no surprise that *American Beauty* screenwriter Alan Ball explicitly identifies the 1950s as a context for his script, noting that "for all of the differences between now and the fifties, in a lot of ways this is just as oppressively conformist a time" (Chumo 8).[8] Schlesinger could be describing *American Beauty*'s construction of the Burnham marriage and its gender dynamic when he writes, "Women seem an expanding, aggressive force, seizing more domains like a conquering army, while men, more and more on the defensive, are hardly able to hold their own and gratefully accept assignments from their new rulers. A recent book bears the stark and melancholy title *The Decline of the American Man*" (238). While Faludi's subtitle is *The Betrayal of the American Man,* and she avoids blaming women for this betrayal, the men she interviews, and the widely repeated cultural narratives that they produce for her, make it clear that masculinity and femininity, men and women, are understood to exist in a delicate balance: when one gender gets (or "seizes") the upper hand, the other loses power. This is, of course, not the only way to understand gender and power, but it was the dominant way in the second half of the twentieth century. The belief that men have "lost something" sets the stage for, and justifies, a recalibrating of the balance in the form of a remasculinization; as Lester says at the outset of the film, "It's never too late to get it back."

Lester gets "it" back by finding his inner adolescent, and the film expects us to applaud this move from "sedated," weak masculinity to mean, buff, self-indulgent, and irresponsible masculinity. In a scene similar to a scene in *Fight Club,* Lester takes revenge on an efficiency expert at the magazine where he works, blackmailing said expert and threatening to file a sexual harassment suit against him. The fact that scenes from the two films express the same kind of fantasy suggests that anxiety over the dominance of "organization" thinking and its consequences for masculinity is widespread and virtually unchanged since mid-century. "I'm an ordinary guy with nothing to lose," Lester tells the expert—a claim that is not supported by what happens in the film but that works to sanction a similar narrative trajectory to the one in *Fight Club*. As Lester drives away, triumphant, from the office, 1969's "American Woman" plays on his car radio, cementing the logic by which women and the feminine are at the heart of the crisis in masculinity as it plays out in the bureaucratic workplace. Lester sings along, predicting his shift in behavior toward both his wife and daughter: "American woman, stay away from me / American woman, mama let me be." That all the workers in Lester's office are men does not keep the film from blaming American women for American men's problems, and, indeed, Lester's rebellion for the remainder of the film remains a rebellion against Carolyn, against the family, and against the protector-provider model of masculinity—rather than against corporate or consumer culture, as *Fight Club* at least tries to have it.

American Beauty opts for individual psychological diagnosis over cultural or political critique; at the same time, however, the film assumes a social context for Lester's story in order to turn him into an Everyman who can illuminate the contemporary social landscape for white middle-class American men. In his review of the film, Paul Arthur points out that this and similar films of the late 1980s and early 1990s (he includes *Fight Club* and *In the Company of Men*) fail to offer a genuinely new take on contemporary conditions, even as they aspire to offer social commentary: "In our giddy climate of public gloating about limitless economic prosperity, there is no denying the surface appeal of movies aiming to skewer vulgar materialism. . . . Of course, rather than directly attack the gospel according to Dow Jones, Hollywood and its indie franchises summon the shopworn ancillary proxies of suburban ennui, the success myth, and heedless consumerism, spiked with trendier evils of oppressive gender roles and sexual dysfunction" (51). As a number of skeptical reviewers opined, however, the oppression of gender applies only to men; the film completely buys into, and reproduces, misogynistic constructions of women that are uncannily similar to those that surfaced at mid-century. Indeed, as Gary Hentzi notes, Carolyn's character "is a familiar—but not necessarily welcome—figure out of the cultural criticism of the immediate postwar era. . . . The ferocious mockery with which she is presented seems to come straight from the yellowed pages of all-but-forgotten jeremiads like Philip

Wylie's *Generation of Vipers*" (47). The strange afterlife of the 1950s once again seeps into late-twentieth-century anti-consumerist discourse.

Carolyn's role in Lester's story is to provoke his rebellion, and the film does not shy away from blaming her for the crisis he is experiencing or his response to that crisis. It is telling that the film contains some knowing references to Ira Levin's 1972 *The Stepford Wives* (made into a film by Bryan Forbes in 1975) that suggest another layer of meaning to the representation of women and suburbia. The references include Carolyn waking up to Lester masturbating beside her in bed (the same thing happens after Walter first visits the sinister Men's Club in Stepford), Carolyn clipping her roses robotically (as does Carol Van Sant when Joanna and Walter first arrive in Stepford), and Carolyn frantically, even hysterically, washing the windows at the house she's trying to sell (the Stepford wives are always frantically cleaning). While both Levin's novel and Forbes's film offer a feminist take on what happens to women in suburbia—and what men want from women—the term *Stepford wife* has entered our cultural lexicon as the embodiment of mindless, passive femininity.[9] The shorthand expressed by the moniker *Stepford wife* includes a blind faith in the promises of consumer culture and a beautiful superficiality.[10] *American Beauty*'s Carolyn fits the bill, and she's represented as robotic and insincere. Indeed, as Richard Alleva notes in his review, despite the film's interest in ways of looking at things and finding a complexity behind them, Carolyn, "as written, is such a collection of neurotic tics, screams, and near-breakdowns that the actress ends up as a cartoon rather than a character" (20). This, too, evokes *The Stepford Wives,* in which picture-perfect female robots (or "normal" robotic housewives, depending on your interpretation) occasionally malfunction to expose the neuroses at the heart of postwar domestic ideology.

Commentary on the film has framed Carolyn as the character who embodies the film's negative construction of suburban consumer culture, and it often buys into Lester's assessment of her as "joyless" and "cold." Even though Lester is just as immersed in consumer culture as is Carolyn, she embodies the inauthenticity of that culture and is understood as the *source* of Lester's, and the era's, discontent: "Carolyn's dominant philosophy represents the American Dream poisoned by the worst aspects of consumerism" (Spector and Wills 281). Even if we were to accept the proposition

that the American Dream is somehow separate from, rather than productive of, consumerism, it's still not clear exactly what "philosophy"
Carolyn is meant to represent. Comparing her to Martha Stewart, a number of reviewers and critics have suggested that she represents an empty
(consumerist) perfection—like the Stepford wives, perhaps. But the film
works hard to present only the beautiful surfaces of the Burnhams' life,
completely erasing the labor that goes into the production of this picture-
perfect domesticity.[11] Although we see Carolyn cleaning the house she is
trying to sell—and she clearly knows what she's doing—we do not see her
performing any domestic labor in her own home. We see the family sitting down to what looks like an elegantly presented dinner, but we don't
see Carolyn preparing that dinner. The only time the film even raises the
questions of who, exactly, produces this domestic lifestyle, it does so only
to portray Carolyn as a bitch; after Jane complains about her mother's
choice of dinner music, Carolyn says, "When you prepare a delicious and
nutritious meal, you can choose the music." This theme gets repeated in
the scene in which Lester wrests control back from the women who aim
to emasculate him; after throwing a plate of asparagus against the wall
and menacingly telling Carolyn, "Don't interrupt me, *honey*," he says that
he will be choosing the dinner music in the future. We are meant to applaud this violent display as a step along Lester's quest to get his authenticity and his masculinity back; we are not meant to side with the woman
whose domestic labor goes unacknowledged by her family and her "perfection" lampooned by the film as a signifier of her superficiality.

The film *needs* Carolyn to be a "representative of nineties Americans
whipping themselves into frenzies of narcissistic will" (Denby 134) in
order to generate sympathy for Lester and to make believable his ultimate
"redemption," his reclamation of something like an authentic self. Yet I
want to suggest that there are moments in the film when Carolyn breaks
out of this frame to become something else, and it is in these moments
that we suspect that Carolyn's repression (her "frigidity," as the film wants
to have it) is in part caused by the misery inflicted on her by Lester—by
his gloomy, and ultimately self-indulgent, insistence that he is a loser and,
later, by his regression to a self-satisfied adolescence, complete with simmering rage. It's interesting to note that critics and reviewers of the film
focus little attention on Carolyn's suffering when, in fact, a number of

scenes show her breaking down in tears. While Lester's awakening, his yearning after freedom, is applauded by critics (even though they also acknowledge that he behaves badly), Carolyn's is ridiculed as false, inauthentic, and "joyless." For example, in reference to the scene where she has sex with (the admittedly smarmy "real estate King") Buddy Kane (Peter Gallagher), Adam Potkay remarks, "Those who have seen the film know, of course, that there is no joy in the life of real-estate brokering and adulterous Carolyn. . . . Their scene of motel sex revs on a mutual narcissism of the most embarrassing sort, with dialogue such as 'You like getting nailed by the King!' and 'Oh yes I love it, fuck me your majesty!' It is painfully clear that, as Lester tells her, property, pleasure, and self-empowerment do not add up to joy" (82).

Like the critics who want to insist that shopping in *White Noise* does not afford the characters "real" or authentic pleasure, many who comment on *American Beauty* want to make a distinction between Lester's and Carolyn's rebellions, their quests for power, their efforts to find meaning. Carolyn does find empowerment when she triumphs at the shooting range—the attendant calls her "a natural"—and when she returns from this experience, triumphantly singing "Don't Rain on My Parade," it's hard to credit Lester's assessment of her as "joyless." This scene mirrors Lester's performance of "American Woman," and Carolyn's choice of the Barbra Streisand anthem of women's resilience in the face of masculine domination presents an interesting counterpart to Lester's anthem of men's rebellion against feminine entrapment. Lester himself notices that Carolyn looks "great" when she returns from her escapades, and he is turned on. The fact that she rejects him does not necessarily mean that she is "joyless," as Lester would have it—or, worse, castrating, as some reviewers suggested. It *might* mean that Lester, in either of his two incarnations, is unappealing to Carolyn, not because she is "frigid" but because he's, well, unappealing. The fact that he lusts after a teenage girl, wants to work in a burger joint, and spends every waking moment improving his body in order to "look good naked" might make him more appealing to the filmmakers and (some members of) the audience, but from Carolyn's perspective, we might understand him as having traded one mode of narcissistic self-indulgence for another. The reading of Carolyn as joyless and castrating depends on her not having a perspective at all; whether we see this as a weakness in the film or a calculated move to center attention on poor Lester, the fact remains that Carolyn is not allowed the redemption or even the metamorphosis that other characters experience.[12] If we were inclined to read against the grain, we might speculate that when Carolyn refuses to join Lester on his journey back to the past—"Whatever happened to that girl I loved?" he asks—it could be because she's tired of Lester and wants to move into a different future.

And what are we to make of that strange moment when Carolyn breaks down, after things fall apart with Buddy, and listens to a self-help tape with the mantra "You are only a victim if you choose to be a victim"? On the one hand, the filmmakers are obviously wanting to lampoon the therapeutic culture that produces the craze for what the tape calls "me-centered living." But, on the other hand, why would Carolyn feel the need to insist that she is not a victim? What might she be the victim of? Her culture? Lester? Her gender? Might Carolyn be experiencing a crisis different in kind from that experienced by Lester? These questions are left unanswered. When, in the denouement of the film, Carolyn makes one more appearance, putting her gun into a closet and weeping as she embraces the clothing hanging there, we are unsure of what exactly she's responding to. Does she know Lester is dead? Is she crying for their lost happiness? Regretting her own choices? Understanding as failed her own quest? We don't know because she is allowed no eleventh-hour revelation such as that experienced by Lester. The truth is that the film cares much more about Lester than it does about Carolyn; it is his story, not hers, his redemption and not hers, his moment of truth and not hers.

Both *American Beauty* and *Fight Club* suggest that, for men, the only possible cure for the crisis in authenticity caused by a materialistic consumer culture is to regress, to revert, to turn back time. Lester's "freedom" is primarily expressed as a freedom from all responsibility, all social contracts; if he is free in the film, he is mostly free to be mean, obnoxious, and narcissistic—all qualities that were earlier repressed. Is a Lester who throws a plate of asparagus against the wall and menacingly tells his wife and daughter to sit down and not interrupt him, a *better*, more "free" Lester than the Lester who cringes in the backseat of the car and listens to his wife and daughter criticize him? Are we to applaud Lester's angry rebuke to his daughter, when she challenges him about his inappropriate lust for her friend, "You better watch out, Janey, or you will become a bitch like your mother"? Is authenticity such an a priori value that being an authentic asshole constitutes a triumph over the false masculinity that is cowed by women and a feminizing system? *American Beauty* does not really take on the question of the cost of Lester's breaking free into the past—in part because it focuses so exclusively on the individual and the personal rather than the social or political; in contrast, *Fight Club* at least forces us to think about how these individual stories of reempowerment and remasculinization might have broader consequences.

Fight Club is a more socially engaged film than *American Beauty*, but rather than offer a historically specific critique of consumer culture, it ultimately opts for replicating a transhistorical narrative about a masculinity endangered by feminizing forces. Contemporary interrogations of the dangers involved in narratives of masculine regression often end up reinforcing the inevitability, the *real*, of male violence even as they regret that real. Even though the film shows what can happen when men try to re-create a pre-consumerist, even pre-cultural, realm of authentic masculinity, it nevertheless buys into the premises of the feminization thesis. The lesson to be learned, for a feminist viewer, is that efforts to return to an authentic masculine selfhood stripped of its social determinations might serve to "liberate" men from consumer culture (and domesticity), but it might well liberate them into violence. Masculine protest against the alienating and feminizing forces of consumer capitalism should be critiqued for its unthinking reproduction of an ahistorical because constantly recurring narrative. That narrative works to resuscitate and stabilize a seemingly unchanging gender system, but it also works to obscure other historical realities. *Fight Club* underlines how seductive this mythical narrative remains and how the unchanging belief in the dangers of feminization have so shaped social critique that masculine protest has been reiterated again and again as the *only* legitimate form of social protest against institutions—whether those institutions be identified as bureaucracy, capitalism, business culture, or their effects identified as the Organization Man, the will-less consumer, the inauthentic poseur. Like so many other attempts to intervene in the "feminization" of American culture, *Fight Club* settles for a countercultural critique that is blindfolded by its own allegiance to a narrative that pits the masculine individual against the feminizing forces of any and all systems that place any limits on a masculinity and an individualism that naturally expresses itself as unfettered power and self-determination. Reviewing *Fight Club* for *Newsweek,* just weeks after the release of her own work on masculinity in crisis, Susan Faludi endorses the film's underlying premise: "Behind the extremities of [the narrator's] character is the modern male predicament: he's fatherless, trapped in a cubicle in an anonymous corporate job, trying to glean an identity from Ikea brochures, entertainment magazines and self-help gatherings. Jack traverses a barren landscape familiar to many men who must contend with a world stripped of socially useful male roles and saturated with commercial images of masculinity" ("It's *Thelma and Louise* for Guys"). The claim that American men are "stripped of socially useful roles" is questionable in a number of ways, and Faludi's *Stiffed* contains many hundreds of such claims. *Are* men (and not women) "stripped" in this way? *Is* there such as thing as the "modern male predicament," and, if so, how is it different from the predicaments of "feminized" masculinity decried in earlier eras? Faludi is seduced by the feminization thesis and, thus, despite her own feminism, endorses a model of social critique that is ahistorical, simplistic, and dependent on a binary notion of sexual difference.

Imagining a masculine authenticity as always *endangered* authorizes a set of cultural meanings and practices that continuously reiterate a normalizing opposition between masculinity and femininity regardless of specific historical and political context. That is, the argument that men are feminized by consumerism, capitalism, celebrity culture, white-collar bureaucracy, the service economy, even "society" itself locks us into a binary logic that will always undermine feminist aims—and, not incidentally, undermine the power of countercultural critique. At the root of the feminization thesis is a deeply seated belief that *real* masculinity depends on men being freed from social determination, freed to embody an unmarked, authentic individualism. Masculine protest against the social forces that work to constrain or limit this masculinity is always a protest not only against feminization but against feminism as well. Because feminism has, to a large extent, been responsible for insisting that masculinity is constructed, that men, too, are subject to the large system of meaning that is gender, films like *Fight Club* and *American Beauty* must also be seen as battling against the marking of masculinity, against the effort to rein in the full expression of an authentic masculinity. "Authenticity" means nothing as a substantive concept; it has no *content*. Instead, it functions structurally and strategically: it does the cultural work of distinguishing between that which is to be valued and that which is to be devalued. Authenticity need not be defined because the concept of inauthenticity is completely elastic: it can be filled with meaning based on any number of signifying systems. "Inauthentic" can mean fake, cheap, commercial, commodified, de-individualized, dependent, low class, and feminine. The very concept of authenticity is produced only as a much-longed-for, but never fully realized, ideal that can be known only through its own absence. This structure means that we are always going to be experiencing a "crisis" in which authenticity is under threat. As I have argued in many instances here, discourses concerned with articulating that threat irresistibly draw on a language of gender. In the next chapter, I turn to a more deliberate and explicit effort to think through the relationship between consumerism and authenticity readable in what I'm calling anti-consumerist consumerism—what some have named "activist consumerism." The engagement with the feminization thesis is more subtle in these discourses but is nevertheless legible in its reliance on the set of oppositions that I have been tracking.

CHAPTER 5

TO SHOP OR NOT TO SHOP

Consumerist Anti-Consumerism and the Production of Guilty Pleasure

The male figures fighting against consumerism and its feminizations in *Fight Club* and *American Beauty* are engaged in an effort to wrest individualism, autonomy, and authenticity from the wastes of consumer culture and its remaking of masculinity. In this chapter, I turn to consumerist anti-consumerism, a form of anti-consumerist critique and activism that understands consumers as empowered to fight the commodification of everyday life and of the self. This form of anti-consumerism is manifested in magazines such as *Adbusters,* the best-selling *No Logo* and other popular texts, self-help guides to "downsizing" and "slowing down," and a growing body of critical literature on the presence of consumerist anti-consumerism in American culture.[1] This anti-consumerism continues the individualist orientation of rebellion that I have tracked in other contexts and is perhaps the best example of how anti-consumerist discourses make moral, rather than economic, arguments and focus on the self instead of the system. Thus, though the anarchist impulses manifested in the soldiers of Project Mayhem occasionally emerge in this body of material, other impulses are more dominant. Consumerist anti-consumerism is articulated through a moralizing framework that distinguishes between good and bad actors, authentic and fake values, and it relies on a familiar set of oppositions that are assumed rather than demonstrated. Like other forms of anti-consumerist critique, these texts utilize a rhetoric of protest, positioning the fighters against advertising, brand culture, and corporate sponsorship of everyday life as heroic and knowing rebels against the status quo. Inevitably, these anti-consumerist critiques, like the critiques of shopping and shoppers I addressed in chapter 3, end up faulting individual consumers for their sheep-like behavior more than the system that might be said to produce this behavior. Consumerist anti-consumerism thus betrays an elitism that distinguishes between savvy, hip, and ethical consumption and unthinking, uncool, and irresponsible consumption.

As might be expected, consumerist anti-consumerism is all about class and culture and about rethinking the sources of cultural capital for an age in which affluence and conspicuous consumption have become the source of guilt. But this guilt is complex, and it is managed by reimagining the (privileged) individual's relation to consumer culture rather than agitating for changes in economic conditions. Many commentators on new versions of anti-consumerism have noted its individualist focus. Kim Humphery puts it clearly when he points out "the extent to which contemporary western anti-consumerism, particularly in its strong focus on the escape from consumer consciousness, does indeed reduce social change to a politics of the purchase. Moreover, this politics is mostly envisaged within recent critique as pursued through the mindful, self-actualizing individual acting as either responsible consumer or frugal non-consumer" (71). The "mindful, self-actualizing individual" is another version of the autonomous self who, as we have seen, is threatened by consumer culture. Consumerist anti-consumerism becomes a way to reinvigorate the self through a fantasy of authenticity that, importantly, can be "publicly expressed" (71) and displayed. As I will argue here, this consumerist anti-consumerism makes possible a kind of guilty pleasure, where guilt is *transformed* into pleasure and social responsibility through ethical consumption becomes a badge of class status. And as we have seen throughout this book, articulations of cultural value may be based on class distinctions, but they also rely on a metaphorics of gender.

The guilty pleasures evident in consumerist anti-consumerism are emphatically *not* the same guilty pleasures that popular culture imagines to be produced by the "shop 'til you drop" version of consumerism. Enthusiastic shoppers, most often women, are meant to feel guilty for their profligate consumer desires and must be disciplined into self-control.

Anti-consumerist discourses aim to transform *this* pleasure into guilt, shame, and social irresponsibility.[2] Those who embrace the pleasures of consumer culture, and fail to feel guilty about it, become the bad actors whose function is to represent a shameful consumption against which a virtuous consumption can be positioned. As I have argued throughout this book, anti-consumerist rebellion most often takes the form of a masculine protest against those forces understood to be feminizing—that is, those forces that are imagined to threaten an autonomous, independent, authentic self.

This chapter takes the argument in a slightly different direction by focusing on texts written by women. The first, Naomi Klein's *No Logo*, will serve as an example of an anti-consumerist consumerism that relies on an us-versus-them rhetoric to differentiate between good consumers, who use their rebellion against consumerism as a badge of honor, and bad consumers, who are almost literally brainwashed by brand culture. Although *No Logo* does not explicitly utilize the language of gender that we have seen functioning in texts by men in the second half of the twentieth century, Klein's rhetoric, nevertheless, builds on and makes sense within the history of masculine protest I have outlined. Like the critiques offered, for example, in books like *The Organization Man* (chapter 2) or accounts of postmodernism as loss (chapter 3), Klein's book can be seen as an updated, and very hip, lament for the loss of an autonomous self, a self not "invaded" by the forces of consumerism. In addition, the rebellions that Klein champions are positioned against feminism and other forms of "identity politics," suggesting that anti-consumerist critiques that focus on how women, people of color, and LGBTQ communities are excluded from, or misrepresented in, consumer culture are naive and ineffective. Klein follows the logic of much anti-consumerist discourse by arrogating to herself the moral authority (and superiority) to stand above consumer culture and criticize its "duped" enthusiasts.

The moralizing elitism that I read in *No Logo* is an explicit target of a very different kind of anti-consumerist text, Judith Levine's *Not Buying It: My Year without Shopping*. Levine shows that resisting consumer culture is not the same as rebelling against it and that a rebellious anti-consumerist posture is more about moral judgment than it is about challenging economic and social conditions. Levine not only avoids the self-righteous attitude of much consumerist anti-consumerism but also actively interrogates the psychological and moral "payoff" that anti-consumerist consumers reap.[3] Where Klein aims to produce guilt in those readers who fail to understand the "real" workings behind the products they buy, or who fail to mount a rebellious protest against the forces of branding that threaten their individuality, Levine meditates on the complex negotiations of guilt and pleasure that arise for a consumer who understands herself as inevitably enmeshed in a system but not, thus, made passive, inauthentic, or de-individualized. In the process, she considers the gendered meanings of consumerism (and anti-consumerism), suggesting that a moralistic rejection of the pleasures of consumption targets women consumers in particular.

Sophie Kinsella's enormously popular "Shopaholic" novels explore in greater detail the complex entwinements of pleasure and guilt in women's shopping. At first glance, these novels would seem far removed from the category of consumerist anti-consumerism, but I read them as something of a rejoinder to the rhetoric of moralism and guilt we can read in those discourses. Kinsella's novels somewhat surprisingly end up short-circuiting the logic of "addiction" that places shopping within a moral narrative about the proper management of the always *female* desire expressed through shopping. The language of addiction, which marks so many discussions of consumerism, foregrounds questions of control and displaces questions of pleasure. Like any number of constructions of consumerism we have attended to, the consumption-as-addiction model represents an effort to wrest an autonomous and authentic self from dissolution and to transform pleasure into guilt.

ANTI-CONSUMERISM AND CULTURAL CAPITAL

Self-righteous forms of anti-consumerism are visible with particular clarity in the consumerist anti-consumerism that has developed in the United States since the early 1990s. Heir to a tradition of consumer activism that has positioned "consumer citizens" as proactive partners in the regulation of markets and in lobbying for product safety, consumerist anti-consumerism ranges from the ethical to the self-congratulatory to the moralistic. Naomi Klein's *No Logo* undertakes to present, analyze, and appreciate a new consumer activism that has become visible in scattered practices, such as culture jamming and adbusters, and in more concerted protests against multinational corporations. In her introduction, she states that the title, *No Logo,* is meant not as a prediction of what might happen if consumers started to rebel against the dominance of brands in contemporary life but as an observation about practices and attitudes that are already emerging. She promises to help the reader see that "anticorporatism is the brand of politics capturing the imagination of the next generation of troublemakers and shit disturbers" (xxxix). Posing this "new" form of activism against what she sees as the "old" form of activism that characterized her college self and cohort (in the 1990s), she chides feminism and other "identity" movements for focusing on specific negative representations of women and other marginalized subjects rather than on a corporate system that is prepared to co-opt and "brand" any oppositional image or representation. In Klein's account, feminism and "identity politics weren't fighting the system, or even subverting it. When it came to the vast new industry of corporate branding, they were feeding it" (113). Klein's narrative, thus, positions feminism as a political program that her generation has outgrown, suggesting that the anti-corporatism she is tracking is a more authentic, more serious, and more effective political stance. The rebellious agents of anti-corporatism are active fighters, where the feminists and "ID warriors" turn out to have been passive dupes of the system or, worse, unwitting collaborators in it. Their cultural capital has been spent.

Klein's reference to this new anti-corporatism as a "brand" without stopping to appreciate the irony of her own language is, perhaps, not a surprise in a book that, as we will see, is unrelentingly hostile not only toward the "web of brands" but also toward irony. To refer to this politics as a *brand* is already to acknowledge that the guerrilla, outsider, rebel position that Klein wants to ascribe to these young activists is not *outside* of the consumerist logic she critiques but fully situated within it. Klein imagines *herself* above the fray, watching both the bad actors (corporations and their consumer dupes) and the good actors (activists and rebels against consumerism)[4] and, in doing so, misses some of the complexities in the networks of individuals, groups, and corporations that challenge her sometimes simplistic construction of this anti-corporatism. And like many other examples of anti-consumerism I have discussed in this book,

No Logo eschews evidence in favor of moralizing, bases its indictment of consumerism on unexamined assumptions, and generally fails to challenge common sense. Klein aims to make unthinking consumers guilty for the pleasures they might take in consumption, and while, perhaps, a little guilt would not be misplaced in the privileged circles in which Klein moves, her self-righteous and often snarky tone makes me skeptical of where her real investments lie. Part of the problem of *No Logo* is its simplistic us-versus-them logic, a logic that betrays an over-simplified notion of agency as well as a cultural and class elitism. As we saw in chapter 1, an all-or-nothing conceptualization of agency cannot account for the complex ways in which individuals participate in consumer culture or how they fight back against that culture. What has become known as "commodity activism"—another name for anti-consumerist consumerism—*can* work to challenge a simplistic "either/or logic of profit versus politics" and to disrupt the "clear distinctions between cultural co-optation and popular resistance" (Banet-Weiser and Mukherjee 3), but it can also further entrench these logics and assumptions in an updated form.

This either-or logic is readable in *No Logo*'s conceptualization of agency: individuals are either actively rebelling against the system or passively constituted by it. For Klein, any practice that blurs the line between active and passive, production and consumption, is illegible as a form of rebellion. This over-simplified notion of agency comes through with particular force in the chapter Klein titles "Alt.Everything: The Youth Market and the Marketing of Cool." This chapter tells the story of corporations, like Nike and Adidas, that have treated the inner city as a marketing laboratory and urban youth as unpaid labor in the construction of the brand. Contextualizing these moves in relation to a history of white culture makers who have looked primarily to black cultures for authenticity, the cool, and the hip, Klein also indicts corporations for selling images of *white* prosperity and happiness to those who are encouraged to tap into racial and class privilege by consuming and identifying with brands like Tommy Hilfiger, Polo, Nautica, and other preppy standards. While Klein is probably not wrong about the motives of these corporations, her analysis gives all agency to the corporations and none to the young men who have themselves appropriated these brands and, in some cases, radically repurposed them. For example, in her discussion of how "hip-hop blows up the brands," Klein makes the point that "young black men in American inner cities have been the market most aggressively mined by the brand-masters as a source of borrowed 'meaning' and identity" (73), underlining the cynicism of this strategy. Klein here creates a one-way, top-down, almost conspiratorial narrative about powerful corporations exploiting disadvantaged youth. In the pursuit of this narrative, and in making her case, she mentions, but does not comment on, the fact that corporations like Hilfiger, Polo, et al. have "refused to crack down on the pirating of their logos for T-shirts and baseball hats in the inner cities, and several of them have clearly backed away from serious attempts to curb rampant shoplifting" (74). As intriguing as this detail is, Klein rushes past it to the conclusion that "like so much of cool hunting, Hilfiger's marketing journey feeds off the alienation at the heart of America's race relations: selling white youth on their fetishization of black style, and black youth on their fetishization of white wealth" (76). Preferring not to take up the challenge of piracy and shoplifting, she prematurely closes down the circuit of meaning that these transactions suggest, granting all agency to the corporations that "feed" and "sell," leaving the consumer with "fetishization" as the only mode of response. But despite Hilfiger's intentions and profit-making goals, might we read the urban youth as themselves practicing a form of appropriation? A form of resistance?

Because Klein's narrative depends not only on a construction of the corporate brand as antithetical to consumer agency but also on the impossibility of that very consumer agency (consumers can't *be* agents), she cannot see that this very interesting detail about the uses these young men make of the brand might point to a more complicated account of agency and action than the conspiratorial narrative allows. For example, might we think about how the dominance of brand culture can be used by disadvantaged actors to derive economic or social benefit? Regardless of the motives of the corporations, don't these young pirates and shoplifters constitute a resistance, if not to the logic of the brand, to the distribution of property and profit? Who's taking advantage of whom here? Who has agency? What meanings and what identities do these consumer-producers imagine through *their* appropriation of the brands that have tried to appropriate *them*? What pleasures are these young "pirates" experiencing? These questions hover above Klein's account, but she is not interested in asking them because, for her, the brand is, by definition, bad; if the young men pirating the Hilfiger logo are getting one over on the corporation, Klein is uninterested in thinking through the implications of this because, for her, the men must remain dupes of the system, not producers within it. Despite the fact that her own account of this set of circumstances muddies the distinction between (active) producers and (passive) consumers, Klein holds fast to this opposition because it enables her to keep in place the concept of agency she needs to make her argument against the machinations of the corporations. The hip-hop appropriators, thus, become unknowing actors whose pleasures are tainted and rendered guilty because they are enmeshed in the system against which they should be rebelling.

If Klein were not so quick to dismiss feminism, she might have found within feminist theory a more complex account of agency. I want to suggest that Klein's belief that only a fully agential subject can adequately rebel against consumer culture and its corporations reveals her reliance on what feminist theorists have called a masculinist concept of the subject. Rebellion, in Klein's account, requires a clearly legible intention to rebel on the part of a subject who, thus, is imagined to be completely in control of his will and actions. It is this subject who either falls prey to the machinations of marketers and branders, if he is not smart or savvy enough; or, in contrast, heroically rebels against those forces by willfully and deliberately defacing billboards or producing parodies of ads. As we saw in chapter 1, in relation to Anne Elizabeth Moore's analysis of the "selling out" of DIY culture, in order to be a legitimate rebel, a subject must be acting "on purpose." Rebellion, thus, depends on a willful agent, a deliberative individual who, in the process of rebelling, constructs for himself a subject position defined by its difference both from those who choose not to rebel and those who resist the forces of the market but without a clearly legible intention to harm the system. Those who do not deliberately rebel, thus, occupy a less than fully agential subject position, their identities constrained by their inability to know how their actions and beliefs are constructed for them, their identities formed by the marketers and branders who are always working to position them as consumers. This kind of subject is less than fully active, if not completely passive; this subject is not fully masculine, if not completely feminine.[5]

Implicit in *No Logo* is a distinction between rebellion and resistance, a distinction that foregrounds a difference between two ways of conceptualizing agency. The hip-hop brand appropriators are practicing forms of resistance, but in Klein's account they don't qualify as rebels because they are not rebelling "on purpose" and, worse, are also promoting the Nike or Hilfiger brand. Resistance might better be thought of as unfolding within a network of relations that includes corporations, consumers, the producers of knockoffs, and the products themselves. These relations are affected by the very social differences that Klein wants to bracket as forever tainted by her youthful romance with "identity politics"—that is, gender, race, ethnicity, and sexual orientation as well as class. Vrajesh Hanspal and Angela McRobbie take Klein to task for relying on a "rather traditional political economy perspective" that is not rich and nuanced enough to account for the *cultural* complexities she means to analyze. For Hanspal and McRobbie, Klein's book enacts the conflict between two forms of cultural critique, a Marxist or neo-Marxist emphasis on political economy and a cultural studies interest in the "economy of signs."[6] They suggest that Klein is "highlighting a contemporary 'renaissance' of brand logic without considering how new forms of resistance take shape, not so much in the hands of an artistic or intellectual elite (the culture jammers), but among those who are supposed to be the key targets of the brands' seductive appeal" (844). Political economy emerges as an effective and genuine—an authentic—form of politics, happily replacing what Klein constructs as a naive identity politics whose calls for positive representations of women and minority subjects were purportedly so easily appropriated by marketers and branders.

These ID warriors, as Klein presents them, were not only innocently feeding the branding machine but, worse, complicit in a host of sins that Klein outlines in her chapter titled "Patriarchy Gets Funky," in which she takes on the campus culture wars and skirmishes over "political correctness." Reading Klein on the culture wars is like entering an alternate reality to the one many of us lived through in those years. Obscuring the fact that Dinesh D'Souza, Roger Kimball, Allan Bloom, and others focused their ire on the "*tenured* radicals" who were politicizing speech and knowledge and "brainwashing" their students, Klein lumps all of the "adults" into one category—neocons and progressives alike—and rewrites the culture wars as a battle between generations: "Despite their claims of living under Stalinist regimes where dissent was not tolerated, our professors and administrators put up an impressively vociferous counteroffensive: they fought tooth and nail for the right to offend us thin-skinned radicals; they lay down on the tracks in front of every new harassment policy, and generally acted as if they were fighting for the very future of Western civilization" (110). This glib and stunning verdict flies in the face of the very careful work done by scholars who painstakingly analyzed what was at stake in the assaults on women's studies and ethnic studies programs. Had Klein taken a moment to actually read the "supposedly subversive theory" (114) she so blithely dismisses, she might have developed a more complex perspective.[7]

The culture wars were a confusing stew of discourse and counterdiscourse, and perhaps Klein can be forgiven for getting some things wrong. But she gets *so much* wrong because she is intent on constructing a narrative about the changing of the political guard, a generational narrative about how one form of ineffective politics gets displaced by a new form of politics. This narrative requires that the complex network that was "identity politics" and "political correctness" in the late 1980s and early 1990s be dismissed as superficial, as merely "insular debates around race, gender and sexuality [that] become nothing other than . . . petty 'image' politics quickly co-opted and sold back to the consumer by the corporate and media establishment" (Hanspal and McRobbie 843). Klein presents herself as fully cognizant of the scholarly work that went hand in hand with the campus debates, claiming that the "political lens for far too many activists *and theorists* was narrowing so dramatically that with the exception of a brief period during the Gulf War, foreign and economic policy were off the radar screen" (123; emphasis added) and taking the time to sneer at Gayatri Spivak for believing that "'great blows are being struck against capitalism in the realm of theory'" (122). But Klein shows no evidence of actually having read Spivak (whose work is not cited), nor does she buttress her claims about theorists' blindnesses. Any theorist, and particularly any feminist theorist, who lived through the PC debacle is likely to be irritated by Klein's dismissive attitude here, her certainty that her view is the only view, her arrogation to herself of a position above the fray. She disowns her youthful naïveté in the service of positioning herself, the self who writes

No Logo, as the real deal, the politico who saw the light and has left all those ID warriors in the dust. As her title "Patriarchy Gets Funky" suggests, it is really feminism that is at fault and must be disavowed. Gender, race, and sexuality all fall away as Klein pursues her cause.

No Logo's problems with agency and Klein's insistence on "real" versus cultural politics also arise in her discussion of the new irony she sees as a dominant mode of response to consumer culture. Like David Foster Wallace, who bemoans the ways that television culture has made postmodern irony the enemy of sincerity, as I discussed in chapter 1, Klein targets "ironic consumption" as a poor substitute for the "real thing"—in Wallace's case good fiction, and in Klein's *authentic* political critique and activism. The problem with hip, ironic consumption is that it plays right into the very logics that it is meant to challenge; the problem with ironic consumption, in other words, is that it is *consumption.* While she is explicitly targeting the "cool hunt"—that is, the strategies by which corporations and brands tap into and commodify alternative cultural groups or formations—she can't help but also chide the consumers of this irony. Granting an agency to the brand but not to the culture it supposedly colonized, Klein charges that "after brands and their cool hunters had tagged all the available fringe culture, it seemed only natural to fill up that narrow little strip of unmarketed brain space occupied by irony with preplanned knowing smirks, someone else's couch commentary and even a running simulation of the viewer's thought patterns" (78). Klein is referring here to the VH1 show *Pop-Up Videos,* as becomes evident in the next paragraph when she suggests that this show, which "adorns music videos with snarky thought bubbles, may be the endgame of this kind of commercial irony. It grabs the punch line before anyone else can get to it, making social commentary—even idle sneering—if not redundant then barely worth the expense and energy" (79). What Klein seems to object to most in this somewhat overblown portrait of brains being "occupied" is the loss of individual agency, autonomy, and creativity. The problem with *Pop-Up Videos* is that it marks the demise of originality: commercial irony is a "fake" version of social commentary, and it positions its viewers as the passive recipients of a pre-packaged set of "thought patterns" and responses. But by what logic is irony, even "commercial" irony, at odds with social commentary? What would Klein say about *Mystery Science Theater*

3000, a precursor to *Pop-Up Videos* and a series whose parodic reframing of classic B-movie sci-fi has generated a huge fan base? What would Klein have to say about fan culture in general? Again, we're faced with her overly simplistic understanding of agency based on a stark division between producers/brands and consumers.

Klein's dismissive discussions of the hip-hop appropriation of the brand and the (a)politics of commercial irony stand in marked contrast to her admiring account of the culture jammers who actively deface and rewrite billboards. These young activists Klein sees as producers rather than consumers, and their more direct attacks on corporate advertising are obviously more appealing to Klein than the hip-hoppers' indirect attacks on corporate profit. This is real rebellion, a more active alternative to the less deliberate resistances of the hip-hoppers. There is a romanticism readable in this discussion of culture jammers, an effort to claim for the artist a privileged space above the consumer fray.[8] Unlike the "cool hunters" whose penchant for "commercial irony" earns Klein's sarcastic disdain, the culture jammers earn her respect. Talking with Rodriguez de Gerada, "widely recognized as one of the most skilled and creative founders of culture jamming," Klein wistfully describes his outsider strategies and status:

> Unlike some of the growing legion of New York guerilla artists, Rodriguez de Gerada refuses to slink around at night like a vandal, choosing instead to make his statements in broad daylight. For that matter, he doesn't much like the phrase "guerilla art," preferring "citizen art" instead. He wants the dialogue he has been having with the city's billboards for more than ten years to be seen as a normal mode of discourse in a democratic society—not as some edgy vanguard act. While he paints and pastes, he wants kids to stop and watch—as they do on this sunny day, just as an old man offers to help support the ladder. (279–80)

Klein's language here is markedly different from her descriptions of the cool hunters, quoted above. There is absolutely no irony here, only a sincere artist whose devotion to democratic values is authentic—"not some edgy vanguard act." This authenticity is readable by the "kids" and the "old man" who stop to watch and help. This is a producer who eschews the cool, the hip, and the commercial. Klein's sharp critical voice completely disappears here as she constructs a romantic image of true, noncommercial artistic agency. It is worth noting that, here, the hip and the cool become the antithesis of the genuine, a construction that contradicts a number of other positions Klein takes and, indeed, her own credentials as the voice of the new and the hip.

Klein is nothing if not a canny rhetorician, and she brings to bear on "brand culture" a range of rhetorical maneuvers that serve to inoculate her polemic against the kind of "uncool" critique I'm practicing here. For example, she litters *No Logo* with personal anecdotes about her logo-crazy youth, her irritation with her socialist parents, and her memories of her (naive) university politics. Such anecdotes function to bolster Klein's credentials as a hip critic of consumerism rather than as a sour, dry, and "academic" killjoy, as do her attacks on academics. In her chapter "The Brand Expands," for example, Klein offers a typical reading of brand culture as substituting the commercial for the artistic and cultural, chiding corporate CEOs and advertising gurus with appropriating such noncommercial values as "transcendence" and "meaningful messages" (28). Trying to make a distinction between the kind of corporate sponsorship that lends financial support to a still autonomous cultural sphere and the kind of corporate sponsorship that aims to make the brand into culture itself, Klein notes that the former type is "frequently overlooked by critics of commercialization, among whom there is an unfortunate tendency to tar all sponsorship with the same brush, as if any contact with a corporate logo infects the natural integrity of an otherwise pristine public event or cause"—the error made, according to Klein, by McAllister's *The Commercialization of American Culture* (31).

Yet it's difficult to see on what grounds Klein herself is making her distinctions, since she does not offer an example of this "positive" partnership between corporations and culture; indeed, her chapter reads very much like what she herself calls a "mostly romantic fiction" about "our culture's lost innocence" (31), as can be seen in the following passage:

> The effect, if not always the original intent, of advanced branding is to nudge the hosting culture in the background and make the brand the star. It is not to sponsor culture but to *be* the culture. . . . [T]his project

has been so successful that the lines between corporate sponsors and sponsored culture have entirely disappeared. But this conflation has not been a one-way process, with passive artists allowing themselves to be shoved into the background by aggressive multinational corporations. Rather, many artists, media personalities, film directors and sports stars have been racing to meet the corporations halfway in the branding game. (30)

When Klein chides artists for their acceptance of corporate sponsorship, one wonders whether *anyone* but Naomi Klein has the power to rebel, the power to distinguish between good and bad forms of commercialization, corporate sponsorship, and the like.

The rhetorical strategies of *No Logo* are reminiscent of the anti-consumerism of Jonathan Franzen's essays in which, as I discussed in chapter 1, he gets to have it both ways: position himself as a critic of "techno-consumerism" *and* as a critic of critics of techno-consumerism. Like Franzen, Klein arrogates to herself a position from which every other attitude can appear as guilty, false, or in bad faith. It is worth noting that Matthew McAllister, writing in a special issue of the journal *Women's Studies Quarterly* on "the market," responds to Klein's usage of him as an "example of overly reductionist Marxist-doctrinaire antiadvertising perspectives," by noting how this encounter with the best-selling *No Logo* has enhanced *his* brand: even a negative reference was "a career booster," McAllister says ("No Logo Legacy" 287). Tongue in cheek or not, McAllister's comment, echoed by many others who have written of Klein's influence and her "brand," points to the slipperiness of *No Logo*'s rhetoric, the trickiness of its investments, and its ambivalent relation to the history of the anti-consumerist critique it attempts to disown.

Like many other anti-consumerist discourses, Klein's book yearns for a "space" outside of the market and a "space" in the individual that is free from the operations of branding. To her credit, she does not seek these spaces in nature, a common strategy among anti-consumerists, but looks for them in the very cultural mix that she yearns to escape from. But what are we to make of this desire to "escape" in the first place? From where does it spring? Klein begins her book by telling the story of how her neighborhood in Toronto is undergoing gentrification, slowly being transformed from the "old industrial Toronto of garment factories, furriers and wholesale wedding dresses" into a "kitschy" version of postindustrial chic, marked by "tragically hip" settings and a "painful new self-consciousness" about this transformation (xxxiii–xxxiv).[9] Yet while Klein seems to want to take some credit for living in "Toronto's ghost of a garment district," and, thus, claim kinship with the likes of Emma Goldman and 1930s garment workers, she is living in this area only because someone has turned these warehouses into apartments, lofts, and condos. Disingenuously, she positions herself against those who would "mine" the "hand-me-downs of industrialization" for "witty fashion ideas," and it's hard to see how a young and hip journalist-writer is somehow more like those erstwhile exploited workers than she is like those Johnny-come-latelys who are buying "condos in secondhand sweatshops, luxuriously reno-ed, with soaking tubs, slate-lined showers, underground parking, skylit gymnasiums and twenty-four hour concierges" (xxxiv). This tricky positioning is evident throughout *No Logo,* perhaps nowhere so much as at the end of the book, where Klein talks about her time with the Worker Assistant Center in the Philippines.

No Logo certainly draws attention to some important issues having to do with sweatshops and corporate exploitation of workers in enterprise processing zones, and Klein is at her most compelling when she focuses on these practices. The book's analysis of brand culture and its destruction of public and private, interiorized, space are less compelling because they are marked by a self-congratulatory posture that, while often witty, is often also self-righteous and irritating. *No Logo* covers a lot of ground, and it is not only about how brand culture has threatened the autonomous self but also shares with other forms of anti-consumerism a narrative of loss and decline that makes this threat legible. Klein is not arguing for a rejection of consumer culture, but the rebellious posture she crafts for herself, and appreciates in other activists, requires a fantasy of independence from a "system" in which less hip, less savvy, and less ethical consumers are enmeshed. Because of her less than full rejection of consumerism, Klein has come in for some pretty hostile critique by Marxist critics who chide her for being insufficiently anti-capitalist. Martin McQuillan, for example, insists that *No Logo* cannot offer a coherent political vision or program for action because, while it calls for a democratic citizenship to replace consumer citizenship, it does not want to overturn capitalism, simply to make it more palatable. In McQuillan's view, the "consumer-based politics" described by Klein and enacted by her book "would appear to only concern itself with designer injustice and fashionable causes. . . . The logic of this politics is not an 'anti-capitalist' one, rather its goal is good-conscience shopping (the desire to consume without guilt). In this sense it is the most fashionable of fashionable trends, a backlash against designer goods and 'Mall culture'" (118).[10]

McQuillan is subjecting Klein to the same kind of moral evaluation to which she submits "ID warriors," transforming the field of anti-consumerist critique into a competition for whose position is the most authentically political. McQuillan's gambit here is a pretty typical rhetorical ploy in anti-consumerist discourse, and its use against Klein reveals the assumption behind so much anti-consumerist rhetoric: the only way to challenge capitalism or to take an authentic political stand against social injustice is to completely reject consumerism and to repeat the moral condemnation of those who fail to embody the preferred form of resistance. Warring anti-consumerisms, thus, vie for political authenticity, with Klein found wanting because she does not complete the gestures required. But why must we adjudicate among competing anti-consumerisms to find the most authentic version? As should be clear by now, my own take on *No Logo* is that its critique follows *too* closely the anti-consumerist narrative that positions authentic (male) rebels against deluded (female) shoppers and reproduces the tried-and-true argument that only producers exercise agency.

Both Klein and her critics reveal the desire at the heart of so much anti-consumerism—that is, the desire to maintain the Manichaean structure that thrives on distinctions between insiders and outsiders, those who fight authentically against consumer culture and those who either refuse to fight at all or, worse, fight in inauthentic ways. That she herself falls victim to this logic is not surprising, given the deeply entrenched but unexamined assumptions about how any connection to consumer culture endangers authenticity—here, political authenticity. To be clear, my critique of anti-consumerist consumerism is *not* the more familiar critique that such anti-consumerism is illegitimate because of the bad faith of its practitioners. My argument is that any anti-consumerism, including

Klein's, that rests on the moralizing distinctions between good actors who reject consumer culture and bad actors who embrace consumer culture—not just because they like to shop but because they literally buy into the belief that consumer culture can deliver authenticity and meaning—can only end up repeating an essentially unchanging master narrative about the feminizations of consumer culture. What McQuillan and other critics of Klein reveal, in my view, is not that she is insufficiently Marxist but that *No Logo* exposes the impossibility of separating the citizen from the consumer, of distinguishing between authentic politics and "good-conscience shopping," between rebellion (or revolution) and resistance. *No Logo* falters on the question of agency because, despite Klein's seeming understanding of the fate of the individual in neoliberalism, she aims to keep in place a romantic concept of the creative, autonomous individual whose independence, will, and power are endangered by brand culture.

TO SHOP OR NOT TO SHOP

Judith Levine's *Not Buying It: My Year without Shopping* is a fascinated and fascinating meditation on consumerism written by someone who has decided to live for a year without buying anything other than the "necessities." Levine decides to undertake this experiment during the Christmas shopping season when her observations of the excesses of anxiety-fueled hyper-consumption prompt her to imagine the possibilities in the book project that turns into *Not Buying It*. She undertakes her experiment, enlisting her partner, Paul, in the project, not because she is sick and tired of consumerism but because she thinks it's a great idea for a book. This point is key, as it sets her apart from the leagues of Voluntary Simplifiers, downshifters, and other anti-consumerist types who decide to opt out of the system as a form of rebellion against the status quo and an attempt to "purify" themselves.[11] Levine is under no illusion that she can "escape" from consumerism and the logics of a market economy. Even when not buying things, she finds that she is always "enmeshed" in the system: "All our lives, we've been operating in the market system. This year we withdrew to its margins in order to observe its workings. But we remain in the gears of the machine, and our personal transactions are lubricated by the familiarity of its rules" (116). Unlike many others who have made similar points, Levine does not see this as cause for despair, nor is she interested in arguing that the system deprives us of our autonomy or distances us from the "real."

Levine divides her book into twelve chapters, one for each month of her not-shopping year, and ties that month's experiences in with some larger concept of relevance to the study of consumer culture: "Surplus," "Scarcity," "Consumer Psychology," "Redistribution of Wealth," "Brand America," "The Ownership Society," and so on. This setup, even if somewhat artificial, allows Levine to make unusual connections between the personal and the political and between the individual and the system. Understanding from the beginning that opting out of consumerism means opting out as well from the version of sociality she is accustomed to in her modestly upscale and intellectually hip circle of friends and colleagues, Levine analyzes not only her own efforts to negotiate survival and happiness without buying anything but also the reactions of those around her who watch with some fascination as she learns how to live without movies and restaurant meals and to figure out how to navigate the social norms that so often center on consumption. The question that she raises, in many different ways, throughout the book is this: "Can a person have a social, community, or family life, a business, a connection to the culture, an identity, even a *self* outside the realm of purchased things and experiences? Is it possible to withdraw from the marketplace? These questions are almost entirely unstudied," despite the "mountains of theory and data" on consumer behavior (7).

Not Buying It contains some pretty smart analysis of the politics of consumer citizenship; Levine has a particularly trenchant analysis of what it means that funding for public libraries has suffered in recent years. The real center of the book, however, has to do with Levine's meditations on pleasure and guilt and on the psychology of both shopping and not shopping, fully participating in consumer culture or trying to escape from it. For example, in the chapter in which she explores the Voluntary Simplicity movement, she presents what is the typical narrative about the use of shopping and buying as a way to bolster identity and well-being. Commenting on Cecile Andrews's *The Circle of Simplicity*, Levine picks up on the commonsense narratives that I have been attending to throughout this book: "Shopping 'saps your energy,' it 'reduces ingenuity,' 'harms your health,' and generally 'makes you unhappy.' . . . Far worse, by supplying a purchasable identity, [Andrews] claims, consuming makes you false, a traitor to the person you really are. Toss out those old clothes and broken tennis rackets at the back of your closet and you will discover your 'authentic self' crushed under the debris" (69). Levine's skepticism here is fueled by her sense that VS is, itself, a commercial enterprise, marketed by "anti-consumerist entrepreneurs" (76). "No two ways about it," Levine says. "Simplicity sells" (77).[12] Unlike the VS group of which Levine remains on the margins, she reaps neither moral currency nor cultural capital through her year without shopping. Commenting on the religious fervor of certain members of the VS group, Levine identifies a discourse of sin and redemption functioning within the VS movement. Levine notes that what "chastity" is to the Right, "anti-consumerism" is to the Left (87).

Levine meditates on guilt and on pleasure, as when she comments that the top stories about hyper-consumerism appeal to us because they make regular consumerism seem "normal": "Like pornography and corruption scandals, these reports trade in both lust and prudery, allowing us to gratify our prurience at the same time as we assuage our guilt" (79). Various versions of *Lifestyles of the Rich and Famous*—now rampant through the expansion of reality TV—also constitute a guilty pleasure, particularly for an audience of middle-class professionals who choose to watch *The Real Housewives* franchise while pledging their allegiance to the slow-food movement. Like many others who meditate on the pleasures, guilt, and guilty pleasures of shopping, Levine understands how attitudes toward shopping reproduce gendered meanings and function to support a gendered hierarchy.

Against the nearly universal condemnation of women's shopping in popular culture and in the critical literature on consumerism, Levine seeks to scrutinize the types of pleasures that shopping provides for women. For example, when she takes a "furlough" from her year of not shopping to purchase an outfit for an upcoming wedding, she attempts to take a critical view of her own behavior. She writes, "And now, having opened myself even gingerly to the small dramas of shopping, the disappointment and triumph, the self-criticism and self-affirmation, I'm like a soldier tasting my first home-cooked meal: I could weep. These feelings may be false consciousness cynically produced by consumer culture. But retail therapy is also therapeutic" (129). We are all familiar with the condemnation of shopping as "therapeutic"; the problem with retail therapy is that it is a poor substitute for "real" therapy—cannot, that is, possibly be "real" therapy because, well, it's *shopping,* and shopping is understood to damage, rather than heal, the authentic self. Would museum or art-appreciation therapy provoke, one wonders, such hostility? In invoking the Marxist vocabulary of the "false consciousness" produced by commodity fetishism, and insisting that her pleasures are real even if "false," Levine severs shopping from the moralistic framework in which it is most often understood. Further, she analyzes how, for women, shopping can serve other functions: it can function as "socially sanctioned 'bad' behavior" that puts into play a "pleasurable tension" between indulging and resisting (129–30). In this scene, Levine mobilizes an irony that is missing in much consumerist anti-consumerism, making fun of the idea that shopping in a non-profit thrift store could transform the experience into a guilt-free pleasure: "If I had to lapse, I've come to the right place: a truly anticonsumerist consumer opportunity, a place to transgress virtuously" (130). Unlike the Voluntary Simplifiers whom Levine represents as sanctimonious, she analyzes the "rational market exchange" she participates in and, simultaneously, exposes the stakes in "virtuous" transgressions. At the end of the episode, she tells us that "secretly, I can't wait to put the clothes on" (130). The performance of virtue is public, and the secret of pleasure must be kept private.

Levine is neither a cheerleader for consumerism nor a sanctimonious rebel against it, and her resistance to taking up either of the two most common positions on consumerism and anti-consumerism allows her to think differently about pleasure and guilt and, in the process, make fun of herself and others who insist on framing shopping as a moral (or immoral) act. In another episode in which Levine "falls," she analyzes the specifically female pleasures to be had in the shopping *"ménage à trois:* salesperson, customer, product." She refers to this exchange as "flirting"—she is flirting with the saleswoman, with the product, and also with herself. "A summer of swimming has made me trim, outdoor chores have made me tan and strong. I look like myself to myself, my best self. I also feel like a woman, doing what women do: preening, flirting in public. Shopping affords a woman this pleasure innocently, like an asexual affair" (161). This idea of shopping as a sensual, even sexual, pleasure will return in my discussion of *Confessions of a Shopaholic,* but for now I want to point out how transgressive Levine is being here, for she is turning guilt into pleasure and, in the process, challenging the self-evident truth that the pleasures of shopping must necessarily pale in comparison with the "real" pleasures of sexual exchange. But there *is* a sexual exchange going on in this scene, and it is mediated in interesting ways by the economic exchange. She is flirting with the saleswoman, flirting with the product (in this case "greenish jacquard silk-polyester blend" pants that achieve just "the right level of dressiness," let her "breathe," and make her "look thin")—and, most important, flirting with her *self,* a self that is revealed through this exchange rather than endangered by it.[13] Mocking both the Voluntary Simplicity credo and her own consumer desires, Levine challenges conventional ideas about authenticity when she wonders, "What if I discover my authentic self, and my authentic self is a shopper?" (70).

This last question is worth dwelling on at some length, for it exposes in eloquent simplicity the assumptions at the heart of so much anti-consumerist discourse. What does it mean, to Levine or to us, to imagine that shopping is a part of one's authentic self? Such a possibility flies in the face of so many self-evident claims and commonsense notions of how consumer culture damages authenticity. Further, Levine's innocent question also puts pressure on the very notion of an "authentic self," a fiction that supports so much anti-consumerist discourse even as its own foundations are precariously rocky. The *Shopaholic* novels have many interesting things to say about these questions because they make the claim that Becky Bloomwood's "authentic self" is, in fact, a shopper. What I hope to show in the analysis that follows is that Kinsella's novels actually explore in surprisingly complex ways what it means to understand as "authentic" a self formed around and through consumer practices. Taking seriously a set of novels that have been relegated to the much-maligned category of "chick lit," that most feminine of genres, I want to argue that Kinsella's protagonist resists the moralistic anti-consumerism I have been tracking and, in doing so, remakes the meanings of shopping, guilt, and pleasure.

DISCIPLINING THE SHOPAHOLIC

The American film adaptation of *Confessions of a Shopaholic* has the protagonist, Becky Bloomwood (Isla Fisher), joining and, then, hilariously subverting a "Shopaholics Anonymous" group. While other participants "share" their challenges in resisting shopping, and their minor triumphs when they do resist, Becky waxes rhapsodic over the pleasures of buying. The other participants speak for guilty pleasure, the pleasure completely entangled with the guilt, while Becky expresses shock over the very fact that anyone should feel guilty about shopping. Her paean to shopping works not to affirm the shopaholic credo but instead to reveal the twelve-step program's destruction of pleasure. At one point, the leader of the group forces Becky to bring some party dresses to a thrift shop, preaching the gospel not only of austerity but of charity as well. While Becky shamefacedly allows herself to be coerced into giving away her dresses, she quickly regrets the donation and returns to the shop in an effort to buy them back. Choosing pleasure over guilt, Becky leaves the group, and the film suggests that the group will be lesser because of her exit. The shopaholics return at the end of the film, when they help Becky resolve her financial woes and make good on her debt by throwing a fantastic auction in which she sells the fruits of her shopping labors. But by this time in the film, even the shopaholics are on Becky's side, and they have learned to take pleasure in the buying, selling, and general consumer exchange that are the subject of Becky's obsession.

Despite its titles, Kinsella's *Shopaholic* series actually works to resist the punitive logic of addiction and recovery that marks efforts to discipline its heroine into austerity. Throughout the series, Becky finds herself in a number of financial jams, and the humor of the books comes from her innovative methods of getting herself out of them. When in *Shopaholic Takes Manhattan,* the second in the series, Becky ends up hired as a "personal shopper" at Barney's, the reader knows that these books are not structured along the trajectory of sin and redemption that we might expect from narratives about addiction and recovery. Indeed, Becky's ethos appears to be *triumphant* at the end of each of the books, and part of the pleasure of reading the novels is that Kinsella allows Becky to get away (mostly) without punishment. While some readers—particularly those of an anti-consumerist bent—might find themselves frustrated by Becky's repeated escapes from the circuit of sin and redemption that marks so many narratives of consumer excess and its consequences, others surely find something subversive in a character who manages to game the system and come out on top. She lands the coveted job, marries the millionaire, resolves family disputes, finds happiness in an expanding circle of family and friends—all despite her profligate habits and the self-delusions that Kinsella often attributes to her. It is thus hard to credit some readings of the novel, which see it as nothing but a grim reenactment of the theory of commodity fetishism, as we see in the following assessment: "Like most chick lit heroines, Becky enjoys the thrill of the new buy, and, as is the case for most of them, her life deteriorates to a point where everything seems to be bleak, until she gives up her commodity fetishism to find happiness. Hence, while fashion allows her to keep up with the consumerist 'Joneses' and briefly bask in the self-confidence it buys her, longer-lasting happiness is achieved only when capitalistic ambition is thwarted and the status quo is restored at the end" (Ghosh 378–79).

Such (mis)readings of the *Shopaholic* series pursue a rote anti-consumerist logic based on the assumption that consumerist pleasure is always and only "false," delusional, or the source of intense personal and social guilt. More important, perhaps, they impose a moralistic narrative on a set of novels, stretching the bounds of the novels themselves to imagine that the heroine is eventually punished and reformed. While Becky's "magical thinking" is, in fact, reminiscent of commodity fetishism, the moralizing impulse that would categorize commodity fetishism as *bad* is missing. When Srijani Ghosh judges that Becky "finds happiness only at the end of the novel once she gives up her conspicuous consumption" (380), she is not paying attention to the novels but instead imposing on them a pre-fabricated anti-consumerist critique. Should Marx or Baudrillard really be the authority on *Confessions of a Shopaholic,* or are there other models to help us understand the desires represented in it, the pleasures it aims to articulate? How can we better understand the series' resistance to the notion that shopping must be understood as something to *give up* as a woman finally gets in line with the (patriarchal) program, giving up her habit in favor of the heterosexual romance plot? Worse, such accounts reveal an elitist desire to take a punitive pleasure in seeing an obsessive shopper get her just deserts. Indeed, there is something familiar in such assessments, which aim to turn pleasure into shame and, perhaps, shame into pleasure. As Judith Levine suggests when she discusses women's shopping as "socially sanctioned 'bad' behavior": "Ricky catches Lucy with a spree-ful of shopping bags and asks her with a wicked gleam in his eye if she has been bad. The pleasurable tension mounts. She is asking for punishment; he is warming up to give it to her" (129).

For fans, the novels are not about exposing commodity fetishism; instead, as Jennifer Scanlon argues, the "books and their readers, through Becky and her shopping adventures, negotiate the romantic, the compensatory, and the resistant: shopping is seductive, it meets women's needs in ways traditional romance does not, and it provides something of an alternative to cultural expectations of womanhood" ("Making Shopping Safe").[14] That alternative has to do with subordinating the heterosexual romance plot to a different kind of romance plot. From a certain point of view, the *Shopaholic* novels seem to support the mythic construction of the out-of-control female shopper who is the cause of so much concern in the mid-twentieth century, but because the novels attempt to liberate this figure from the moralistic narrative in which she is embedded, something different emerges. Take, for example, the following description of the pleasures of shopping in which Kinsella has Becky compare shopping to food and to sex. While we might expect such a description to confirm the moralistic reading of Becky as pursuing the "false" promises of consumer culture rather than the "real" promises of heterosexual romance, what actually emerges here is a challenge to the opposition between the false and the real, the inauthentic and the authentic: "That moment. That instant when your fingers curl round the handles of a shiny, uncreased bag—and all the gorgeous new things inside it become yours. What's it like? It's like going hungry for days, then cramming your mouth full of warm buttered toast. It's like waking up and realizing it's the weekend. It's like the better moments of sex. Everything else is blocked out of your mind. It's pure, selfish pleasure" (*Confessions* 29–30). Like women's shopping, women's eating has also long been the target of discipline, and Western culture is riddled with representations of both dangerous and guilty eating. What's so striking here is the lack of guilt—guilt for eating, for shopping, for women indulging in *selfish* pleasure. Note how Becky references the "*better* moments of sex," rather than sex, period—suggesting that, while it is possible to experience sex that is not so great, the sensual pleasures of shopping, like the sensual pleasure of cramming buttered toast into one's mouth, are more transgressive because focused entirely on the self.

Critical response to the *Shopaholic* novels demonstrates the difficulty of severing representations of enthusiastic consumption from a moralizing narrative. It also reveals the persistence of a self-evident truth about how consumer culture endangers authenticity. Becky unapologetically pursues consumption as a mode of identity construction, often imagining how the purchase of a particular item of clothing will transform her into another kind of person. She fantasizes about being known as "the Girl in the Denny and George scarf" (*Confessions* 16), for example. Jessica Lyn Van Slooten argues that such episodes indicate that Becky turns to conspicuous consumption and the purchase of "opuluxe" clothing and accessories to fill a void in her life—thus suggesting that Becky's mode of identity construction is inauthentic, her desires shallow: "In London, and more intensely in Manhattan, Becky uses fashion to create both costumes and imitations of celebrity culture. Becky's creation of both suggests dissatisfaction with the actual self" (226). What that "actual self" might be is never identified. Additionally, because she must acknowledge that the novels fail to end with Becky fully "cured" of the disease of trivial status seeking, Van Slooten shies away from arguing that Kinsella is offering a critique of Becky's supposed delusions. She concludes that the novels are "not particularly critical of" Becky's spending and that Kinsella is "not wholly indicting this culture of conspicuous consumption" (220, 225). What I find interesting here is that the critics who want to assimilate these novels to a particular narrative about consumerism must position themselves *above* not only Becky but also Kinsella. Although never saying so directly, both Van Slooten and Ghosh imply either that Kinsella is herself as guilty as Becky or that she is not completely in control of her own narrative. Either way, this response signals that chick-lit authors cannot be taken seriously or, worse, are just passively channeling the bad impulses of consumer culture.

Against this problematic construction of Kinsella's authorship, and against the knee-jerk anti-consumerism that marks readings of the novels, I want to argue that Kinsella's novels consistently offer a challenge to the cultural imperative to make women feel guilty for their shopping and feel inadequate for seeing fashion as a way to construct and enact identity. Kinsella keeps guilt and pleasure in separate compartments, suggesting that it is not shopping or even overspending that make Becky feel guilty, and it is certainly not her pleasure that produces the guilt.[15] Becky feels guilty only when she endangers her interpersonal relations by lying or failing to follow through on promises made to family and friends. Against the view that the novels "lack a moral center,"[16] I want to argue that Kinsella endows Becky with a clear moral code—it's just not the moral code that opposes indulgence to thrift and sees shopping (even for identity) as a necessarily degraded form of self-realization or of pleasure. For instance, nearly everyone who writes about these novels reproduces a description from *Shopaholic Takes Manhattan* as evidence to support the claim that the novels replace an authentic sense of self and of community with one constructed through the practices of shopping; when Becky discovers the existence of sample sales in New York, she declares, "These are my people. I've found my homeland" (184). As I noted in chapter 3, the idea that one can create identity or community through shopping is anathema to anti-consumerist discourse: any identity or community created through consumption is always, and necessarily, a *lesser,* false, or inauthentic community or identity. Even if Becky does use fashion as a way to imagine new versions of her self, as she clearly does, why must such efforts be dismissed as "illusory" or "delusional"? Why must the pleasures that come from literally fashioning a self be read as mere fantasies, mere dreams that must always "come crashing down" (Van Slooten 229)? Is it "immoral" to imagine one's self through fashion? Why must this be a *guilty* pleasure?

The only times that Becky experiences guilt are at those moments when she fails to live up to her own goals or when she disappoints a friend or family member. For example, after failing as a shop assistant in an upscale retail store, Becky does console herself by going shopping and later regrets her spree. "I'm well aware," she tells us, "that at the back of my mind, thumping quietly like a drumbeat, are the twin horrors of Guilt and Panic. . . . If I let them, they'd swoop in and take over. I'd feel completely paralyzed with misery and fear. So the trick I've learned is simply not to listen. My mind is very well trained like that" (*Confessions* 154). On the one hand, this passage suggests that Becky does, in fact, feel guilty for indulging in retail therapy, but taken in the context of the novels' overall moral schema, I want to read this passage as *mocking* the idea that Becky must feel guilty. Note the capital letters (Guilt and Panic); note, also, the fact that these "twin horrors" are imagined like cartoon characters that "swoop in and take over." In fact, the language here brings to mind count-less comics, their humor directed at women surrounded by shopping bags, who worry that their husbands will catch them indulging in their guilty pleasures. Elsewhere in the novel, Kinsella contrasts this represen-tation of "Guilt" with a capital G to Becky's guilt over steering her parents' neighbors into losing a windfall from a bank merger: "A nasty cold feeling is creeping over me. They took the decision to switch their money based on my advice, didn't they? They asked me if they should switch funds, and I said go ahead. But now I come to think of it . . . hadn't I already heard a rumor about this takeover? Oh God. Could I have stopped this?" (250–51; ellipsis in the original). Becky's failure to give the proper advice to Janice and Martin cannot be attributed to her "shopaholism," her leisure activi-ties, but instead is owed to her lackadaisical attitude toward her *work* in an unsatisfying sector of the publishing industry. Ironically, Becky writes fluff pieces for a magazine called *Successful Saving,* a job to which she is ill-suited but the only job for which her college degree seems to have qualified her. Becky is bad at her job because her job is unfulfilling and boring, not because she is so easily distracted by the promises of shopping and consumption.

It's worth noting that Becky consumption is not the out-of-control, buy-anything-at-all consumption that the concept of addiction would suggest. For example, she has no interest in home improvement or in pursuing "respectable" middle-class modes of success. Although she knows she is "supposed" to take the "successful singles" route toward upward mobility with "property ladders and growth funds, too," she balks at this expec-tation. "Oh God, I'm missing the gene which makes you grow up and buy a flat in Streatham and start visiting Homebase every weekend." In a moment of rebellion, Becky wonders, "Who defines 'real life'? Who says 'real life' is property ladders and hideous pearl earrings?" (196). According to middle-class norms, buying property and shopping for the home and family are the "right" kinds of consumerism, while shopping for the self and pursuing fashion are the "wrong" kinds. The *Shopaholic* novels do, in fact, offer an alternative to property ladders and pearl earrings; unlike her friend Elly, who leaves journalism to become a fund manager, Becky seeks (throughout the entire series) alternative ways to shift career tracks and find more fulfilling work.

In *Confessions of a Shopaholic,* Becky takes her guilt over her bad advice to Janice and Martin and turns it into a career change. She writes an exposé of Flagstaff Life's scam against investors, finds herself being treated like a "real" financial expert rather than a "faux" expert, and lands herself a job on a morning television program. It is this happy ending that troubles critics of the novel, who have a hard time coming to terms with the fact that Becky essentially remains not only unpunished for her "bad" behavior but also rewarded for it: she makes enough money from her new gig to get out of debt. But there is another narrative arc here, not about shopping or debt or the pursuit of fantasy: it's about job opportunities for women and about sexist attitudes toward women who care about fashion and shopping. Part of what motivates Becky to stand up for Janice and Martin, and to carve a more fulfilling career out of the experience, is her memory of not being taken seriously by the successful Luke Brandon and his kind. After discovering that Luke earlier sought her advice and consumer expertise not to make a purchase for himself but for his girlfriend, Becky feels like the butt of a joke. This passage, not once cited in any article or review, foregrounds the cultural construction of the superficial shopper, the woman who pursues shopping instead of the authentic things in life: "I swallow hard, feeling sick with humiliation. For the first time, I'm realizing how Luke Brandon sees me. How they all see me. I'm just the comedy turn, aren't I? I'm the scatty girl who gets things wrong and makes people laugh. The girl who didn't know SBG and Rutledge Bank had merged. The girl no one would ever think of taking seriously" (182).

One cannot help but hear in Becky's complaint about never being taken seriously her creator's subtle jab at the cultural position of "chick lit." Sneering at the "pinkness" of these book covers—and the fact that the pinkness advertises the novels as commodities—critics of the genre draw on the "common sense" of cultural and gender hierarchy and name as "guilty" any pleasures to be found in their consumption. Maureen Dowd, who ought to know better, articulates the hackneyed Dwight MacDonald–esque protest against the arrival of this upstart, feminine, genre on the shelves of bookstores: "'Looking for Mr. Goodbunny' by Kathleen O'Reilly sits atop George Orwell's '1984.' 'Mine Are Spectacular!' by Janice Kaplan and Lynn Schurnberger hovers over 'Ulysses.' Sophie Kinsella's 'Shopaholic' series cuddles up to Rudyard Kipling." Dowd, in good anti-consumerist style, arrogates to herself a superior position above the "sea of pink," and is it any wonder that *all* of the writers she worries are being "edged out" by chick lit are men? Is it really possible that a feminist-leaning columnist for the *New York Times* could actually pen the following comments in 2007? "I realized with growing alarm, chick lit was no longer a niche. It had staged a coup of the literature shelves. Hot babes had shimmied into the grizzled old boys' club, the land of Conrad, Faulkner and Maugham. The store was possessed with the devil spawn of 'The Devil Wears Prada.' The blood-red high heel ending in a devil's pitchfork on the cover of the Lauren Weisberger best seller might as well be driving a stake through the heart of the classics." As Cheryl A. Wilson points out in a welcome article on Kinsella's interest in "using Becky's shopping to raise larger questions about twenty-first century conceptions of culture and assignments of value" (223), common responses to chick lit resonate with a history of not taking writing by women seriously.[17] They also, of course, reproduce the feminization thesis in raising alarm about how these commercial texts "drive a stake through the heart of the classics" of the masculine tradition.

Becky's anger at not being taken seriously is ignored by critics, perhaps because it might complicate the easy moral condemnation of her character. Later, after Becky writes her article exposing the fraud at Flagstaff Life, she finds herself set up to look foolish because the formidable Luke, whose public relations firm represents the company, has been booked to challenge her narrative and to provide drama for the television audience. But Becky shines in this context and successfully defends both her article and the investors who lost out because of the company's deliberate attempts to deceive and cheat them. This spotlight on corporate greed functions to put Becky's own "moral lapses" into perspective. The fact that, in the midst of this heated debate, Becky takes the time to "hope [her] legs look OK" (311) does not take away from her triumph. As the series develops, Becky often attempts to remake herself, not only through the purchase of consumer goods and the pursuit of fashion but also through discovering what kind of work she is good at and suited to—and she always endeavors to do so without Luke's help, as a way to assert her independence from him and his money. *Confessions of a Shopaholic* ends with Luke and Becky in bed in a posh hotel and, thus, would seem to suggest that romance with Luke will replace her romance with shopping. But not so. After Luke leaves, Becky finds herself drawn to a television shopping channel and is happy to congratulate herself for resisting the NK Malone sunglasses on sale; "the new Rebecca'" she boasts, "has more self-control than this. The new Rebecca isn't even *interested* in fashion" (346).

Luckily for the fans of the series, self-control is not the a priori value in the world of the shopaholic, and Becky's indulgence in the sunglasses promises that she is still interested in fashion and will remain so. As the fans whom Jennifer Scanlon interviewed confirm, the ending of the novel does *not* subordinate Becky's desire to shop to her desire for a romance with Luke; as one fan puts it, "Shopping was her 'one true love' before she met Luke, and she can't bring herself to abandon it just because she met a man" ("Making Shopping Safe"). Scanlon concludes that fan response to the novels reinforces the idea that "Becky Bloomwood shops compulsively but also shops, for the most part, not to compete with another woman, or to look a certain way to attract a man, but rather to please herself. Her fans acknowledge and celebrate this."

There are now eight novels in the *Shopaholic* series, and each one follows Becky through her shopping adventures at different stages of her life, producing something like a consumer bildungsroman: moving to New York, getting married, finding out that she has a half sister, having a baby, moving to Los Angeles to relaunch her career, and, finally, traveling throughout the western United States to track down her father and best friend Suze's husband, Tarkie, who have disappeared on some mysterious mission. It's important to point out that these books are hilarious, and Kinsella has developed a particular brand of humor that makes it nigh impossible for any but the most resistant readers to maintain a moralistic, judgmental distance from Becky. The final novel to date, *Shopaholic to the Rescue,* published in 2015, offers an interesting twist on the series' exploration of the complex stew of women's guilt and pleasure around shopping. In this novel, Becky is deeply troubled by what she sees as the unaccountable disintegration of her friendship with Suze, her own failed career aspirations, and anxiety over how her father's inexplicable behavior threatens to undermine the family's sense of themselves and their history. Rather than turn to retail therapy as she has done previously, however, Becky rejects shopping—something that critics of the series might applaud but something that her family and friends find troubling. Suze cries out in horror when Becky confesses that she's "slightly gone off shopping" (183) and worries to Luke that "Bex has gone all weird" (203). Her mother, Luke, Suze, and everyone else in this traveling band of rescuers are appalled at the "flatness" of the new Becky, her lack of drive and enthusiasm (184). What they are noticing is that the Becky whose "authentic self" *is* a shopper has disappeared, leaving behind a void.

Kinsella does not leave Becky in her non-shopping funk for long, and once our protagonist realizes that she is not responsible for all the bad things that happen to her loved ones, she starts shopping again—much to the relief of those loved ones. In an earlier scene in the novel, Kinsella suggests that Becky, even when not buying things, is read by others as an expert shopper—and the series takes seriously that Becky's shopping expertise is "authentic." While on the trip to Las Vegas, Becky visits a souvenir shop, and the reader expects her to go on a wild shopping spree because she is particularly susceptible to the temptations of the souvenir. Following her usual practice, Becky purchases a number of items, but when faced with a customer satisfaction survey, she finds herself unable to tick off the "Awesome" box to characterize her experience. Feeling something like an existential crisis at this moment—she tells us, "To my horror, tears are suddenly trembling on my lashes" (*Rescue* 72)—she ends up deciding to return her purchases. Watching the "expert" behave in this way, the other shoppers follow suit: "Down the lines, I can see other women listening in and looking in their baskets and taking things out. It's like some contagious wave of unshopping hits the crowd" (75). The cashier panics and asks Becky to leave the store. On reflection Becky tells us, "Honestly. You'd think I'd been single-handedly trying to bring down capitalism or something" (76). What is so significant here is that the reaction to Becky's not shopping is virtually identical to the reaction to Becky's "over-shopping": the female shopper is made to feel guilty for her consumer behavior, no matter what it is, and to bear the responsibility for the health or disease of consumerism. As we have seen throughout this book, overblown representations of female shoppers make women responsible for both the excesses of consumerism and its failures.

This scene also contains one of many parodies of consumerist anti-consumerism Kinsella offers throughout the series. When Becky decides to return her items, she does so with the encouragement of another woman in line, who spouts the doctrine of the "meaningful" shopping course Becky herself completed at Golden Peace, a New Agey California spa. This spa, featured in *Shopaholic to the Stars,* the previous entry in the series, offers a range of courses Becky selects to get in the groove of the California lifestyle: "I do self-esteem group on Mondays, Compassionate Communication on Tuesdays, The Transitive Self on Wednesdays, and this brilliant class called Tapping for Well-Being on Fridays. Right now it's a Thursday morning, and I'm in Mindfulness for a Positive Life" (148). Becky drinks the Kool-Aid and ventriloquizes her anti-consumerist coach: "'Going shopping can often be a way of boosting low self-esteem,' I say knowledgeably. 'So, I have to boost my self-esteem with affirmations'"— like "I approve of myself and feel great about myself," typed on "positive thought-cards" (167). Of course, Golden Peace also sells T-shirts with these slogans printed on them and other upscale merchandise, tempting Becky away from "meaningful" shopping and also enabling Kinsella to underline the hypocrisy of Golden Peace's philosophy. An earlier parodic treatment of consumerist anti-consumerism has Becky pledging to make herself over into what her anti-consumerist self-help books tell her she should be: "Frugality. Simplicity. These are my new watchwords. A new, uncluttered, Zen-like life, in which I spend nothing. Spend *nothing.* I mean, when you think about it, how much money do we all waste every day? No wonder I'm in a little bit of debt. And really, it's not my fault. I've merely been succumbing to the Western drag of materialism—which you have to have the strength of elephants to resist. At least, that's what it says in my new book" (*Confessions* 64). Kinsella lampoons this attitude, just as she makes fun of the notion that the female consumer has the power to "bring down capitalism."

The *Shopaholic* novels challenge the critical commonplace that marks so much of anti-consumerist critique (along with consumerist anti-consumerism): consumer culture, the marketplace, and commodification necessarily destroy authenticity. They offer an almost direct rejoinder to the anti-consumerist crazes that Levine discusses. The "philosophy" at the heart of Voluntary Simplicity, for example, imagines not-shopping as the road not only to virtue but also to creativity, health, and even salvation. To recall, reading Cecile Andrews's *The Circle of Simplicity,* Levine relays this piece of self-help advice: "Toss out those old clothes and broken tennis rackets at the back of your closet and you will discover your 'authentic self' crushed under the debris. After that, Heaven's the limit: VS, writes Andrews, 'is a life that allows the individual's soul to awaken'" (69). *Shopaholic* mocks this philosophy—which makes shopping just as important as does Becky's retail philosophy—when Kinsella has Becky try out and try on various schemes to curb her shopping impulses. At one point, in *Shopaholic Takes Manhattan,* she follows this VS advice when, at Suze's urging, she agrees to "declutter" her room. Suze insists that "it completely transforms your life!" (328), but Becky, unable to do it, instead stuffs all of her goods into Space Bags (which compress when the air is sucked out of them by a vacuum cleaner). Inevitably, they explode, and Becky literally finds herself "crushed under the debris" at the back of her closet, but that self, that involuntarily simplified self, is false. Becky's "authentic self" is a shopper.

The fantasy of authenticity that underwrites so much anti-consumerism can be seen with particular clarity in those texts, like *No Logo,* that attempt to make consumerism safe for elite consumers who seek to position themselves against "ordinary" consumers, those mindless dupes who allow themselves (ourselves) to be seduced by the false promises of consumer happiness. While exposés of unethical business practices (sweatshops, environmental destruction) are necessary components of contemporary forms of consumer activism, so much of consumerist anti-consumerism makes moral arguments about good and bad selves instead of political arguments about economic conditions. Klein's book does a little of both, but, in my estimation, her main goal is to identify a new class of anti-consumerist activists who are distinguishable, in the first instance, from the previous generation of feminist and other critics of the politics of representation; in the second, from mindless consumers who allow ourselves to be pawns of corporations and advertisers; and, in the third, from those savvy, if morally suspect, architects of "brand culture." Klein herself floats above all players and above the sociocultural field she surveys, pronouncing judgment on all. Is it any wonder, then, as she wryly notes in the introduction to the tenth anniversary edition of *No Logo,* that she was offered consulting jobs by corporations who saw her as a "kind of anti-corporate dominatrix, making overpaid executives feel good by telling them what bad, bad brands they were" (iii)? Indeed, *No Logo* has made Naomi Klein into a brand, and the complex network of actors invested in that brand should (but does not) prompt her to think in more complicated ways about the complicities among the different actors she observes (herself included). Klein's book aims to produce guilt and suggests that the only pleasure to be had from consumer culture is in taking up a rebellious posture against it.

Unlike Judith Levine's book, which is interested in resistance rather than rebellion, *No Logo* has no patience for complex analysis. *Not Buying It* analyzes the motives both of consumers and of anti-consumers, acknowledging the complicated circuits of desire, responsibility, pleasure, and guilt that inevitably attach to practices of shopping (and not-shopping). Rejecting the idea that consumer culture endangers the "real" self, Levine wants to ask the Voluntary Simplifiers and culture jammers, the adbusters and downshifters, "What if I discover my authentic self, and my authentic self is a shopper?" (70). Like the *Shopaholic* novels, Judith Levine's *Not Buying It* takes seriously the pleasures of being immersed in consumer culture, even as it offers a sharp critique of the excesses of American materialism at the close of the twentieth century. I do not categorize the *Shopaholic* novels as "anti-consumerist," but they have sometimes been read as "Exhibit A" in the indictment of consumer culture or, perhaps more accurately, in the indictment of *consumers*. When readers and critics try to assimilate Kinsella's novels to a moralistic discourse of sin and redemption, indulgence and denial, they do so because the anti-consumerist narrative I have tracked throughout this entire book is self-evident, not subject to demonstration. It is, in fact, *ideological,* a construction masquerading as a description of the "way things are."

CODA

Throughout this book, I have drawn attention to the ways in which the discourse of anti-consumerism can stage a competition to determine what is the most authentic expression of rebellion and who is the most virtuous practitioner of it. Competitive anti-consumerism and conspicuous authenticity are the signs that the rhetoric of rebellion against consumerism has gone off the rails, but they are also the signs that what William Whyte many years ago sarcastically identified as "keeping down with the Joneses" has become the new normal. The rhetoric of rebellious anti-consumerism always draws attention to the rebel, to his virtue, to his countercultural credentials, to his lonely quest for an individualism not tainted by commodification. "Authenticity Guaranteed" is the false promise of anti-consumerism, if also of certain consumer products, and this is just one of many ironies I have found here. I have resisted identifying an *authentic* mode of anti-consumerism, a better way of articulating the rebellion against consumerism, because the posture of rebellion and its fetishization of "authenticity" is the problem to which I wanted to draw attention. One conclusion that emerges from my analysis is that a wide variety of cultural, intellectual, and commercial forces have rendered the concept of "authenticity" virtually unusable as a critical lever with which to challenge consumer capitalism. Because anti-consumerist critique is a moral, rather than an economic, discourse, it too often ends up denouncing as false the activities of consumer culture in general and consumers in particular. Further, its often unintended effect is to preserve a hierarchical relationship between different groups or classes of individuals by constructing a set of oppositions that include masculine and feminine, authentic and inauthentic, savvy and deluded. Anti-consumerism, as it has been articulated in the United States over the past fifty years, is a form of *masculine* protest, even when it is articulated by women.

As I was completing final revisions of this book in the spring and summer of 2017, I kept experiencing an almost irresistible impulse to litter
the text with comments and endnotes connecting my argument, and the
rhetoric of anti-consumerism, to the rhetoric of Donald Trump's presiden-
tial campaign and the early days of what we must call the "Trump era."
I did resist those impulses, but I want to take this space to start to think
through, in a spirit of speculation, some of those connections. I do not mean
to suggest that the anti-consumerist critics I have analyzed here are the
cousins of Donald Trump or that the dominance of anti-consumerism in
American culture has somehow produced the backlash that is Trumpism.
What I do want to do is to urge us to consider how the language in which
we couch our social critique and the narratives we construct to tell the
story of American culture can feed, rather than ameliorate, the social inequalities we aim to contest. Trumpism has brought home to me just how
powerful masculine protest can be and brought home to me, as well, the
absolute bankruptcy of the concept of "authenticity."

Donald Trump succeeded, in part, by mobilizing the concept of "authenticity." Targeting globalization rather than shopping, and cultural
elites rather than deluded consumers, Trump's rhetoric nevertheless exposed the underside of a concept that, at best, positions the individual
against the social and, at worst, legitimates a worldview in which the
forces of conservative reaction, racism, and misogyny can be justified by
virtue of their "authenticity" and their arrogation of an "outsider" position.
The structure of the anti-consumerist narrative, with its identification of
insiders and outsiders, its calculus about authenticity and inauthenticity, and its complicity with a gender system that values the masculine
and derogates the feminine, can easily be turned on its head so that the
forces of conservative reaction can occupy the position of the "alternative" or the "countercultural." The Trump campaign took advantage of
this structure. It eagerly embraced the feminization thesis, and it used the
language of a righteous rebellion against the status quo. And while no one
would claim that the "Make America Great Again" campaign was in any
way a call to define America against the values of consumerism, *globalization* functioned as a code word for a host of imagined ills afflicting "ordinary" Americans whose values, the narrative goes, had been destroyed
in the rush to make everything a commodity on the global market. The

rhetoric of Trumpism reinforced the distinctions between authenticity and inauthenticity, finding an America "softened" by the rise of global, consumerist values and the decline of industrial production and self-made manhood. That Trump's slogan actually meant "Make America White Again" was not lost on anyone—not his supporters and not his detractors. The powerful conjunction of white resentment, anti-elitism, and anger at the perceived erosion of male dominance and heteronormativity has produced a toxic "rebellion" that threatens to become violent at any moment.

What is so striking about the discourses around authenticity that came to the forefront through the Trump phenomenon is the fact that they are so predictable and recursive. As I have argued, a master narrative about how large social systems function to feminize men, and by extension the nation, by destroying authenticity has long served to justify and legitimate a symbolic gender order in which all things masculine "trump" all things feminine. And the language of gender also works to naturalize other social differences, so that class and even racial differences get sucked up into the feminization thesis and its calculus for determining value. We see this most clearly and explicitly through responses to the poor in U.S. culture, but we can also see it in recent spectacular displays of white supremacist masculine protests, which begin from the premise that the "Nanny State"—nurtured by liberals and the forces of "political correctness"—has made America weak and, in depriving white men of what is "rightfully" theirs, has also destroyed the very foundations that prop up white supremacy and male privilege. When the *New York Times* reported on the white supremacist demonstrations in Charlottesville, Virginia, in August 2017, the article noted that "the far right, which has returned to prominence in the past year or so, has always been an amalgam of factions and causes, some with pro-Confederate or neo-Nazi leanings, some opposed to political correctness or feminism" (Feuer). While it is not surprising that white supremacists make common cause with anti-feminists, it is striking that the conjunction "political correctness and feminism" could provoke the kind of rage and violence that was on display in Charlottesville and elsewhere. Further, the logic expressed by this conjunction makes pro-Confederate and neo-Nazi forces the "authentic" expression of American identity and "heritage," while feminism, anti-racism, and the fight for LGBTQ rights are inauthentic, signs only of "political correctness."

Narratives about how American culture and American citizens have been feminized are on the rise in the Trump era. When Preston Wiginton, a self-described "white nationalist," expressed his ire that his efforts to stage a "White Lives Matter" rally on my own campus, Texas A&M University, were thwarted, he did so in the familiar language of feminization. Assessing blame for the threatened "extinction" of white nations, Wiginton settled on a version of the argument I have been tracking here. "Part of that is the white race's fault," he told *Rolling Stone.* "They bought into consumerism and feminism. Women would rather have careers than children, and men would rather have boats than children." Wiginton here evokes the rhetoric of "race suicide" that has been around at least since the nineteenth century, but his identification of *consumerism* as a source not only of the decline of masculinity but also of whiteness suggests that the so-called "alt-Right" has taken a page from countercultural rebellions, locating authenticity in rebellion against consumerism. Indeed, as *New York Times* writer John Herrman suggests in an article entitled "Why the Far Right Wants to Be the New 'Alternative' Culture," the Right's appropriation of the label "alternative" can be seen as another turn of the screw in the battle over who gets to claim "authentic" outsider status:

> An essential feature of the rise of Trumpism has been the brazen inversion, that trusty maneuver in which you wield your critics' own values against them—say, borrowing the language of social justice to argue that the "oppressor" is actually oppressed or suddenly embracing progressive social causes in the service of criticizing Islam. It's a blunt but effective rhetorical confiscation, in which a battle-ready right relishes its ability to seize, inhabit and neutralize the arguments and vocabularies of its opponents, reveling in their continued inability to formulate any sort of answer to the trusty old "I know you are, but what am I?" (279–80)

As I have argued, bemoaning the "co-optation" of a discourse and rhetoric as an illegitimate move toward de-authenticating cultural critique—as in advertising's promotion of countercultural themes, for example—is not a particularly effective strategy. Submitting others' utterances to something like an authenticity meter directs attention away from the substance of those utterances to the speaker of them. Again, the Trump campaign masterfully demonstrated this process and did so through the use of so-called political correctness, which has long been shorthand for inauthentic or insincere. Drawing on the self-evident truth that anyone who makes anti-racist, anti-sexist, anti-Islamophobic, anti-homophobic claims is necessarily and always insincere and inauthentic, this political narrative legitimated the most offensive utterances and behavior by understanding them as "authentic" and, in the process, earned for its "heroes" an outsider position. This outsider position granted a moral authority that, as I have argued here, seems always to attach to rebels in American culture. While many commentators challenged the racism and sexism of the Trump campaign, nearly everyone implicitly endorsed the claim that "political correctness" endangers authenticity and so implicitly supported the narrative that re-energized dangerous reactionary speech and behaviors. David Boyle is right to note that the "demand for authenticity is inevitable and probably unstoppable, but it is also extremely dangerous. Unmet demands for something 'real' are emerging in some very scary forms—in fundamentalist interpretations of the Bible and the Koran, in bizarre new kinds of nationalism and authoritarianism, in brutal backlashes against women, asylum-seekers or outsiders" (262).

Authoritarianism is worth fighting, and so is consumerism. But if the greatest sin of consumerism is its erosion of individualism, masculinity, and authenticity, then for whom is this fight really fought? The rhetorics of rebellious anti-consumerism I have analyzed here are elitist in the literal sense of thriving on distinctions: if you are an authentic person, someone else is not; if your position is authentically political, someone else's is not. These are ultimately moral distinctions, and the discourses of anti-consumerism construct a moral economy in which there are always "good" and "bad" actors—whether bad means inauthentic, deluded, passive, feminine, or whatever. That we use the language of gender to further entrench these distinctions, to make them more legible, is the problem that I aimed to illuminate here. I ended with the *Shopaholic* novels, in what might seem to suggest an uncritical embrace of consumerism as a way to fight against the moralistic anti-consumerism that was the object of my analysis. But that was not my intention, nor is it the position I am espousing. If the "ordinary" readers who flock to these novels find in them a relief from the hackneyed cultural narratives about consumerism (and about femininity), who's to say that "ordinary" citizens contesting the hackneyed cultural narratives about rebellious masculinity purveyed by Trumpism might not succeed in creating a counternarrative? It is the *structure* of the anti-consumerist narrative that we need to contest, just as we need to contest the *structure* of the narratives about authenticity that propelled Donald Trump to victory. Articulated from the Left or from the Right, rhetoric about the "feminization" of America and contests over authenticity can only ever reproduce the essentially ahistorical narrative that pits the real against the fake and, in doing so, finds moral justification for assigning individuals a place in a hierarchy of value. As I have argued here, such narratives are never only symbolic, are never *just* narratives. They are also schemas for organizing the world into insiders and outsiders, winners and losers, with often unwitting, but also dangerous, consequences.

NOTES

INTRODUCTION

1. Fraiman is discussing Ross's "Weather Report: The World Cup," published in *Artforum* (September 1994).

2. Andrew Slack is the founder of the HPA, whose website makes the following promises: "THE HARRY POTTER ALLIANCE TURNS FANS INTO HEROES. We're changing the world by making activism accessible through the power of story. Since 2005 we've engaged millions of fans through our work for equality, human rights, and literacy" (http://www.thehpalliance.org). See also Slack.

3. Sophie Kinsella is the pen name of Madeline Wickham, and although she is British, her books are enormously popular in the United States and, as I will argue, offer an interesting commentary on the "Americanness" of anti-consumerism.

CHAPTER 1: FANTASIES OF AUTHENTICITY

1. For work on advertising, some of which discusses gender, see Lears, *Fables of Abundance;* Leach; Ewen; Miller; and Nickles.

2. This is made explicit by the title of Christopher Breward's book *The Hidden Consumer: Masculinities, Fashion and City Life, 1860–1914.*

3. Pendergast quotes from an editorial titled "Never Underestimate the Power of a Man" to flesh out editor Bill Williams's strategy of promoting men as the *true* consumers, the subjects in control of the home and of women, ending thus: "And we're going to continue giving you strong men's fare for reading material every month. And any time we meet a cartoonist who has turned out a henpecked husband gag, we're going to punch him in the nose. After all, who signed the Declaration of Independence? Were there any women there?" (234).

4. See also Bill Osgerby's discussion of how *Playboy* managed to "masculinize" cookery as one mode of its "business of colonizing the feminine" (129).

5. The rise of reality television has also put some strain on the feminization thesis, as numerous shows focus on men being involved in designing and decorating home spaces and participating in various kinds of consumer-mediated "makeovers." HGTV and other networks such as A&E, however, work to differentiate

between feminine and masculine forms of consumer behavior, with shows like *Storage Wars, Pimp My Ride, American Chopper,* and *Date My House* working in various ways to safeguard heterosexual masculinity from the threat of feminization. Brenda Weber suggests that in "Makeover Nation," *all* subjects, regardless of gender, are positioned as "feminized," and when men are ensnared in the "makeover machine," the shows utilize various strategies (not all of them successful) to protect the male subject from becoming feminine. Such strategies include allowing men to "resist" the ministrations of the largely female and gay male makeover "gurus" and to recoup self-made manhood through a set of discourses and conventions that insist on the makeover only ever discovering the natural, essential, and "real" man inside the makeover subject, rather than constructing a new man through artificial, consumerist means. In addition to Weber, see also Cohan, "Queer Eye for the Straight Guise."

6. A possible exception to this is Lionel Trilling's *Sincerity and Authenticity,* which does not offer an account of the quest for authenticity. Rather, Trilling is interested in understanding how the concepts of sincerity and authenticity have shifted in response to major literary and philosophical-theoretical developments.

7. In addition to Golomb's discussion of authenticity in philosophy, see Vannini and Williams as well as Bendix for accounts of the quest for authenticity and sociology and folklore studies, respectively.

8. Colin Campbell, in *The Romantic Ethic and the Spirit of Modern Consumerism,* a title riffing on Weber, argues that the romantic ethic was from the start completely entangled with consumerism. For Campbell, the principle driving modern consumerism is a "self-illusory hedonism" characterized by a "longing to experience in reality those pleasures created and enjoyed in the imagination." Campbell argues that "romantic teachings concerning the good, the true and the beautiful, provide both the legitimation and the motivation necessary for modern consumer behavior to become prevalent throughout the contemporary industrial world" (205–6).

9. Sarah Thornton titles a full chapter "Authenticities from the Record Hop to the Rave" in her *Club Culture: Music, Media and Subcultural Capital* and makes the case that "authenticity is arguably the most important value ascribed to popular music" (26).

10. See Keir Keightley for an account of rock's sometimes contradictory constructions of authenticity, "authentic individualism," the "mainstream," and the "commercial." See Weisethaunet and Lindberg for an account of how rock criticism has enshrined "the idea of artistic independence as 'refusal' or 'purity.' . . . This version of 'authenticity' seems to indulge in some of the core myths of the rock field, especially that of the image of the artist as a rebel" (472).

11. See Lawrence Grossberg for an analysis of "authentic inauthenticity" (224) in rock and roll—a kind of postmodern meta-authenticity he sees in performers like Madonna and David Bowie.

12. See Marilyn Halter for an analysis of how American consumers seek such authenticity in ethnically marked products and festivals. Halter paints a complex picture of how both marketers and members of ethnic communities have interests in defining which products and festivals are "authentically" ethnic, and while noting that when "market forces are at play, authenticity is a hot commodity" (18), she does not enforce a distinction between the "pure" and the "commercial" because, in her research, she has found that the distinction does not hold.

13. Moore is citing punker Jane Stebbins's comments as reported in Ann Powers's book *Weird Like Us* (230; qtd. in Moore 12).

14. Although Potter does not make this point, Mailer's paean to the hipster as "white negro" is one chapter in a history of associating racial otherness with authenticity. It is also worth mentioning that within African American popular and literary cultures, the question of "racial authenticity" has a long and complex history that connects with, but is not solely determined by, white efforts to appropriate blackness as the sign of authenticity. For analyses of politically problematic appeals to black authenticity—problematic for their anti-feminist, anti-woman, and homophobic assumptions—see Thomas as well as Johnson. For an analysis of the place of authenticity in criticism and theory of American multicultural literature, see Karem.

15. Franzen would do well to read Stephen King's 1987 novel *Misery,* which articulates a complex critique of the high-low culture divide as it characterizes attitudes toward "serious" versus "popular" fiction. King's author figure, Paul Sheldon, makes fun of himself for his own literary pretensions, his desire to distance himself from his (female) audience and his (feminine) genre fiction by making himself over into a "Serious Writer."

16. These comments, widely quoted, come from a *Fresh Air* interview, October 13, 2001. There has been a great deal written about how the Franzen-Oprah episode reveals a cultural divide still operative in U.S. culture. See T. Edwards; G. Snyder; and L. Miller for discussions of the episode in the popular press; and Ingraham; B. Smith; Ribbat; and Green for scholarly treatments. While Franzen seems to be posing "literary fiction" against mass culture, what he is really trying to come to terms with is his position in *middlebrow* culture, a category that best describes both the books Oprah selects and the way her club models reading. In a 2011 article published in *GQ*, titled "Middlebrow: The Taste That Dare Not Speak Its Name," Devin Friedman makes a comment that one can imagine haunting Jonathan Franzen: "I would gladly sit listening to Sting while I consume a three-pound fajita burrito at Chipotle wearing a J.Crew suit and reading Jonathan Franzen with *Friday Night Lights* on in the background. These are all things that make me happy to consume. And they are all middlebrow." Friedman blithely rejects the very basis for most distinctions between high, low, and middle—that is, the distinction between art and commerce, between the artwork and the "product." We can guess how Franzen might respond to being denoted as the J.Crew of literary production.

CHAPTER 2: AUTHENTIC INDIVIDUALS AND ORGANIZATION MEN

1. See Steinle for an excellent and thorough account of the controversies over the censorship of *Catcher*.

2. I have located only one feminist essay on *Catcher*, by Mary Suzanne Schriber. She delivers a devastating blow to the assumptions behind the lionization of Salinger's novel as a story about *the* adolescent, *the* American character, and *the* tradition of American literature. The recent Routledge Guides to Literature volume on *Catcher*, edited by Sarah Graham, is a welcome addition to criticism of the novel. Along with a much shorter version of this chapter, the volume includes two other essays on gender and sexuality, by Pia Livia Hekanaho and Clive Baldwin.

3. Of course, the commercial success of *Catcher* and the consequent ridicule it received from aggrieved highbrow critics put an ironic spin on this dynamic. See Medovoi, "Democracy, Capitalism, and American Literature," for an interesting discussion of how the novel and its reception prompted a great deal of rhetorical gymnastics on the part of Cold War liberal intellectuals.

4. Alan Nadel argues that the novel is an allegory about McCarthyism, with Holden playing the part of an ambivalent "Red Hunter" seeking out "phonies"— that is, Communists masquerading as Americans.

5. See Duane Edwards for just such a reading; see also Baldwin.

6. See Cohen, especially chapter 7, "Segmenting the Masses," for an analysis of how market segmentation worked alongside a broader cultural identity politics in the 1960s and 1970s.

7. Bareiss also connects the Beats to Whyte, Riesman, and Salinger.

8. For example, Manuel Luis Martinez argues that the Beats' lauded rebellion against "conformism" is more accurately read as an anxiety-ridden response to the imagined threat to individualism posed by collectivism or, in Martinez's phrasing, communalism. Martinez reads the Beats' penchant for "movement" as signifying an individualist, masculinist, imperialist frontier spirit radically at odds with the collective sense of social "movement" gathering force in the 1950s and '60s. Several other critics have identified in *On the Road* the centrality of the imperialist impulse toward conquering the frontier, with Sal and Dean taking the part of the rugged individualists who stake out their territory. See also Elmwood.

9. Nabokov clearly subscribes to the gendered high-low scale of cultural production and consumption, enthusiastically detailing the difference between Lo's feminine taste and Humbert's masculine response to that taste.

10. Reviews from *Commonweal*, *Newsweek*, *Time*, *Atlantic Monthly*, *Harper's*, *Playboy*, and the *Nation* are available in facsimile at the University of Virginia Crossroads Project: http://xroads.virginia.edu/~ugoo/lambert/ontheroad/taking.html. Included is also a spoof penned by John Updike for the *New Yorker*, titled

"On the Sidewalk." Updike lampoons the "revolutionary" rhetoric of the novel, while also suggesting that it is childish.

11. In addition to Martinez, Jon Panish offers a persuasive critique of the bias toward individualism and the consequent misreading by the Beats of jazz. He attributes the general white appropriation of jazz as marred by the ideology of "color blindness." On the Beats' racial appropriations, see Ligari and also Holton.

12. This phrase comes from George Lipsitz.

13. An early reviewer, who sees Kerouac's "handling of this episode" with Terry as the "major flaw in the book," chides the author for the insincerity of his character's appeal to "white sorrows" as an explanation for his abandonment of Terry: "It won't do. If Paradise had thought, it got cold, I got tired and I wanted to finish that book I was writing without the burden of that Mexican girl [sic] and her son, that would have been honest. To blame his treachery on the color of his skin or the culture he has inherited is a bit thick" (Curley 596).

14. Carden also sees Sal and Dean's behavior as a form of consumer behavior, linking the novel's representation of the quest for sex and movement to letters between Kerouac and Cassady: "All this frenetic motion and frantic sex seem as driven and anxiety-ridden as more conventional forms of consumption, and like other, capitalist, forms, provide returns in elevated status" (84).

15. The craze for authenticity and the anti-consumerism that animates the myth of the Beats gets further entrenched in the years that follow when, as Rossinow points out, "alienation" replaces "exploitation" as the primary wrong of the American political system. Particularly for the white male activists of the New Left that are Rossinow's main subject, "alienation" becomes a rallying cry and heralds a shift away from a materialist political analysis to a more psychologized and existential analysis. Such a shift does not require that gender, racial, and class realities be forgotten, but the new and growing interest in the alienation of the individual did enable the mostly white and middle-class college-educated male leaders of sixties movements to put their own experiences at the center of countercultural critique. Rossinow writes, "They felt their own alienation was an estrangement less from dominant social norms, or from conventional political activity"—as, for example, it might have been for black activists—"than [an estrangement] from their own real selves" (4).

16. *The New Individualists* is one of a number of books written for a wide audience and disconnected from literary study, cultural studies, and "high" theory that, nevertheless, find "postmodernism" useful as a way to describe a paradigm shift in experiences of individualism and individuality, in responses to products and consumer culture more generally, and in changing ideas about authenticity. The chapter called "The End of Authenticity" is the most sustained analysis of how pervasive the logic of postmodernism is.

CHAPTER 3: SHOPPING FOR THE REAL

1. In an article arguing that Franzen "at present most embodies the figure of the compromised and conflicted white male liberal writer" (191), Colin Hutchinson notes that despite the novel's representation of female characters who struggle with the same conflicts as the male characters, "Franzen is addressing a substantially white, male left-liberal position. That *The Corrections* goes to some lengths to hide the possibility that feminism might offer 'transgressive' alternatives that present a potential for left-liberal solidarity is revealing. There are two expressly feminist characters in the novel: the college lecturer Venda O'Fallon and Chip's former girlfriend Tori Timmelman. O'Fallon is portrayed as the purveyor of a shallow politics of identity and emotion, while Timmelman is dismissed as a helpless neurotic who is 'throttled by rage.' It appears that when white male dissenters are unable to escape their complicity with consumerist individualism, no one else is permitted to do so either" (206n14).

2. There has been surprisingly little work on gender in DeLillo. See Nel; Helyer; and Longmuir.

3. I say "fantasized" modernism in order to question the validity of this narrative about modernism—indeed, as many recent critics have done. See Outka for a very interesting analysis of modernism's fascination with the "commodified authentic."

4. See, especially, Frow; Duvall; and Lindner.

5. Alice Jardine's *Gynesis* is exemplary of this skepticism. See McRobbie, *Postmodernism and Popular Culture,* for a valuable retrospective look back on debates about feminism, postmodernism, and Marxism. She has more recently disavowed this earlier position and joined in the critique of "commodity feminism" as "postfeminism." See her "Postfeminism and Popular Culture."

6. In her critique of Fredric Jameson, McRobbie argues that the version of postmodernism that focuses on depthlessness and fragmentation fails to ask questions about the politics of representation: "Who gets to be able to express their fragmentation?" Acknowledging that fragmentation has always marked the subjectivity of "subaltern" groups allows us to see that "fragmentation can be linked to a politics of empowerment." However, "for Jameson (and for white middle-class masculinity?) it means disempowerment, silence, or schizophrenic 'cries and whispers'" (*Postmodernism and Popular Culture* 29).

7. *Agency panic* is Timothy Melley's term for the anxieties readable in a wide range of literary and social discourses in the postwar period.

8. What compromises the Gladneys' "kinship" for Ferraro is the extra-textual suggestion that this family harmony is always temporary, given the "fact" that both Jack and Babette have a habit of dissolving and reforming families. While granting that "the kind of intercourse conducted in the market generates an effect of kinship that pushes beyond mere semblance to genuine warmth and mutual need" (35),

Ferraro argues that, thanks to "no-fault-no-shame divorce," the Gladney family's "relatively efficacious, even compelling domesticity" is based on "quicksand" (20). The logic here is rather odd: since the family cements its kinships through shopping, and this is a family that is not stable, then shopping necessarily endangers the family. Or alternatively: since the family seeks kinship in shopping, then it is a family that's bound to splinter. Neither of these positions seems warranted by the novel.

9. See Taylor for a discussion of how postmodern culture has eroded authenticity.

10. An exception to this is David J. Alworth, who is interested in bridging the gap between sociological and fictional-artistic accounts of the supermarket, rather than making a particular argument about DeLillo. However, his comments on *White Noise* as a "microethnographic treatment" of consumer culture are intriguing, particularly his idea that DeLillo, à la Latour, is "responding to a certain relay between human and nonhuman agency that manifests itself in the postmodern supermarket" (308).

11. See Campbell for an interesting discussion of the differences between male and female modes of shopping, based on interviews he conducted with shoppers in Leeds, England, in 1992 and 1993. Campbell concludes that, for women, shopping serves "expressive" needs and is a form of leisure, whereas for men, shopping serves "instrumental" needs and is more a form of work. Interestingly, Campbell also concludes that it is women's shopping that is more in tune with a "postmodern consumer society" and wonders whether men will be left behind as "old-fashioned" consumers, while women emerge as "modern and sophisticated consumers" ("Shopping, Pleasure and the Sex Wars" 175).

12. Frank Lentricchia suggests that Murray and Jack are "ironic cultural critics" in the supermarket (100), and Ferraro notes that "the dazzling inventiveness of the talk" in the supermarket supports Murray's contention of the space as full of energy and "psychic data" (34). Both critics, however, suggest that this talk and this criticism are somehow compromised by both its topic and its location.

13. The image on the cover of this book, titled *Repetition*, can be seen as an ironic homage to Baudrillard's *The Consumer Society*, whose Sage Publication edition cover (1999) features a line of shopping carts. His are meant, I think, to signal a self-evident homogeneity and triviality, the shopping cart as epitome of mindless consumption. As I was thinking about cover images for the book, I came across a book called *The Stray Shopping Carts of Eastern North America: A Guide to Field Identification* by Julian Montague. The book is meant to bring attention to the abandoned shopping cart as an "integral part of the urban and suburban landscape. . . . To the average person, the stray shopping cart is most often thought of as a signifier of urban blight or as an indicator of a consumer society gone too far. Unfortunately, the acceptance of these oversimplified designations has discouraged any serious examination of the stray shopping cart phenomenon" (6). Montague aims to challenge this understanding by publishing this lushly photographed "field guide,"

complete with its "Linaean taxonomy." Tongue in cheek or not, the book renders the stray shopping cart a serious object of cultural analysis and appreciation.

14. Interestingly, Hoberek has backed away from this evaluation of *White Noise*, in an excellent recent article analyzing *White Noise* as offering something like a marriage of Vietnam War fiction and the 1970s–'80s minimalism known to focus on the domestic and the personal, rather than a textbook exemplification of "postmodernism." Reading the novel against the backdrop of "modernization theory"—and as a "domestic rewriting" of *The Names*—Hoberek argues against an "abstract" account of the novel (exemplified by John Frow) and for a reading of it as "privileging . . . discrete individual objects as a kind of counterweight to abstract theory, mobilized in response to what we might call the competing aesthetics of U.S. foreign policy" ("Foreign Objects" 108). In other words, *White Noise* critiques the abstractions of foreign policy of the era through analogy with the novel's representation of the "commonplace as a vexed but nonetheless potentially rich site of meaning" (114).

15. In an interesting reading of *White Noise* as a critique of the "new class" of white-collar experts and knowledge workers, particularly within academia, Stephen Schryer argues that the novel counters the "omnipresence of new-class culture" with "whatever is left of traditional know-how in contemporary society." Schryer suggests that that "know-how" is "embodied in the artisanal working class" exemplified by Vernon Dickey: "Unlike the novel's scientists and humanists, he is not alienated from the world of objects around him; he has a hands-on knowledge of how to build and fix things" (186). Acknowledging that DeLillo "ironizes Vernon just as he ironizes all of the redemptive figures in his fiction" (187), Schryer nevertheless poses Vernon as the authentic embodiment of an ethos centered on production. That this ethos is also clearly coded as *masculine* goes unremarked by Schryer. See Weekes for a discussion of Vernon as representing a "way of life that has passed as well as a gender stereotype to which Jack may not consciously subscribe but to which he is still vulnerable" (291).

16. As the titles of typical reviews of Franzen's collections of essays suggest, he is as self-absorbed a literary figure as it is possible to be, analogizing his own personal despair and distress to the state of the nation and, more specifically, the nation's literature: "All Me, All the Time" (*Christian Science Monitor*), "Advertisements for Himself" (*New Republic*), and "I Feel Your Pain: The Difficulty of Being Jonathan Franzen" (*New Statesman*). In an article on post-postmodernist American fiction writers, Catherine Toal notes the attraction of melancholy narratives to late-twentieth-century white male writers, including Franzen, Rick Moody, and David Foster Wallace. These novels "betray the symptoms of a specifically 'American' cultural ideology, which takes all processes of formation for mechanisms of control, and any advocacy of particular ones for the illegitimate arrogation of authority. Thus, even as they anatomize an individual and a general debility, the narratives . . . also tend—justifying their surrender to the side-effects of contemporary culture—to create substitute objects of condemnation and blame" (306).

17. It is telling that as many reviewers and critics find it to be a *failed* critique as find it a successful one. See, particularly, Annesley, who sees *The Corrections* as a fatally flawed effort to write a "novel of globalization."

18. It is tempting to read the Chip-Alfred relationship as semi-autobiographical, especially in light of Franzen's discussion of his father's afflictions in "My Father's Brain" (in *How to Be Alone*). Indeed, reading this essay also suggests that Enid is more than a little bit based on Franzen's own mother. Oddly, no critics have taken this tack.

19. For a discussion of Franzen's ambivalence (what else?) about the Midwest, see Poole. Franzen has some interesting things to say about the Midwest in "Meet Me in Saint Louis," his account of being filmed returning "home" by Oprah's crew (reprinted from the *New Yorker* in *Being Alone*).

CHAPTER 4: THE REAL DEAL

1. I say "men" here since the film has no interest in women. The one female character, Marla, interestingly, identifies against the corporate consumer culture that the film wants to displace. She's more at home in the anti-consumer, anti-domestic space of the house on Paper Street where "Tyler Durden" lives than she would be in the clean domestic space that is the narrator's home at the beginning of the film. We see her attitude toward consumption when she breezes into a Laundromat, takes jeans out of several dryers, and sells them at a secondhand shop. Later, she lampoons a kind of commodity fetishism when she describes her dress as a bridesmaid's dress, worn once and discarded, "like the victim of a sex crime"—and purchased by her for one dollar. The fact that Marla is closer to Tyler's position than to the narrator's might suggest that she's an essential part of the narrator's transformation—*might* suggest, if, that is, the film has anything other than a passing interest in her character. It seems clear, as well, that she functions as a heterosexual alibi for what are so obviously the homoerotic connections among the men.

2. Here is a sampling of what reviewers of the film interpret as the narrator's problem and the film's attitude toward it: His life an "amalgam of boredom and consumer lust" (Enright 10), this "wage slave . . . alienated from his life" (77) is a figure for the "hysterical male response to the perceived emasculation in contemporary corporate society" (Romney 43). "*Fight Club* is a 'grande' molotov cocktail pitched at the comfort zone of consumer culture, the cozy capitalism of Starbucks and Ikea," as one reviewer put it (Johnson 86); "too much of a postindustrial cipher to even have a name," the narrator's "Everyman no longer has any licit means of self-expression beyond shopping and twelve-step programs. He is neutered" (Klawans). Responding to the narrator's affectless recitation of the meaningless details of his everyday life, these viewers acquiesce to the seemingly self-evident "commonsense" wisdom uttered by Tyler Durden (Brad Pitt, the narrator's alter

ego): "The things we own end up owning us." Regardless of whether they like the film, these reviewers, in other words, find unproblematic the film's premise that consumer culture is at the root of the narrator's problem, his penchant for furniture, clothing, and accessories what alienates and numbs him.

3. See S. Clark; J. Clark; and Friday.

4. See Ta; Lizardo; and Giroux.

5. In a provocative analysis of the film, Claire Sisco King takes on the question of how it is that the film attracts and repels in almost equal measure and argues that this doubleness is built into its representation of the "abject hegemony" of masculinity. Arguing that the main characters are both attracted to and repulsed by the feminine (particularly maternity), King traces the strategies by which hegemonic masculinity utilizes the "abject" as a way to gather into itself, to absorb, any and all differences—and, thus, to be "both everything and nothing."

6. In Chuck Palahniuk's novel, the fat comes not from a liposuction clinic but from the refrigerator at the Paper Street house, put there by Marla, whose mother sends it to her to used as a "collagen trust fund"—as a hedge against the process of (female) aging. Female vanity is at issue in the novel's representation, but Fincher's addition of the raid on the clinic provides an opportunity to position its male characters as "rebelling" against consumer culture by undermining its own premises.

7. For an interesting and compelling analysis of how the special edition DVD of *Fight Club* works to erase the homoerotic meanings of the film, see Brooky and Westerfelhaus. They argue that the "extra text" offered on the DVD draws on a residual ideology of auterism to delegitimize the film's obvious homoerotic aspects.

8. The film literally brings the 1950s onto the screen (and the soundtrack) when we see the Fitts at home, watching a black-and-white Ronald Reagan movie on an old console television, dressed in vaguely retro garb, and when Carolyn plays tunes from mid-century musicals during dinner.

9. *American Beauty* also references "Lolita"—by which I mean the figure that has been constructed within American popular culture, not the novel or film by that name. Like "Stepford Wife," "Lolita" as a figure has been reconstructed from her original context and come to signify a crass, sexually voracious teenager. Witness the references to Amy Fisher as the "Long Island Lolita." It is worth noting that Alan Ball indicates that the Amy Fisher case, and the media coverage of it, was one of his inspirations for the screenplay. See Chumo's interview with Alan Ball (4).

10. Interestingly, Chuck Palahniuk wrote an introduction to a recent British edition of *The Stepford Wives*. Titled "Revisionist Herstory: Everywhere Is Stepford," the essay appreciates Levin's novel as a warning about how men might respond to the feminist gains of the 1970s and ends up chiding feminists for abandoning feminist goals in the 1990s. Although he makes some good points about how current "chick lit" novels represent women as, once again, focused on male approval, and now also represent other *women* as tormentors, he also trots out the snide dismissal of consumer culture that always manages to make women look inauthentic,

superficial, and, well, Stepford-like. Applauding Levin for warning us that the backlash was coming, he laments, "Nevertheless, it's odd how the bookshelves are filling with pretty dolls. Those glazed pretty dolls wearing their stylish designer outfits—Prada and Chanel and Dolce—swilling their martinis and flirting, flirting, flirting in their supreme effort to catch a rich husband. Always a *rich* husband. Instead of political rights, they're fighting for Jimmie Choos. In lieu of protest, they express themselves through shopping" (viii). Palahniuk also suggests that Martha Stewart is a real-life Stepford Wife, to be blamed for setting the women's movement back. Although *American Beauty* is not worried about feminism, its reviewers also evoke the figure of Martha Stewart in describing Carolyn.

11. The DVD contains a version of the film with "insightful commentary with director Sam Mendes and writer Alan Ball." While Ball's very sparse comments tend to be focused on what the characters' behavior signifies, Mendes is almost completely focused on the look of the film, the way the light is used, how the scenes are staged, and so on. In his comments on the scene in which Carolyn resists Lester's sexual come-on, Ball makes a point about how the living room contains so much "stuff," and both men laugh about the feminine bad taste the scene is meant to highlight.

12. Paul Arthur, who very much dislikes the film for its shopworn narrative and metaphysical pretensions, notes that the "two characters excluded from the orgy of redemption [are] Carolyn and Mrs. Fitts, the only adult women in the film, neither of whom has a clue about the path to enlightenment" (52).

CHAPTER 5: TO SHOP OR NOT TO SHOP

1. David Boyle identifies the "authenticity" elements that anti-consumerist forms of consumption are seeking—including "green" consumption, the slow-food movement, eco-tourism, and culture jamming. Those authenticity elements include the ethical, the natural, the simple, the honest, the unspun, the sustainable. Boyle's book is another entry in what has become a boom market in popular accounts of consumerism and anti-consumerism. For Boyle, the new quest for authenticity is an often cynical quest to find the "real" that has been damaged by the rush to globalization. While he is not really interested in challenging the logic behind this quest, he does a good job of unearthing some of the contradictions at its core.

2. Anthropologist Mary Douglas pens a spirited "defense of women's shopping, of the time they take over it and the money they spend on it. It is meant to rebut the ideas that men have about shopping as an activity and to indict a consumer theory that demeans consumer choice." This consumer theory, according to Douglas, is "a one-sided theoretical approach to shopping with crashingly obvious limitations" (15).

3. Jo Littler helpfully makes distinctions between "moral," "ethical," and "moralistic" strains of anti-consumerist consumption. She also uses the telling phrase "sanctimonious shopping."

4. Perhaps the most interesting take on the "rebel consumer" can be found in Lawrence B. Glickman's *Buying Power,* in which he devotes a chapter to the consumer activism of the "nonintercourse" movement that, in the antebellum South, aimed to boycott all products associated with the North. Glickman makes the point that these political consumer activists share a history with more contemporary "rebel consumers": "Nineteenth-century white Southern supporters of slavery and secession would appear to have nothing in common with contemporary ethical shoppers and 'green consumers.' The comparison is surprisingly apt, however, for notwithstanding enormous differences in outlook and in political orientation, both sets of rebel consumers share a defining characteristic: a tendency to treat consumption as heroic political action and indeed to frame their actions in the marketplace as alternatives to base consumption" (91–92).

5. In the late 1980s, feminist theorists from a number of different disciplines focused attention on how conceptualizations of the subject (as of the self) relied on a masculinist notion of agency—a model that was never meant to apply to women. This critique includes Luce Irigaray's engagement with Freud, Donna Haraway's reading of "myths of origins," and Jane Flax's challenge to philosophical conceptualizations of consciousness. Some representative essays are collected in Linda Nicholson, ed., *Feminism/Postmodernism.* It is worth noting that this conversation was happening at the same moment that Klein identifies as dominated by identity politics.

6. Tellingly, Klein has been heralded both as a good Marxist and as a wannabe Marxist who "invokes the material as if that in itself were enough to understand the material and cites the need for action as if that itself were an adequate action" (McQuillan 120). See Matthew Sharpe for an assessment of "Marxist themes" in *No Logo.* When I presented a version of this chapter to my department, one of my colleagues mentioned that, on a certain segment of the conference circuit (concerned with neoliberalism and globalization), Klein is often mocked as a less than serious voice, a Marxist wannabe. My colleague suggested that there might be a gendered dimension to this response, her work considered "soft" rather than "hard" social analysis. Juliet Schor would agree. She suggests that there is a feminist lesson to be learned from the reception of *No Logo* by academics: "When Naomi Klein published *No Logo,* she was a woman in her twenties without a graduate degree, venturing into territory fully occupied by a left-wing intellectual elite that was overwhelmingly male" (301).

7. See *PC Wars: Politics and Theory in the Academy,* edited by Jeffrey Williams.

8. See Christine Harold as well as Henry Jenkins for analyses of shifts in the forms and meanings of "culture jamming."

9. Sharon Zukin analyzes waves of gentrification and neighborhood "renewal" in New York in her "Consuming Authenticity." An evenhanded analysis of the costs and benefits (for old and new residents) of such changes, Zukin's article makes the important point that "authenticity is a resilient concept in consumer

society," one that unevenly serves the interests of privileged versus underprivileged residents (745). Although Klein does not invoke "authenticity" in her nostalgic paean to Emma Goldman's era, her narrative nevertheless plays on the idea of such spaces as, in Zukin's words, "oases of authenticity in a Wal-Mart wasteland" (725).

10. Similarly, Judith Williamson argues that *No Logo* is, "at heart, a sort of *Bildungsroman*—the story of young North America's disillusion with capitalism, and its outrage at discovering the inequities which fuel its own lifestyle" (211). Along with this outrage comes a sense of "betrayal," a belief that capitalism has failed to live up to its own promises—not, in Williamson's estimation, a belief that capitalism's promises have always been false. She also chides Klein for suggesting that the economic inequities she tracks were "virtually created in the 1990s" (214).

11. Scott Dannemiller's *The Year without a Purchase: One Family's Quest to Stop Shopping and Start Connecting* is also a recent book that reports on a couple who decide to stop buying things and then must learn to negotiate life as non-consumers in consumer culture. Dannemiller's experiment and his narrative are motivated and framed by Christianity, and the book proffers the perhaps predictable "conclusion" that separating oneself from materialism brings one closer to spirituality, integrity, and caring for others.

12. Michael Maniates and others have argued that there is a glaring contradiction at the heart of anti-consumerist movements like VS. More importantly, there is an unacknowledged class dimension to such movements: only those who are not experiencing *involuntary* simplicity brought on by economic hardship can afford the luxury of making choices to "downshift" and to buy the products that will help them in this effort. See the essays collected in *Confronting Consumption*, edited by Pincen, Maniates, and Conca, for a range of perspectives on these efforts.

13. I am reminded here of a wonderful essay by Iris Marion Young, titled "Women Recovering Our Clothes." Young meditates on female pleasure in clothes—in shopping for clothes, in wearing clothes, in talking about clothes with other women, and in using clothes to fantasize alternative selves—even while acknowledging that fashion is a semiotic system that can reduce women to objects and that the female desire to display clothes plays into the visual system in which a male gaze positions women as objects. "Patriarchal fashion folds create a meticulous paradigm of the woman well dressed for the male gaze, then endows with guilt the pleasure we might derive for ourselves in these clothes. Misogynist mythology gloats in its portrayal of women as frivolous body decorators. Well trained to meet the gaze that evaluates us for our finery, for how well we show him off, we then are condemned as sentimental, superficial, duplicitous, because we attend to and sometimes learn to love the glamorous arts" (203).

14. Scanlon's analysis of the fan culture around the Shopaholic novels makes it clear that readers do *not* read the novels as an exercise in Baurdrillardian analysis, as Ghosh suggests they be read. Interestingly, these fans stress the ways in which the novels subordinate the romance plot to an exploration of the female pleasures

of consumerism. Noting that Kinsella avoids representing Becky's physical body and eschews the typical chick-lit emphasis on diet and weight, Scanlon reads in fans' responses an appreciation of the novels' lack of "attention to the intricacies of the measured and manipulated body" ("Making Shopping Safe").

15. The discourse around "shopaholism" understands "guilt" as a signal of a woman's dangerous "addiction" to shopping. For example, Carolyn Wesson in *Women Who Shop Too Much* offers a checklist to determine whether a particular woman (presumably the reader) is or is not a "shopaholic" or "addicted shopper." For Wesson—a therapist who draws on her own experience, her therapy sessions with women, and the examples of famous "shopaholics" Imelda Marcos, Jackie Kennedy Onassis, Princess Diana, and Mary Todd Lincoln (!)—a key indicator of addiction is feeling guilty and ashamed about one's shopping. For Wesson, the guilt always comes from inside the women, and, thus, she is uninterested in thinking about how social constructions of "women who shop too much" might also be at the root of these guilty feelings.

16. Wilson surveys reviewers who "decry the materialism and absent moral center" of chick lit more generally (216).

17. See also Rita Felski's chapter in *Doing Time,* titled "Judith Krantz: The Author of the Cultural Logics of Late Capitalism," in which she takes seriously the importance to postmodern culture of the "money, sex, and power novel." And, of course, Janice Radway's landmark *Reading the Romance* (should have) forever changed the way academics and cultural elites respond to "trivial" feminine genres.

WORKS CITED

Alleva, Richard. "No *Leave It to Beaver: American Beauty*." *Commonweal*, vol. 126, no. 19, November 5, 1999, pp. 19–20.

American Beauty. Directed by Sam Mendes. DreamWorks, 1999.

Andrews, Cecile. *The Circle of Simplicity: A Return to the Good Life*. Harper, 1997.

Annesley, James. "Market Corrections: Jonathan Franzen and the 'Novel of Globalization.'" *Journal of Modern Literature*, vol. 29, no. 2, Winter 2006, pp. 111–28.

Ansen, David. "A Fist Full of Darkness." Review of *Fight Club*. *Newsweek*, October 18, 1999, p. 77.

Arthur, Paul. "*American Beauty*." *Cineaste*, vol. 25, no. 2, 2000, pp. 51–52.

Auslander, Leora. "The Gendering of Consumer Practices in Nineteenth-Century France." *The Sex of Things: Gender and Consumption in Historical Perspective*, edited by Victoria de Grazia, with Ellen Fourlough, U of California P, 1996, pp. 79–112.

Baldwin, Clive. "'Digressing from the Point': Holden Caulfield's Women." *J. D. Salinger's "The Catcher in the Rye,"* edited by Sarah Graham, Routledge, 2007, pp. 109–18.

Banet-Weiser, Sarah. *Authentic™: The Politics of Ambivalence in a Brand Culture*. New York UP, 2012.

Banet-Weiser, Sarah, and Roopali Mukherjee. "Introduction: Commodity Activism in Neoliberal Times." *Commodity Activism: Cultural Resistance in Neoliberal Times*, edited by Sarah Banet-Weiser and Roopali Mukherjee, New York UP, 2012, pp. 1–17.

Barber, Benjamin. *Consumed: How Markets Corrupt Children, Infantilize Adults, and Swallow Citizens Whole*. W. W. Norton, 2007.

Bareiss, Warren. "Middlebrow Knowingness in 1950s San Francisco: The Kingston Trio, Beat Counterculture, and the Production of 'Authenticity.'" *Popular Music and Society*, vol. 33, no. 1, February 2010, pp. 9–33.

Barker, Jennifer. "'A Hero Will Rise': The Myth of the Fascist Man in *Fight Club* and *Gladiator*." *Literature/Film Quarterly*, vol. 36, no. 3, 2008, pp. 171–87.

Baudrillard, Jean. *The Consumer Society: Myths and Structures.* Translated by Chris Turner, Sage, 1998.

Baym, Nina. "Melodramas of Beset Manhood: How Theories of American Literature Exclude Women." *American Quarterly,* no. 33, 1981, pp. 123–39.

Begley, Adam. "The Art of Fiction CXXXV: Don DeLillo." *Conversations with Don DeLillo,* edited by Thomas DePietro, UP of Mississippi, 2005, pp. 86–108.

Bendix, Regina. *In Search of Authenticity: The Formation of Folklore Studies.* U of Wisconsin P, 1997.

Bennett, Amanda. *The Death of the Organization Man.* William Morrow, 1990.

Berkley, George. *The Administrative Revolution: Notes on the Passing of the Organization Man.* Prentice Hall, 1971.

Berman, Marshall. *The Politics of Authenticity: Radical Individualism and the Emergence of Modern Society.* Atheneum, 1970.

Berrett, Jesse. "Feeding the Organization Man: Diet and Masculinity in Postwar America." *Journal of Social History,* vol. 30, no. 4, Summer 1997, pp. 805–25.

Bordo, Susan. "Reading the Slender Body." *Body/Politics: Women and the Discourse of Science,* edited by Mary Jacobus, Evelyn Fox Keller, and Sally Shuttleworth, Routledge, 1990, pp. 83–112.

Bowlby, Rachel. *Carried Away: The Invention of Modern Shopping.* Columbia UP, 2001.

Boyle, David. *Authenticity: Brands, Fakes, Spin and the Lust for Real Life.* HarperCollins, 2003.

Breazeale, Kenon. "In Spite of Women: *Esquire* Magazine and the Construction of the Male Consumer." *The Gender and Consumer Culture Reader,* edited by Jennifer Scanlon, New York UP, 2000, pp. 226–44. Originally published in *Signs,* vol. 20, no. 1, 1994, pp. 1–22.

Breward, Christopher. *The Hidden Consumer: Masculinities, Fashion and City Life, 1860–1914.* Manchester UP, 1999.

Brooky, Robert Allan, and Robert Westerfelhaus. "Hiding Homoeroticism in Plain View: The *Fight Club* DVD as Digital Closet." *Critical Studies in Media Communication,* vol. 19, no. 1, March 2002, pp. 21–43.

Brown, Bill. "Commodity Nationalism and the Lost Object." *The Pathos of Authenticity: American Passions of the Real,* edited by Ulla Haselstein, Andrew Gross, and Maryann Snyder-Korber, Universitätsverlag Winter, 2010, pp. 33–55.

Campbell, Colin. *The Romantic Ethic and the Spirit of Modern Consumerism.* Basil Blackwell, 1987.

———. "Shopping, Pleasure and the Sex War." *The Shopping Experience,* edited by Pasi Falk and Colin Campbell, Sage, 1997, pp. 166–76.

Carden, Mary Paniccia. "'Adventures in Auto-Eroticism': Economies of Traveling Masculinity in *On the Road* and *The First Third.*" *What's Your Road, Man? Critical Essays on Jack Kerouac's "On the Road,"* edited by Hilary Holladay and Robert Holton, Southern Illinois UP, 2009, pp. 77–98.

Chatterjee, Srirupa, and G. Neelakantan. "'Forever Fearful of a Crash': Family Vis-à-Vis Materialism in Jonathan Franzen's *The Corrections.*" *Notes on Contemporary Literature,* vol. 37, no. 4, September 2007, pp. 6–9.

Cheever, Abigail. *Real Phonies: Cultures of Authenticity in Post–World War II America.* U of Georgia P, 2010.

Chumo, Peter N. "*American Beauty:* An Interview with Alan Ball." *Alan Ball: Conversations,* edited by Thomas Fahy, UP of Mississippi, 2013, pp. 3–13. Originally published in *Creative Screenwriting,* vol. 7, no. 1, January–February 2000, pp. 26–35.

Clark, J. Michael. "Faludi, *Fight Club,* and Phallic Masculinity: Exploring the Emasculating Economies of Patriarchy." *Journal of Men's Studies,* vol. 11, no. 1, Fall 2002, pp. 65–76.

Clark, Suzanne. "*Fight Club:* Historicizing the Rhetoric of Masculinity, Violence, and Sentimentality." *Journal of American Culture,* vol. 21, no. 2, 2001, pp. 411–20.

Cohan, Steven. *Masked Men: Masculinity and the Movies in the Fifties.* Indiana UP, 1997.

———. "Queer Eye for the Straight Guise: Camp, Postfeminism, and the Fab Five's Makeovers of Masculinity." *Interrogating Postfeminism: Gender and the Politics of Popular Culture,* edited by Yvonne Tasker and Diane Negra, Duke UP, 2007, pp. 176–200.

Cohen, Lizbeth. *A Consumer's Republic: The Politics of Mass Consumption in Post-war American Culture.* Alfred A. Knopf, 2003.

Collins, Jim, ed. *High-Pop: Making Culture into Entertainment.* Blackwell, 2002.

Confessions of a Shopaholic. Directed by P. J. Hogan. Touchstone Pictures, 2009.

Conroy, Mark. "From Tombstone to Tabloid: Authority Figured in *White Noise.*" *Critique,* vol. 35, no. 2, Winter 1994, pp. 97–110.

Corber, Robert J. *Homosexuality in Cold War America: Resistance and the Crisis of Masculinity.* Duke UP, 1997.

———. *In the Name of National Security: Hitchcock, Homophobia and the Political Construction of Gender in Postwar America.* Duke UP, 1993.

Curley, Thomas. "Everything Moves, but Nothing Is Alive." Review of *On the Road, Commonweal,* September 13, 1957, pp. 595–97.

Dannemiller, Scott. *The Year without a Purchase: One Family's Quest to Stop Shopping and Start Connecting.* Westminster John Knox Press, 2015.

Davidson, Michael. *Guys Like Us: Citing Masculinity in Cold War Poetics.* U of Chicago P, 2004.

DeCurtis, Anthony. "'An Outsider in This Society': An Interview with Don DeLillo." *Conversations with Don DeLillo,* edited by Thomas DePietro, UP of Mississippi, 2005, pp. 52–74.

De Grazia, Victoria, with Ellen Fourlough, eds. *The Sex of Things: Gender and Consumption in Historical Perspective.* U of California P, 1996.

DeLillo, Don. *White Noise.* Penguin, 1985.

Denby, David. "Transcending the Suburbs." Review of *American Beauty. New Yorker,* September 20, 1999, pp. 133–35.

DePietro, Thomas, ed. *Conversations with Don DeLillo.* UP of Mississippi, 2005.

Dery, Mark. *Culture Jamming: Hacking, Slashing and Sniping in the Empire of Signs.* Pamphlet no. 25, Open Magazine, 1993.

———. Foreword to *Culture Jamming: Activism and the Art of Cultural Resistance,* edited by Marilyn Delaure and Moritz Fink, New York UP, 2017, pp. xi–xv.

doCarmo, Stephen N. *History and Refusal: Consumer Culture and Postmodern Theory in the Contemporary American Novel.* Lehigh UP, 2009.

Donohue, Kathleen G. "What Gender Is the Consumer? The Role of Gender in Defining the Political." *Journal of American Studies,* vol. 33, no. 1, 1999, pp. 19–44.

Douglas, Ann. *The Feminization of American Culture.* Avon Books, 1977.

Douglas, Mary. "In Defense of Shopping." *The Shopping Experience,* edited by Pasi Falk and Colin Campbell, Sage, 1997, pp. 15–30. Originally published in Mary Douglas, *Objects and Objections,* Toronto Semiotics Circle, 1992, pp. 66–87.

Dowd, Maureen. "Heels over Hemingway." *New York Times,* February 10, 2007, http://select.nytimes.com/2007/02/10/opinion/10dowd.html.

Duvall, John N. "The (Super)Marketplace of Images: Television as Unmediated Mediation in *White Noise.*" *Arizona Quarterly,* vol. 50, no. 3, Autumn 1994, pp. 127–53.

Edwards, Duane. "'Don't Ever Tell Anybody Anything.'" *Major Literary Characters: Holden Caulfield,* edited by Harold Bloom, Chelsea House Publishers, 1990, pp. 105–13. Originally published in *ELH,* 1977.

Edwards, Thomas. "Oprah's Choice." *Raritan,* vol. 21, no. 4, 2002, pp. 75–86.

Ehrenreich, Barbara. *The Hearts of Men: American Dreams and the Flight from Commitment.* Anchor Books, 1983.

Elmwood, Victoria. "The White Nomad and the New Masculine Family in Jack Kerouac's *On the Road.*" *Western American Literature,* vol. 42, no. 4, Winter 2008, pp. 335–61.

Engles, Tim. "Connecting *White Noise* to Critical Whiteness Studies." *Approaches to Teaching DeLillo's "White Noise,"* edited by Tim Engles and John Duvall, MLA, 2006, pp. 63–72.

Enright, Robert. "Iron Jerk." Review of *Fight Club. Border Crossings,* vol. 18, no. 4, November 1999, pp. 10–11.

Epstein, Joseph. "Surfing the Novel." *Commentary,* January 1, 2002, pp. 32–37.

Ewen, Stewart. *Captains of Consciousness: Advertising and the Social Roots of Consumer Culture.* Basic Books, 1971.

Faludi, Susan. "It's *Thelma and Louise* for Guys." Review of *Fight Club. Newsweek,* October 25, 1999, p. 89.

———. *Stiffed: The Betrayal of the American Man.* William Morrow, 1999.

Felski, Rita. *Doing Time: Feminist Theory and Postmodern Culture.* New York U Press, 2000.

Ferraro, Thomas. "Whole Families Shopping at Night!" *New Essays on "White Noise,"* edited by Frank Lentricchia, Cambridge UP, 1991, pp. 15–38.

Feuer, Alan. "Far Right Plans Its Next Move with New Energy." *New York Times,* August 14, 2017, https://www.nytimes.com/2017/08/14/us/white-supremacists-right-wing-extremists-richard-spencer.html.

Fight Club. Directed by David Fincher. Twentieth Century–Fox. 1999.

Fight Club. Promotional website. Twentieth Century–Fox, 1999, http://www.foxmovies.com/fightclub/.

Fiske, John. "Popular Discrimination." *Modernity and Mass Culture,* edited by James Naremore and Patrick Brantlinger, Indiana UP, 1991, pp. 103–16.

Flax, Jane. *Thinking Fragments: Psychoanalysis, Feminism, and Postmodernism in the Contemporary West.* U of California P, 1990.

Fraiman, Susan. *Cool Men and the Second Sex.* Columbia UP, 2003.

Frank, Thomas. *The Conquest of Cool: Business Culture, Counterculture, and the Rise of Hip Consumerism.* U of Chicago P, 1997.

Franklin, Ruth. "Impact Man." *New Republic,* September 22, 2010, https://newrepublic.com/article/77903/impact-man.

Franzen, Jonathan. *The Corrections.* Picador, 2001.

———. *How to Be Alone: Essays.* Farrar, Straus and Giroux, 2002.

———. "I'll Be Doing More of the Same." *Review of Contemporary Fiction,* vol. 16, no. 1, Spring 1996, pp. 3438.

Friday, Krister. "'A Generation of Men without History': *Fight Club,* Masculinity, and the Historical Symptom." *Postmodern Culture,* vol. 13, no. 3, 2003, doi:10.1353/pmc.2003.0016.

Friedman, Devin. "Middlebrow: The Taste That Dare Not Speak Its Name." *GQ,* June 20, 2011.

Frow, John. "The Last Things before the Last: Notes on *White Noise.*" *Introducing Don DeLillo,* edited by Frank Lentricchia, Duke UP, 1991, pp. 175–91.

"The Ganser Syndrome." Review of *On the Road. Time,* September 9, 1957.

Ghosh, Srijani. "*Res Emptito Ergo Sum:* Fashion and Commodity Fetishism in Sophie Kinsella's *Confessions of a Shopaholic.*" *Journal of Popular Culture,* vol. 46, no. 2, 2013, pp. 378–93.

Gilmore, James H., and B. Joseph Pine II. *Authenticity: What Consumers Really Want.* Harvard Business School Press, 2007.

Gilmore, Paul. *The Genuine Article: Race, Mass Culture, and American Literary Manhood.* Duke UP, 2001.

Giroux, Henry A. "Private Satisfactions and Public Disorders: *Fight Club,* Patriarchy, and the Politics of Masculine Violence." *Journal of American Culture,* vol. 21, no. 1, 2001, pp. 1–31.

Glickman, Lawrence B. *Buying Power: A History of Consumer Activism in America.* U of Chicago P, 2009.

Goldberger, Paul. "Cuddling up to Quasimodo and Friends." *New York Times,* June 23, 1996, http://www.nytimes.com/1996/06/23/movies/cuddling-up-to-quasimodo-and-friends.html.

Golomb, Jacob. *In Search of Authenticity: From Kirkegaard to Camus.* Routledge, 1995.

Gould, Philip. "Revisiting the 'Feminization' of American Culture." *differences,* vol. 11, no. 3, 1999–2000, pp. i–xii.

Graham, Sarah, ed. *J. D. Salinger's "The Catcher in the Rye."* Routledge, 2007.

Green, Jeremy. *Late Postmodernism: American Fiction at the Millennium.* Palgrave Macmillan, 2005.

Grossberg, Lawrence. *We Gotta Get Out of This Place: Popular Conservatism and Postmodern Culture.* Routledge, 1992.

Halter, Marilyn. *Shopping for Identity: The Marketing of Ethnicity.* Schocken Books, 2000.

Hanspal, Vrajesh, and Angela McRobbie. "Logo Love and Its Critics." *Media, Culture, and Society,* no. 22, 2000, pp. 841–45.

Haraway, Donna. *Simians, Cyborgs, and Women: The Reinvention of Nature.* Routledge, 1991.

Harold, Christine. "Pranking Rhetoric: 'Culture Jamming' as Media Activism." *Culture Jamming: Activism and the Art of Cultural Resistance,* edited by Marilyn Delaure and Moritz Fink, New York UP, 2017, pp. 62–112.

Heath, Joseph, and Andrew Potter. *Nation of Rebels: Why Counterculture Became Consumer Culture.* Harper Business Press, 2004.

Hekanaho, Pia Livia. "Queering *Catcher*: Flits, Straights, and Other Morons." *J. D. Salinger's "The Catcher in the Rye,"* edited by Sarah Graham, Routledge, 2007, pp. 89–97.

Helyer, Ruth. "DeLillo and Masculinity." *The Cambridge Companion to Don DeLillo,* edited by John Duvall, Cambridge UP, 2008, pp. 125–36.

Hentzi, Gary. "*American Beauty.*" *Film Quarterly,* vol. 54, no. 2, Winter 2000–2001, pp. 46–50.

Herrman, John. "Why the Far Right Wants to Be the New 'Alternative' Culture." *New York Times Magazine,* June 27, 2017, p. 11.

Hoberek, Andrew. "Foreign Objects; or, DeLillo Minimalist." *Studies in American Fiction,* vol. 37, no. 1, 2010, pp. 101–25.

———. *The Twilight of the Middle Class: Post–World War II American Fiction and White-Collar Work.* Princeton UP, 2005.

Hoffman, Meredith. "The Battle over White Nationalism at Texas A&M." *Rolling Stone,* August 23, 2017, http://www.rollingstone.com/politics/features/the-battle-over-white-nationalism-at-texas-am-w498905.

Holt, Douglas B. *How Brands Become Icons: The Principles of Cultural Branding.* Harvard Business School Press, 2004.

Holton, Rob. "'Real Country and Real People': The Countercultural Pastoral, 1948–1971." *European Contributions to American Studies,* no. 42, 1999, pp. 93–106.

Humphery, Kim. *Excess: Anti-consumerism in the West.* Polity Press, 2010.

Hutcheon, Linda. "Irony, Nostalgia, and the Postmodern." *Methods for the Study of Literature as Cultural Memory,* edited by Raymond Vervliet and Annemarie Estor, Rodopi, 2000, pp. 189–207.

———. *The Politics of Postmodernism.* Routledge, 1989.

Hutchinson, Colin. "Jonathan Franzen and the Politics of Disengagement." *Critique,* vol. 50, no. 2, 2009, pp. 191–207.

Huyssen, Andreas. *After the Great Divide: Modernism, Mass Culture, Postmodernism.* Indiana UP, 1986.

Ingraham, Chris. "Talking (about) the Elite and the Mass: Vernacular Rhetoric and Discursive Status." *Philosophy and Rhetoric,* vol. 46, no. 1, 2013, pp. 1–21.

Interview with Jonathan Franzen. *Fresh Air.* National Public Radio, October 13, 2001.

Irigaray, Luce. *This Sex Which Is Not One.* Cornell UP, 1985.

Irwin, William. *Free Market Existentialist: Capitalism without Consumerism.* Wiley Blackwell, 2015.

Jameson, Fredric. *Postmodernism; or, The Cultural Logic of Late Capitalism.* Duke UP, 1991.

Jardine, Alice. *Gynesis: Configurations of Woman and Modernity.* Cornell UP, 1987.

Jenkins, Henry. "From Culture Jamming to Cultural Acupuncture." *Culture Jamming: Activism and the Art of Cultural Resistance,* edited by Marilyn Delaure and Moritz Fink, New York UP, 2017, pp. 133–58.

Johnson, E. Patrick. *Appropriating Blackness: Performance and the Politics of Authenticity.* Duke UP, 2003.

Johnston, Allan. "Consumption, Addiction, Vision, Energy: Political Economies and Utopian Visions in the Writings of the Beat Generation." *College Literature,* vol. 32, no. 2, Spring 2005, pp. 103–26.

Karem, Jeff. *The Romance of Authenticity: The Cultural Politics of Regional and Ethnic Literatures.* UP of Virginia, 2004.

Keightley, Keir. "Reconsidering Rock." *The Cambridge Companion to Pop and Rock,* edited by Simon Frith, Will Straw, and John Street, Cambridge UP, 2001, pp. 109–42.

Kerouac, Jack. *Dharma Bums.* 1958. Penguin Books, 2006.

———. *On the Road.* 1955. Penguin Books, 1976.

King, Claire Sisco. "It Cuts Both Ways: *Fight Club,* Masculinity, and Abject Hegemony." *Communication and Critical/Cultural Studies,* vol. 6, no. 4, December 2009, pp. 366–85.

Kinsella, Sophie. *Confessions of a Shopaholic.* Dell, 1999.

———. *Shopaholic Takes Manhattan.* Dell, 2001.

———. *Shopaholic to the Rescue.* Dial Press, 2015.

———. *Shopaholic to the Stars.* Dial Press, 2014.

Klawans, Stuart. Review of *Fight Club. Nation,* vol. 269, no. 15, November 8, 1999.

Klein, Naomi. *No Logo.* 10th anniversary ed. Picador, 2000.

Knight, Peter. *Conspiracy Culture: From Kennedy to the "X-Files."* Routledge, 2001.

Leach, William. *Land of Desire: Merchants, Power, and the Rise of a New American Culture.* Pantheon Books, 1993.

Lears, T. J. Jackson. *Fables of Abundance: A Cultural History of Advertising in America.* Basic Books, 1994.

———. *No Place of Grace: Antimodernism and the Transformation of American Culture, 1880–1920.* U of Chicago P, 1981.

Leinberger, Paul, and Bruce Tucker. *The New Individualists: The Generation after the Organization Man.* Harper Collins, 1991.

Lentricchia, Frank. "Tales of the Electronic Tribe." *New Essays on White Noise,* edited by Frank Lentricchia, Cambridge UP, 1991, pp. 87–113.

Levine, Judith. *Not Buying It: My Year without Shopping*. Free Press, 2006.

Ligari, Rachel. "When Mexico Looks Like Mexico: The Hyperrealization of Race and the Pursuit of the Authentic." *What's Your Road, Man? Critical Essays on Jack Kerouac's "On the Road,"* edited by Hilary Holladay and Robert Holton, South Illinois UP, 2009, pp. 139–54.

Lindner, Christoph. *Fictions of Commodity Culture: From the Victorian to the Postmodern*. Ashgate, 2003.

Lipsitz, George. *The Possessive Investment in Whiteness: How White People Profit from Identity Politics*. Temple UP, 1998.

Littler, Jo. *Radical Consumption: Shopping for Change in Contemporary Culture*. Open UP, 2009.

Lizardo, Omar. "*Fight Club;* or, The Cultural Contradictions of Late Capitalism." *Journal for Cultural Research*, vol. 11, no. 3, July 2007, pp. 221–43.

Longmuir, Anne. "Genre and Gender in Don DeLillo's *Players* and *Running Dog*." *Journal of Narrative Theory*, vol. 37, no. 1, Winter 2007, pp. 128–45.

MacDonald, Dwight. "Masscult and Midcult." *Against the American Grain*, Da Capo Press, 1962, pp. 3–75. Originally published in *Partisan Review* (1960).

Maniates, Michael. "In Search of Consumptive Resistance: The Voluntary Simplicity Movement." *Confronting Consumption*, edited by Thomas Pincen, Michael Maniates, and Ken Conca, MIT Press, 2002, pp. 199–235.

Martinez, Manuel Luis. *Countering the Counterculture: Rereading Postwar American Dissent from Jack Kerouac to Tomás Rivera*. U of Wisconsin P, 2003.

McAllister, Matthew P. *The Commercialization of American Culture: New Advertising, Control and Democracy*. Sage Publications, 1995.

———. "'No Logo' Legacy." *Women's Studies Quarterly*, vol. 38, nos. 3–4, Fall–Winter 2010, pp. 287–92.

McQuillan, Martin. "Spectres of Poujade: Naomi Klein and the New International." *Parallax*, vol. 7, no. 3, 2001, pp. 114–30.

McRobbie, Angela. "Postfeminism and Popular Culture: Bridget Jones and the New Gender Regime." *Interrogating Postfeminism: Gender and the Politics of Popular Culture*, edited by Yvonne Tasker and Diane Negra, Duke UP, 2007, pp. 27–39. Originally published in *Feminist Media Studies*, vol. 4, no. 3, 2004, pp. 255–64.

———. *Postmodernism and Popular Culture*. Routledge, 1994.

Medovoi, Leerom. "Democracy, Capitalism, and American Literature: The Cold War Construction of J. D. Salinger's Paperback Hero." *The Other Fifties: Interrogating Midcentury American Icons*, edited by Joel Foreman, U of Illinois P, 1997, pp. 255–87.

———. "Mapping the Rebel Image: Postmodernism and the Masculinist Politics of Rock in the U.S.A." *Cultural Critique*, no. 20, Winter 1991–92, pp. 153–88.

Melley, Timothy. *Empire of Conspiracy: Paranoia in Postwar American Culture.* Cornell UP, 2000.

Merish, Lori. *Sentimental Materialism: Gender, Commodity Culture, and Nineteenth-Century America.* Duke UP, 2000.

Miller, Daniel. *Material Culture and Mass Consumption.* Basil Blackwell, 1987.

———. *A Theory of Shopping.* Cornell UP, 1998.

Miller, Laura. "Book Lovers' Quarrel." *Salon*, October 26, 2001, http://www.salon.com/2001/10/26/franzen_winfrey/.

Mills, C. Wright. *White Collar: The American Middle Classes.* 1951. 50th anniversary ed. Oxford UP, 2002.

Modleski, Tania. *Feminism without Women: Culture and Criticism in a "Postfeminist" Era.* Routledge, 1991.

Montague, Julian. *The Stray Shopping Carts of Eastern North America: A Guide to Field Identification.* Harry N. Abrams, 2006.

Moore, Anne Elizabeth. *Unmarketable: Brandalism, Copyfighting, Mocketing, and the Erosion of Integrity.* New Press, 2007.

Morris, Meaghan. "Things to Do with Shopping Centres." *Grafts: Feminist Cultural Criticism*, edited by Susan Sheridan, Verso Books, 1988, pp. 193–225.

Morrow, Lance. "Are Men Really That Bad?" *Time*, February 14, 1994, pp. 53–59.

Mukherjee, Roopali, and Sarah Banet-Weiser, eds. *Commodity Activism: Cultural Resistance in Neoliberal Times.* New York UP, 2012.

Nadel, Alan. *Containment Culture: American Narratives, Postmodernism, and the Atomic Age.* Duke UP, 1995.

Naidotti, Maria. "An Interview with Don DeLillo." *Conversations with Don DeLillo*, edited by Thomas DePietro, UP of Mississippi, 2005, pp. 109–18.

Nava, Mica. *Changing Cultures: Feminism, Youth and Consumerism.* Sage Publications, 1992.

Nel, Philip. "Amazons in the *Underworld*: Gender, the Body, and Power in the Novels of Don DeLillo." *Critique*, vol. 42, no. 4, Summer 2001, pp. 416–36.

Nicholson, Linda, ed. *Feminism/Postmodernism.* Routledge, 1990.

Nickles, Shelley. "More Is Better: Mass Consumption, Gender, and Class Identity in Postwar America." *American Quarterly*, vol. 5, no. 4, December 2002, pp. 581–622.

Osgerby, Bill. *Playboys in Paradise: Masculinity, Youth and Leisure-Style in Modern America.* Berg, 2001.

Osteen, Mark. *American Magic and Dread: Don DeLillo's Dialogue with Culture.* U of Pennsylvania P, 2000.

Outka, Elizabeth. *Consuming Traditions: Modernity, Modernism, and the Commodified Authentic.* Oxford UP, 2008.

Packard, Vance. *The Hidden Persuaders.* Pocket Books, 1957.

Palahniuk, Chuck. *Fight Club.* Henry Holt, 1996.

———. "Revisionist Herstory: Everywhere Is Stepford." Introduction to *The Stepford Wives*, by Ira Levin, Constable & Robinson, 2011, pp. v–ix.

Panish, Jon. *The Color of Jazz: Race and Representation in Postwar American Culture.* UP of Mississippi, 1997.

Pendergast, Tom. *Creating the Modern Man: American Magazines and Consumer Culture, 1900–1950.* U of Missouri P, 2000.

Pincen, Thomas, Michael Maniates, and Ken Conca, eds. *Confronting Consumption.* MIT P, 2002.

"*Playboy's* Penthouse Apartment." *The Gender and Consumer Culture Reader*, edited by Jennifer Scanlon, New York U Press, 2000, pp. 94–99. Originally published in *Playboy*, 1956.

Poole, Ralph. "Serving the Fruitcake; or, Jonathan Franzen's Midwestern Poetics." *Midwest Quarterly*, vol. 49, no. 3, Spring 2008, pp. 263–83.

Potkay, Adam. "The Joy of *American Beauty*." *Raritan*, vol. 25, no. 1, Summer 2005, pp. 69–86.

Potter, Andrew. *The Authenticity Hoax: Why the "Real" Things We Seek Don't Make Us Happy.* Harper Perennial, 2010.

Radway, Janice. *A Feeling for Books: The Book-of-the-Month Club, Literary Taste, and Middle-Class Desire.* U of North Carolina P, 1997.

———. *Reading the Romance: Women, Patriarchy, and Popular Literature.* U of North Carolina P, 1984.

Ribbat, Christoph. "Handling the Media, Surviving *The Corrections:* Jonathan Franzen and the Fate of the Author." *Amerikastudien/American Studies*, vol. 47, no. 4, 2002, pp. 555–66.

Riesman, David. *The Lonely Crowd.* Yale UP, 1950.

Roberts, Martin. "The Fashion Police: Governing the Self in *What Not to Wear*." *Interrogating Postfeminism: Gender and the Politics of Popular Culture*, edited by Yvonne Tasker and Diane Negra, Duke UP, 2007, pp. 227–48.

Roberts, Mary Louise. "Review Essay: Gender, Consumption, and Commodity Culture." *American Historical Review*, vol. 103, no. 3, June 1998, pp. 817–44.

Robinson, Sally. *Marked Men: White Masculinity in Crisis.* Columbia UP, 1999.

Romney, Jonathan. "Boxing Clever." *New Statesman*, November 15, 1999, pp. 43–44.

Rossinow, Doug. *The Politics of Authenticity: Liberalism, Christianity, and the New Left in America.* Columbia UP, 1998.

Salinger, J. D. *The Catcher in the Rye*. 1945. Little, Brown, 1991.

Salzberg, Joel. Introduction to *Critical Essays on Salinger's "The Catcher in the Rye,"* edited by Joel Salzberg, G. K. Hall, 1990, pp. 1–22.

Scanlon, Jennifer. "Making Shopping Safe for the Rest of Us: Sophie Kinsella's Shopaholic Series and Its Readers." *Americana*, vol. 4, no. 2, Fall 2005, http://www.americanpopularculture.com/journal/articles/fall_2005/scanlon.htm.

———. "What's an Acquisitive Girl to Do? Chick Lit and the Great Recession." *Women's Studies*, vol. 42, no. 8, 2013, pp. 904–22.

Schlesinger, Arthur. "The Crisis of American Masculinity." *The Politics of Hope*, Houghton Mifflin, 1963, pp. 237–46. Originally published in *Esquire*, November 1958.

Schor, Juliet. "Combating Consumerism and Capitalism: A Decade of *No Logo*." *Women's Studies Quarterly*, vol. 38, nos. 3–4, Fall–Winter 2010, pp. 299–301.

Schriber, M. S. "Holden Caulfield, C'est Moi." *Critical Essays on Salinger's "The Catcher in the Rye,"* edited by Joel Salzberg, G. K. Hall, 1990, pp. 227–38.

Schryer, Stephen. *Fantasies of the New Class: Ideologies of Professionalism in Post–World War II American Fiction*. Columbia UP, 2011.

Sernovitz, Gary. "What 'the Organization Man' Can Tell Us about Inequality Today." *New Yorker*, December 29, 2016, http://www.newyorker.com/business/currency/what-the-organization-man-can-tell-us-about-inequality-today.

Sharp, Matthew. "The Logo as Fetish: Marxist Themes in Naomi Klein's *No Logo*." *Cultural Logic*, vol. 6, 2003, http://clogic.eserver.org/2003/sharpe.html.

Slack, Andrew. "Case Study: The Harry Potter Alliance." *Beautiful Trouble: A Toolbox for Revolution*, edited by Andrew Boyd and Dave Oswald Mitchell, OR Books, 2012, pp. 322–25.

Smith, Bonnie Kathryn. "Branded Literacy: The Entrepreneurship of Oprah's Book Club." *Women and Literacy: Local and Global Inquiries for a New Century*, edited by Beth Daniell, Peter Mortensen, and Min-Zhan Lu, Routledge, 2007, pp. 157–70.

Smith, Caroline J. *Cosmopolitan Culture and Consumerism in Chick Lit*. Routledge, 2008.

Snyder, Gabriel. "When Oprah Stomped on Franzen, It Revealed a Vast Culture Split." *New York Observer*, November 5, 2011, http://observer.com/2001/11/when-oprah-stomped-on-franzen-it-revealed-a-vast-culture-split/.

Snyder, Katherine. "A Paradise of Bachelors: Remodeling Domesticity and Masculinity in the Turn-of-the-Century New York Bachelor Apartment." *Prospects*, vol. 23, October 1998, pp. 247–84.

Spector, Judith A., and Katherine V. Tsiopos Wills. "The Aesthetics of Materialism in Alan Ball's *American Beauty*." *Midwest Quarterly*, vol. 48, no. 2, Winter 2007, pp. 279–96.

Steinle, Pamela H. *In Cold Fear: "The Catcher in the Rye" Censorship Controversy and Postwar American Character*. Ohio State UP, 2002.

Swiencicki, Mark A. "Consuming Brotherhood: Men's Culture, Style and Recreation as Consumer Culture, 1880–1930." *Journal of Social History*, vol. 31, no. 4, Summer 1998, pp. 773–808.

Ta, Lynn M. "Hurt So Good: *Fight Club*, Masculine Violence, and the Crisis of Capitalism." *Journal of American Culture*, vol. 20, no. 3, 2006, pp. 265–77.

Tasker, Yvonne, and Diane Negra, eds. *Interrogating Postfeminism: Gender and the Politics of Popular Culture*. Duke UP, 2007.

Taylor, Charles. *The Ethics of Authenticity*. Harvard UP, 1991.

Thomas, Kendall. "'Ain't Nothin' Like the Real Thing': Black Masculinity, Gay Sexuality, and the Jargon of Authenticity." *Representing Black Men*, edited by George P. Cunningham and Marcellus Blount, Routledge, 1996, pp. 55–69.

Thornton, Sarah. *Club Cultures: Music, Media and Subcultural Capital*. Wesleyan UP, 1996.

Toal, Catherine. "Corrections: Contemporary American Melancholy." *Journal of European Studies*, vol. 33, nos. 3–4, 2003, pp. 305–22.

Trilling, Lionel. *Sincerity and Authenticity*. Harvard UP, 1971.

van Elteren, Mel. "The Subculture of the Beats: A Sociological Revisit." *Journal of American Culture*, vol. 22, no. 3, Fall 1999, pp. 71–99.

Vannini, Phillip, and J. Patrick Williams, eds. *Authenticity in Culture, Self, and Society*. Ashgate, 2009.

Van Slooten, Jessica Lyn. "Fashionably Indebted: Conspicuous Consumption, Fashion, and Romance in Sophie Kinsella's Shopaholic Trilogy." *Chick Lit: The New Woman's Fiction*, edited by Suzanne Ferriss and Mallory Young, Routledge, 2006, pp. 219–38.

Walker, Joseph S. "Criminality, the Real, and the Story of America: The Case of Don DeLillo." *Centennial Review*, vol. 43, no. 3, 1999, pp. 433–66.

Wallace, David Foster. *Consider the Lobster, and Other Essays*. Little, Brown, 2006.

———. *A Supposedly Fun Thing I Will Never Do Again: Essays and Arguments*. Little, Brown, 1997.

Weber, Brenda. *Makeover TV: Selfhood, Citizenship, and Celebrity.* Duke UP, 2009.

Weekes, Karen. "Consuming and Dying: Meaning and the Marketplace in Don DeLillo's *White Noise.*" *Literature Interpretation Theory,* vol. 18, no. 4, 2007, pp. 285–302.

Weisethaunet, Hans, and Ulf Lindberg. "Authenticity Revisited: The Rock Critic and the Changing Real." *Popular Music and Society,* vol. 33, no. 4, October 2010, pp. 465–85.

Wesson, Carolyn. *Women Who Shop Too Much: Overcoming the Urge to Splurge.* St. Martin's Press, 1990.

Whitfield, Stephen J. "Cherished and Cursed: Toward a Social History of *The Catcher in the Rye.*" *New England Quarterly,* vol. 70, no. 4, December 1997, pp. 567–600.

Whiting, Cecile. *A Taste for Pop: Pop Art, Gender and Consumer Culture.* Cambridge UP, 1997.

Whyte, William. *The Organization Man.* Doubleday Anchor Books, 1957.

Wilcox, Leonard. "Baudrillard, DeLillo's *White Noise,* and the End of Heroic Narrative." *Contemporary Literature,* vol. 32, no. 3, 1991, 346–65.

Williams, Colin C. *A Commodified World? Mapping the Limits of Capitalism.* Zed Books, 2005.

Williams, Jeffrey, ed. *PC Wars: Politics and Theory in the Academy.* Routledge, 1995.

Williamson, Judith. "An Anti-capitalist *Bildungsroman.*" *New Formations,* no. 45, Winter 2001, pp. 210–14.

Wilson, Cheryl A. "Becky Bloomwood at the V&A: Culture, Materialism, and the Chick Lit Novel." *Journal of Popular Culture,* vol. 45, no. 1, 2012, pp. 214–25.

Woolcott, James. "Advertisements for Himself." *New Republic,* December 2–9, 2002, pp. 36–40.

Wylie, Philip. *Generation of Vipers.* Dalkey Archive Press, 1996. Originally published 1942.

Yost, Milo, and Jeff Wilser. *The Man Cave Book.* Harper, 2011.

Young, Iris Marion. "Women Recovering our Clothes." *On Fashion,* edited by Shari Benstock and Suzanne Ferriss, Rutgers UP, 1994, pp. 197–210.

Zukin, Sharon. "Consuming Authenticity: From Outposts of Difference to Means of Exclusion." *Cultural Studies,* vol. 22, no. 5, September 2008, pp. 724–48.

———. *Point of Purchase: How Shopping Changed American Culture.* Routledge, 2004.

INDEX

www.ingramcontent.com/pod-product-compliance
Lightning Source LLC
Chambersburg PA
CBHW020345270326
41926CB00007B/319